The Evolving Landscape of Media and Communication in Hong Kong

# The Evolving Landscape
# of Media and Communication in Hong Kong

Yu HUANG and Yunya SONG

CITY UNIVERSITY OF
HONG KONG PRESS
香港城市大學出版社

| Editor | Joanna PIERCE | |
| Cover Design | Carrie YU |  Création 城大創意製作 |
| Book Design | LAU Wai Chun | |

ISBN: 978-962-937-351-1

Published by
      City University of Hong Kong Press
      Tat Chee Avenue
      Kowloon, Hong Kong
      Website: www.cityu.edu.hk/upress
      E-mail: upress@cityu.edu.hk

Printed in Hong Kong

A timely and important pulse-taking of the state of media conditions in what is touted as an East-West meeting point and a hub of globalization, currently facing a confluence of severe challenges from technological change, creeping authoritarian control, and decline of public trust.

Prof. Chin-Chuan LEE
Chair Professor (Emeritus), City University of Hong Kong

Huang Yu, Song Yunya and their collaborators are to be congratulated on the production of this invaluable text. In a series of clearly written and painstakingly researched case studies the authors present a comprehensive account of the state of the media twenty years after Hong Kong's return to China. Everyone who is interested in the media in Hong Kong will find the book indispensable.

Prof. Colin SPARKS
Chair Professor, Hong Kong Baptist University

This volume is a timely review of the fast changing media landscapes in post-handover Hong Kong. Comprehensive in approach, its reports and analyses cover various sectors, including traditional media, new media, advertising, public relations, and some special issues in public communication. Informative and insightful, the volume makes a useful reference for academics, communication professionals and students who are interested in understanding how the Hong Kong media and communications have been transformed in the last two decades.

Prof. Joseph M. CHAN
Chair Professor (Emeritus), The Chinese University of Hong Kong

The media landscape in Hong Kong has shifted dramatically with changes in the political environment and information technology. This book provides a comprehensive description of content production, distribution and media market. Providing an effective way to understand Hong Kong media and their role in society.

Dr. Luwei Rose LUQIU
Former TV Journalist and Assistant Professor, Hong Kong Baptist University

# Table of Contents

Introduction ⸻ 1

## Part I  Traditional Media

1. The Landscape of Newspapers in Hong Kong ⸻ 13
   *Bess WANG and Tin Chi WONG*

2. An Overview of Telecommunications,
   English Press and Magazines in Hong Kong ⸻ 31
   *C. K. LAU and Siu Wai CHEUNG*

3. Allies and Foes: The Impact of Technological Convergence
   and Public Participation on TV Journalism in Hong Kong ⸻ 47
   *Florin C. SERBAN*

4. The State of the Radio Sector in Hong Kong ⸻ 63
   *Jenny LAM*

## Part II  New Media

5. The Emergence of Internet Media in Hong Kong ⸻ 85
   *Alice Y. L. LEE*

6. Social Media in Hong Kong's Changing Ecology
   of News Production and Consumption ⸻ 99
   *Roselyn DU and Alex TANG*

7. Social Media Use in Hong Kong ⸻ 115
   *Ke ZHANG and Yunya SONG*

## Part III  Media Credibility

8.  A Report on Public Evaluations of Media Credibility
    in Hong Kong ——————————————————————— 135
    *Steve GUO*

9.  Feel Real, Feel Credible: Animated News and Credibility ———— 151
    *Wai Han LO and Benjamin K. L. CHENG*

## Part IV  Public Relations and Advertising

10. Public Relations Developments in Hong Kong:
    Twenty Years after the Handover ————————————————— 169
    *Angela K. Y. MAK, Regina Y. R. CHEN, Lennon L. L. TSANG
    and Hyun Jee OH*

11. Media Change and the State of the Advertising Industry
    in Hong Kong ——————————————————————————— 193
    *Kineta H. K. HUNG*

12. Contemporary Advertising Industry:
    Profiling Top Advertisers in Hong Kong ————————————— 201
    *Terri H. CHAN*

13. Creative Professionals' Perceptions of Creativity
    in Hong Kong ——————————————————————————— 213
    *Vivienne S. Y. LEUNG*

14. Attitudes towards Advertising ———————————————————— 225
    *Kara CHAN*

15. Public Complaints against Advertising
    on Licensed Broadcasting Services in Hong Kong ———————— 235
    *Maggie S. K. FUNG*

# Part V  Communication and Society

16. Media and Populations in Hong Kong ———————————— 251
   *Tien Ee Dominic YEO*

17. An Overview of Health Communication Research
   in Hong Kong ———————————————————————— 267
   *Timothy K. F. FUNG, Terri H. CHAN, Yu-Leung NG,*
   *Sice WU and Jun LAM*

18. Post-Democratic and Pre-Democratic Movements:
   From "Sunflower" in Taiwan to "Umbrella" in Hong Kong ———— 281
   *Ringo MA*

# Introduction

*Yu HUANG and Yunya SONG*

The year 2017 marked the twentieth anniversary of Hong Kong's return to Chinese sovereignty. Round-number anniversaries like this one are good moments for scholars to look back and analyse what has changed and what has stayed the same since the important event. For researchers at Hong Kong Baptist University's School of Communication, the two-decade mark provides a good opportunity to examine the state of the territory's media today. "One country, two systems"—the coexistence of China's communism and Hong Kong's free-market capitalism—has been the governing principle for Hong Kong, and this pairing of opposites has resulted in fluctuating levels of cooperation and tension. This applies to the media and communication sectors as much as any other areas of life in Hong Kong.

The main task of this edited volume is a difficult one: to capture the current state of Hong Kong's media and communications development, media education, advertising and public relations (PR) research, and evaluate their application. The problem is not so much in the themes themselves but in the major changes witnessed by Hong Kong society, in general. As the contributors to this volume aptly highlight, what is happening in the media has its roots in the deep and diverse changes that are taking place in society, politics, ideology, economics and technology. The difficulty in discussing the transformations of media and communication professions themselves—such as journalism, PR, advertising and so on—is compounded by the complexity of its causes.

Providing an in-depth analysis for the main communication and media sectors in Hong Kong, this volume identifies the difficulties and opportunities of media professionals to engage with their audiences. At the same time, some of the authors highlight how the audience—through their rituals of consumption—have an evolving role in deciding the fate of media and communication industries.

Researchers from the Anglo-American realm point to technology and economics as the main basis for the media transformation of recent years. The process in the Western sphere involves the decrease in revenue for traditional media industries due to the shift from the one-to-many model of communication to a many-to-many model in which the public can circumvent established media outlets. In Hong Kong, which has, as the authors of this volume point out, one of the highest penetration rates of technological convergence and the world's freest economy, the processes of change have been further complicated by the social tumult that erupted in in the autumn of 2014, when the students took to the streets in a mass protest known as Occupy Central and dubbed by the international media the Umbrella Revolution. These political developments have added extra layers to the task of analysing media changes in the territory, making it particularly difficult to take a snapshot of the current situation. With digital technology bringing about extreme changes in the ways media is produced, distributed and consumed, journalists and other communication professionals are striving hard to stay up-to-date, but sometimes this is not enough to keep their media profitable or even to keep their jobs.

## The State of Hong Kong's Media Twenty Years On

In recent months, one of the most respected media institutions in Hong Kong—Cable News—has been struggling with what are, on the surface at least, financial problems. The parent company announced it will not be able to finance Cable's operations in the future because television is becoming less and less profitable. We have yet to see whether the business can be saved in the long run, but there are voices suggesting the issue is not just a question of audience and profitability. The reporters of this television station are known not to hide their criticism of the Beijing government when necessary, and some think the parent company wishes to sell in order to protect its other business interests from possible political backlash. This is a prime example of how media development in Hong Kong operates at levels and in contexts that are much more nuanced than in the Anglo-American context.

The question of how China would deal with Hong Kong after 1997 dominated the public sphere both before and immediately after the handover.

Fears of fast changes in cultural policies proved to be unfounded, and, twenty years later, Hong Kong looks robust in its ability to maintain a high level of freedom of speech. The media today remains outspoken in its criticism of the local administration. Nevertheless, the autonomy of Hong Kong remains a hot topic of discussion, with a growing presence of political groups calling for localism. One could argue this is the direct result of the failure of political and electoral reform packages offered by Beijing. As highlighted by the Occupy Central social movement, those who were very young in 1997 are today at the forefront of political groups calling for Hong Kong's independence. The older generation, expecting worse, were just relieved that freedom of speech was maintained after 1997. The new generation, very young at the time or not even born then, have experienced the territory's high educational standards and been able to learn about the liberties and rights that are present in functional democracies around the world but missing in Hong Kong. Thus, the transformations Hong Kong has gone through in the past twenty years and the challenges it faces today are related to the coming of age of this younger generation. As we will see in the chapters of this volume, they have different media consumption habits, both in terms of the news they consume and the technological devices they use to receive, create and distribute content. Just as important for media producers and advertisers, the young have very different media preferences from their parents.

## Introducing the Chapters

This book provides case studies and analyses in several fields of Hong Kong's communication sector: traditional media, new media, PR and advertising, media education, media credibility, health communication and street movements. The articles are written from a vast array of theoretical standpoints and rely on both quantitative and qualitative methodologies. The contributors are all specialists in their fields of research and have strong voices in the local research realm. Their contributions are clustered into themes.

Part I starts with a chapter authored by Bess Wang and Tinchi Wong who provide an overview of the distribution and consumption of newspapers in Hong Kong. Their analysis shows that young people do not read newspapers in high numbers. There is also a gap in which newspapers different generations read, with young people tending to read *Apple Daily* and older people *Oriental Daily News*. Thus, we can argue that the polarisation of politics is also visible in the choice of newspaper, as *Apple Daily* is perceived as a pro-democracy newspaper, though with low credibility, and *Oriental Daily News*, once pro-Kuomintang in stance in its early years, is perceived as being pro-establishment since the handover.

C. K. Lau and Siu Wai Cheung present an overview of the telecommunications, magazines and English-language newspapers in Hong Kong. The telecommunications market in Hong Kong remains a liberal one, with a free flow of information. The government imposes no control on the number of service providers and no restrictions on foreign investment in media outlets. The high state of deregulation sped up the penetration of mobile services, with, at the end of 2016, 16.72 million subscribers in a population of just over 7 million. The news magazine industry in Hong Kong is also facing financial turmoil. All three types of magazines—local, political gossip and international—face shrinking revenues. The owners of these magazines are concerned and anxious as they face unprecedented challenges in a city that moves faster and faster, allowing less and less time for the reading of long-form stories. There is also media saturation in this segment of the media business, and it is difficult to imagine that many of the magazines currently available on the market will survive in the long term. The English-press market was once dominated by the *South China Morning Post* (*SCMP*), which back in the day built up a domestic and international reputation as a trustworthy source of news on China. Today, despite a decline in its reputation due to its perceived support of the pro-Beijing camp, it continues to be an important source of information for those who live in Hong Kong but are not literate in Chinese. Recently, the online version of the *SCMP* removed its paywall, so anyone can access its news at no cost. Other competitors are the free newspaper *The Standard* and also Hong Kong Free Press (HKFP), an online-only media outlet which finances itself mostly from the donations of its readers. It is interesting to notice that the main competitors for the English-language market in Hong Kong are a newspaper with a long history and a new media website with an online-only business model. It is worth paying attention to see which one will dominate the market in the years to come.

Florin C. Serban provides a first-hand examination of the difficulties faced by television journalists who must deal with technological convergence and public participation. These two processes are affecting the journalistic work, but perhaps surprisingly, they are not as disruptive in Hong Kong as they are elsewhere in the world. This is because Hong Kong journalists are early adopters of technological gadgets and, especially television journalists, have extensive experience with using technology in their daily work. Instead of making the journalistic practices more complicated, technological convergence may help journalists to better connect with their audiences.

In "The State of the Radio Sector in Hong Kong", Jenny Lam thoroughly examines the radio market in Hong Kong. Radio Television Hong Kong is highlighted as the most trusted of the electronic media, thus fulfilling its mission as a public service broadcaster. However, less than 5% of the population listen to radio news regularly, a problem which radio companies will have to tackle in the near future if they want to keep themselves in the market. It is interesting to note that the audience is clearly segmented between those older than fifty, who listen to programmes on analogue radio sets, and younger listeners, who tend to use their smartphones to tune in. Radio stations in Hong Kong also face the challenge of having to digitise their operations—an extremely high cost given the low revenues—at a time when their audience is declining. It is likely that radio operators will have to cater to younger audiences if they want to survive in the long run.

The second part of the book examines new media in Hong Kong. Compared to Part I, which deals mainly with traditional media, the outlook for new media is not as bleak. As Alice Lee points out, internet media in Hong Kong are positioning themselves as strong rivals to old mainstream media, and do a much better job in reaching a younger audience. There is a connection between the arrival of many alternative new media sites and the social movements Hong Kong is getting used to. One of them, InMedia Hong Kong, was established in October 2004 by a group of social activists and public intellectuals. These new outlets are perceived by their public (especially the young ones) as addressing problems that are closer to their interests, unlike the traditional media, which mostly discuss social themes of concern to the establishment. The main challenges faced by these new media outlets are: to be recognised as professional entities in the field and financing themselves without corporate support, like that offered to traditional media sources.

The chapter by Roselyn Du and Alex Tang examines the role of social media in Hong Kong's changing ecology of news production and consumption. According to their research, Facebook is the first place of contact for reading breaking news in Hong Kong. This should not be surprising, as the average daily time spent on social media by locals is 1.5 hours, a situation that has come about largely because of the fast penetration of digital technologies in the territory. In terms of news production, they examine the use of digital and social media by mainstream journalists. Television Broadcasts Limited (TVB) distinguishes itself by having a much stronger social media presence than any of its competitors. In fact, many of the social media accounts of mainstream news outlets have little engagement with users. One reason for this is the lack of dedicated staff to push content out on social media platforms. The article also points to some very interesting online behaviour of traditional media: in an attempt to reach a younger audience, some radio stations set up Instagram accounts, which are for posting pictures. This is very interesting because the audio nature of the medium is displaced in the online realm to cater to the visual needs of the younger audience.

Ke Zhang and Yunya Song discuss the public's use of social media, noting that WhatsApp and Facebook are the two most used platforms in Hong Kong. The authors point out that social media platforms popular in Mainland China, such as WeChat and Weibo, have yet to gain traction in the Hong Kong market. In turn, this could explain why content originating in China on these social platforms is not popular in Hong Kong.

Part III deals with the credibility of media in Hong Kong. In his contribution, Steve Guo takes an off-the-beaten-track perspective as he examines what media credibility means for the audience, rather than what it means for academics and journalists themselves. Based on focus groups and surveys, his research shows that readers' perceptions of credibility are very tied to the perceived ideology of the newspaper. Thus, a rise in a newspaper's readership can be explained not by a paper's credibility, but by its stance — pro-democracy or pro-Beijing. It is also very interesting to note that media credibility is a marginal issue in people's choice of what to read. For example, although *Ming Pao* is perceived to be one of the most credible media outlets in Hong Kong, it does not have the same number of readers as other newspapers—especially *Apple Daily*—that score low in credibility. Thus, although it might seem surprising, especially given the previous research on this topic, it seems that, in Hong Kong, media credibility is not the main gratifier for audiences. Everyday people do not take these processes into account in their daily decisions of what to read, what radio station to listen to, or what television channels to watch.

Wai Han Lo and Benjamin Cheng investigate how animation, as a presentation feature, influences perceived credibility, its relationship with the concept of "presence" and with media dependency and use. They first illustrate the recent development of melodramatic animated news and how media use and dependency may interact with animation to influence perceived news credibility. Then, they discuss why the concept of presence can be the mediator of the relationship between animation and perceived news credibility. Finally, a discussion of two research findings and their implications for future research is provided.

Part IV is concerned with the development of PR and advertising in Hong Kong. Relying on interviews with local PR leaders, the authors—Angela Mak, Regina Chen, Lennon Tsang and Hyun Jee Oh—describe the main challenges PR professionals are facing in detail. Remarkable in this article is the information given the by PR "gurus", providing both a list of challenges and several proposals for guidelines that could fix the current problems. The PR industry is under severe stress because the business environment, the employment environment, the new media environment and the relationships with stakeholders are all changing. The Hong Kong PR industry is changing from being a stepping stone for companies that wish to enter Mainland China for business to one that works primarily for the local market. Technology is also a game changer for PR as the public become more engaged with gadgets and spend less time reading and watching traditional media. To address these issues, PR professionals should learn how to talk with the public, and not just limit themselves to talking to it. Interactivity might be a buzzword, but it is identified as a crucial feature that will have to be taken into account by future PR professionals if they want their organisation to succeed. This can in fact be easily done with the help of digital and networked gadgets that Hong Kong people enjoy using so much. Thus, PR companies will have to build on their localised marketing strategies, recruit local talent and find clients with a proper understanding of the role of a PR company.

Advertising in Hong Kong is also discussed in this part. Kineta Hung points out that, now more than ever, advertisers must reconsider their practices as they must share the stage with the audience. For revenue reasons, the industry must now follow the audience, with the desirable demographics now online more than ever. Given the decline of print, advertisers are spending more and more time and money on social media, and the figures show that interactive and mobile ads gathered more than three times the amount of revenue compared with that spent on radio advertising, for example. Although the numbers for TV advertising (31% in 2015) and newspaper advertising (29% in 2015) are still high, it is expected that more and more will be spent in coming years on interactive and mobile ads. A quarter of the jobs currently available in advertising are for social media. Thus, the industry is in growing need of professionals who have the skills and knowledge to carry out advertising in the online realm. Also, given the high number of tourists in Hong Kong, those entering the advertising business will need to have insights not only into local residents but also inbound visitors.

In their contributions, Terri Chan and Vivienne Leung argue that the ad industry must find better ways to connect and engage with a digital-native audience. The top spender in the advertising industry is the Hong Kong government, which invested close to HK$2 billion in public campaigns. Financial companies, such as banks and investment funds, are close behind, ahead of pharmaceutical and health companies. Local advertising agencies like to distinguish themselves based on the awards they receive, and for this they need to be more resourceful. Based on qualitative interviews with several creative professionals in the advertising sector, the article finds that creativity is crucial for advertising. However, creativity should not be carried out for the sake of itself, but must be anchored in practicality. The interviewees point out that advertising is more creative in the Hong Kong market than in Mainland China, with strategic planning being a key driver to promotional effectiveness. It is important to strike a balance between creativity and practicality, especially in the Chinese culture with its high value on harmony and personal prestige.

Kara Chan shifts the focus as she looks at attitudes towards specific advertisements in Hong Kong, examining consumers' reactions to them. Generally, consumers have a positive outlook towards television advertising, with less than 10% considering it to be bad. Furthermore, younger respondents are neutral towards advertising in general, while older generations show some liking of advertising. It is worth pointing out that the level of income is an important variable as well. The higher the income of those interviewed, the higher the possibility that they would consider advertising a good thing.

Maggie Fung assesses public complaints made to the advertising standards and regulatory body—the Communication Authority. Though Hong Kong has a liberal approach to advertising, any individual can file a complaint.

In 2014 and 2015, the regulatory body received sixteen advertising-related complaints, with an overwhelming number of grievances related to the embedding of advertising material within TV and radio programmes and the extensive display of sponsored material. However, with the expansion of social networking platforms, more complaints are being voiced in the online realm, thus not ending up with the regulatory body. In Hong Kong, there is no legislation or regulation for online media, and this could encourage some advertisers to explore advertising practices as they wish.

The final part of this volume deals with communication and society in Hong Kong. The themes discussed are media and populations, the state of health research and the pro-democratic movements. Dominic Yeo discusses media-related issues and problems that are faced by some minority populations (i.e., sexual minorities, ethnic minorities, youth and the elderly) in Hong Kong. He examines their relationships with both traditional and new media over the last decade. The public still has limited and biased exposure to LGBT issues given the lack of coverage in the local media, while the rise of social media brings more opportunities for LGBT individuals to stay connected and raise public awareness. Ethnic minorities in the city also experience negative media coverage, and the media often shape people's understanding of the ethnic groups they report on. More than 80% of the population of Hong Kong has access to the internet, with the local mobile penetration rate exceeded 230%. Yeo's study also examines two age groups—the young and the elderly, by revealing some of their experiences when navigating the internet.

The medical system in Hong Kong relies on a mix of Chinese and Western values. Timothy Fung, Terri Chan, Yu-Leung Ng, Sice Wu, and Jun Lam systematically review health communication literature in the territory to see which journals publish Hong Kong-based research; what the prevailing theoretical and methodological approaches are; and what countries, media and diseases scholars focus on. The results show that almost 150 journal articles were published in the past twenty-five years, with 40% focused on the Hong Kong region, and they used both quantitative and qualitative approaches. Survey and content analysis were the preferred research methods for local scholars. This study highlights the low presence of theory building and comparative research for local scholars as well as the significance of health communication in the unique cultural context present in Hong Kong.

The final article of this volume is authored by Ringo Ma and draws a comparison between the street movements that took place in Taiwan and Hong Kong in 2014. Ma argues that although the two events have plenty of similarities at first glance, they were quite different in nature. This is because the political and cultural contexts for both territories were quite different: while Taiwan had already experienced two significant changes in power and in 2014 was a full democracy, Hong Kong did not have a fully democratic system. The Sunflower Movement in Taiwan aimed to trigger an awakening of its citizens, a reaction to the shortcomings of the representative system in their democracy. On the other hand, Hong Kong's Occupy Central can only be considered a democratic movement within a dictatorship. Thus, both social movements occurred in different stages of democratic development, with the Taiwan movement being, of course, more advanced. Despite the numerous similarities in the objectives of the two movements, Ma argues that Occupy Central should not be perceived as a replica of the Sunflower Movement, as it was very different in nature. Instead, the two movements taking place in the same year should be seen more as a coincidence and as special cases for research into multi-society movements.

It is impossible to envision how Hong Kong media will develop over the next twenty years. Nevertheless, the safest bet is to assume that media professionals in Hong Kong should expect both exciting and difficult times in the near future. A continuous decline in audience will likely push media professionals to envision new ways of connecting with their public. Technological developments will continue to influence the media and communications landscape. This will have consequences in the way media professionals are trained, the performance of their daily duties, and the role they play in society as communication leaders. Just as well, as there is no indication that the influence of Mainland China will decline in these sectors. It is up to media and communication professionals in the territory to find the best ways to remain relevant in an ever-growing competitive market. It is our hope that this edited volume will stand the test of time and provide a reference point in a time when the media and communication sectors were at a crossroad in their developments.

# Part I

Traditional Media

# Chapter 1

# The Landscape of Newspapers in Hong Kong

*Bess WANG and Tin Chi WONG*

## Introduction

Despite the increasing penetration of digital news media, newspapers are still important in Hong Kong. In the second half of 2016, Hong Kong had a population of about seven million and there were eleven major paid newspapers, namely *Apple Daily, Oriental Daily News, Ming Pao, Sing Tao Daily, Sing Pao Daily News, The Hong Kong Economic Journal, Hong Kong Economic Times, South China Morning Post, Wen Wei Po, Ta Kung Pao* and *Hong Kong Commercial Daily*. In addition, there was a weekly paid newspaper, *HK01*, and five free newspapers: *Metro Daily, AM730, Headline Daily, Sky Post* and *The Standard*. All are in Chinese except *South China Morning Post* and *The Standard*, which are in English. This chapter describes the landscape of paid newspapers and the basic features of their readership.

## Political Stance

Since the handover of Hong Kong's sovereignty to China in 1997, political, economic and social interaction between Hong Kong and Mainland China has increased, resulting in cooperation but also producing tension and polarising politics into camps supportive of Beijing on one side and supportive of greater democracy on the other. The major newspapers may be categorised in a similarly dichotomous manner, into, for example, pro-local versus pro-China

(Chan & Lee, 2011; Lee & Lin, 2006), pro-democracy versus pro-establishment, or leftist versus rightist. Among the newspapers, *Apple Daily* is normally regarded as pro-local and pro-democracy and sometimes called rightist, while *Wen Wei Po*, *Ta Kung Pao* and *Hong Kong Commercial Daily* are pro-China and pro-establishment, sometimes called leftist. Other newspapers take a more centrist stance and many practice neutrality and objectivity as a strategy in the face of political pressure (Lee, 2007a, 2007b). Critics of self-censorship on the part of these papers accuse them of implementing "a set of editorial actions ranging from omission, dilution, distortion, [and] change of emphasis, to choice of rhetorical devices" (Lee, 1998) to avoid trouble. When it came to coverage of the controversial legislation proposed in 2003 to implement security measures under Article 23 of the Basic Law—eventually shelved after massive protests—a content analysis found that the pro-China papers were, as expected, significantly supportive of the legislation, the centrist papers were more neutral in their coverage and occasionally tilted towards a more critical stance, while *Apple Daily* explicitly advocated social action against the legislation (So, 2003). Similar observations may be made about more recent issues such as the Occupy Central movement, the 2014 protests which called for universal suffrage.

## Readership

According to a survey (n=1,012) conducted in 2016 by the Hong Kong Baptist University School of Communication, newspapers (both print and digital) are still the most frequently used source of news in Hong Kong, if by a small margin. Among the people surveyed, 35.9% reported using newspapers to get news, while the figure for television was 35.1%, and for other platforms—radio, non-press websites and social media—27%.

*Apple Daily* was the most popular newspaper, with 35.3% of respondents saying they read it (Table 1.1). The second most read paper was *Oriental Daily News* (22.8%). *Ming Pao* came third with 9.1%. The two financial papers had very few readers—*The Hong Kong Economic Journal* was read by 1.4% of respondents and *Hong Kong Economic Times* by 2.4%. As for the free papers, more than 20% of respondents reported reading them. Overall though, the reality is that many people do not read newspapers at all: 15.9% reported they never read any, whether printed or digital. Of respondents who reported reading newspapers (n=851), 27.5% read news on websites, while 28.8% used

**Table 1.1**

**Newspaper Readership**

| | Number of Respondents who Read the Outlet | Percentage of All Respondents (%) |
|---|---|---|
| *Apple Daily* | 357 | 35.3 |
| *Oriental Daily News* | 231 | 22.8 |
| *Ming Pao* | 92 | 9.1 |
| *Sing Tao Daily* | 43 | 4.2 |
| *Hong Kong Economic Journal* | 24 | 2.4 |
| Free newspapers | 214 | 21.1 |
| *South China Morning Post* | 10 | 1.0 |
| *Wen Wei Po and Ta Kung Pao* | 8 | 0.8 |
| Not reading any newspapers | 161 | 15.9 |

mobile apps. Notably, nearly half of all respondents read printed papers, indicating that the print platform is still important.

The time spent on reading newspapers is another indicator of Hong Kong people's dependence on them. About 60% of the respondents reported spending fifteen minutes to an hour daily reading newspapers, and 20% more than an hour daily.

## Demographic Factors

A series of statistical tests was conducted to examine the demographic factors shaping people's experience of news reading, including age, family income and education level. The results in Table 1.2 indicate that readers from different demographics tended to select different newspapers and platforms (print, websites or mobile apps). Education was an important factor in choice of platform. Respondents with primary-level education tended to read printed newspapers, while those educated to university level were more likely to use digital platforms. Of all respondents using websites, 46.5% had tertiary education. Among those reporting that they used mobile apps, 52.1% were university graduates.

Age was also significantly related to the respondents' selection of media platforms. Of all those using print media, only 8.2% were 29 years old or younger. Of all of the respondents using websites, only 7.9% were 60 years old or older. Of those using mobile apps, only 5.9% were 60 or older. This indicates that many young people have abandoned traditional print media.

The same demographic factors also contribute to people's choice of newspapers. The three most read papers—*Apple Daily*, *Oriental Daily News*

**Table 1.2**

**News Platforms, Education Levels,
Age and Monthly Family Incomes of the Respondents**

|  | Print | Websites | Mobile Apps |
|---|---|---|---|
| **Education** | | | |
| Primary | 20.0% | 5.3% | 4.2% |
| Secondary | 57.4% | 48.2% | 43.8% |
| University | 22.4% | 46.5% | 52.1% |
| N/A | 0.2% | 0.0% | 0.0% |
|  | $n=465, \chi^2=78.80$** | $n=228, \chi^2=31.86$** | $n=240, \chi^2=59.61$** |
| **Age** | | | |
| 18–29 | 8.2% | 26.9% | 34.7% |
| 30–59 | 57.0% | 65.2% | 59.4% |
| 60 or above | 34.8% | 7.9% | 5.9% |
|  | $n=463, \chi=142.47$** | $n=227, \chi^2=39.00$** | $n=239, \chi^2=79.80$** |
| **Monthly Family Income** | | | |
| $9,999 or below | 15.4% | 5.3% | 2.5% |
| $10,000–19,999 | 19.9% | 11.9% | 12.5% |
| $20,000–39,999 | 28.1% | 32.2% | 31.3% |
| $40,000–59,999 | 10.5% | 20.7% | 20.0% |
| $60,000 or above | 8.1% | 18.5% | 18.3% |
| N/A | 18.0% | 11.5% | 15.4% |
|  | $n=467, \chi^2=69.78$** | $n=227, \chi^2=32.39$** | $n=240, \chi^2=37.65$** |

*\*\*p<.001, \*p<.05*

and *Ming Pao*—were tested. The results suggest that people 60 years old or above are less likely to read *Apple Daily* (only 13.8% did so), and young people tend not to read *Oriental Daily News* (only 8.0% said they did). In terms of education, readers of *Apple Daily* and *Ming Pao* were more highly educated than those reading *Oriental Daily News*. The family income of readers of *Oriental Daily News* was also lower than that of readers of *Apple Daily* and *Ming Pao*, as shown in Table 1.3.

**Table 1.3**

**Demographic Factors and Choice of Newspapers**

|  | *Apple Daily* | *Oriental Daily News* | *Ming Pao* |
|---|---|---|---|
| **Education** | | | |
| Primary | 6.9% | 20.1% | 5.8% |
| Secondary | 52.6% | 63.8% | 37.2% |
| University | 40.5% | 16.1% | 57.0% |
|  | $n$=363, $\chi^2$=52.71** | $n$=249, $\chi^2$=39.44** | $n$=86, $\chi^2$=30.05** |
| **Age** | | | |
| 18–29 | 30.1% | 8.0% | 29.4% |
| 30–59 | 56.1% | 62.8% | 50.6% |
| 60 or Above | 13.8% | 29.2% | 20.0% |
|  | $n$=362, $\chi^2$=78.24** | $n$=250, $\chi^2$=22.44** | $n$=85, $\chi^2$=8.45* |
| **Monthly Family Income** | | | |
| $9,999 or below | 4.4% | 13.3% | 3.5% |
| $10,000–19,999 | 14.0% | 20.1% | 11.6% |
| $20,000–39,999 | 32.0% | 32.1% | 24.4% |
| $40,000–59,999 | 20.1% | 10.4% | 16.3% |
| $60,000 or above | 13.8% | 8.0% | 20.9% |
| N/A | 15.7% | 16.1% | 23.2% |
|  | $n$=363, $\chi^2$=52.34** | $n$=249, $\chi^2$=13.70* | $n$=86, $\chi^2$=17.44** |

**$p<.001$, *$p<.05$

## Major Newspapers

### Apple Daily

*Apple Daily* was launched by Jimmy Lai Chee-ying on 20 June 1995. The newspaper is published by the company Next Digital, previously known as Next Media. Considered as having a brash and blunt reporting style, *Apple Daily* holds an anti-government political stance, which is almost unseen in other major newspapers (Li, 2014). Despite being subjective in reporting, having low credibility (Centre for Communication and Public Opinion Survey, 2014) and even being suspected of faking (Chen Jiankang, 1998) and exaggerating news, *Apple Daily* is still the most read newspaper in Hong Kong. Most of its readers are pro-democracy in their political views. However, the political stance of the newspaper has affected its revenue from advertisements. Several major local property developers stopped advertising in it in 2003 because of its support for the protests against the proposed Article 23 legislation, and when Jimmy Lai openly supported the Occupy Central movement in 2014, three major banks cancelled their advertisements as well ("Tamed Hounds", 2014).

Jimmy Lai left his position in the company after being arrested during the Occupy Central movement, and Ip Yut-kin became the new editor-in-chief (Kwok & Jim, 2014). In March 2015, Chan Pui-man succeeded Ip and became the first female editor-in-chief of the newspaper (Kwok, 2015). The sharp loss in revenue, mainly from advertising, is believed to have led to a downsizing of the breaking news team and the editorial department in 2016 (Pingguo, 2016).

*Apple Daily* was among the first newspapers in Hong Kong to introduce news-in-motion, which features news with animations. It manages a Facebook page which had around two million likes in September 2016. Yet, according to the *South China Morning Post*, the paper has been considering charging readers for its online content due to the decline in the paper's online and offline advertisements (Lam, 2018).

### Hong Kong Commercial Daily

The *Hong Kong Commercial Daily* is a business-oriented newspaper founded on 11 October 1952. During the early years of its establishment, the newspaper aimed to provide accurate information about local and Chinese commerce. It is one of the few newspapers authorised to publish the Hong Kong government's legal announcements, and one of the few Hong Kong newspapers allowed to circulate freely in Mainland China.

In December 1989, the Joint Publishing (HK) Company Limited became the largest shareholder of the newspaper. In 1999, the Shenzhen Press Group, a Mainland publisher, acquired the newspaper. The Beijing government positions the *Hong Kong Commercial Daily* as "China's window to the international media", promoting the Mainland to foreign readers and reporting international affairs for Chinese readers (Guanyu Shangbao, n.d.).

As a result of its positioning, the paper's readers are mostly investors and businesspeople in Hong Kong and Mainland China, especially in the Pearl River Delta region and special economic zones, such as Shenzhen. The online version of the newspaper can be read without payment.

## Ta Kung Pao

*Ta Kung Pao* is the oldest active Chinese-language newspaper in China, having been founded in 1902 in the late Qing Dynasty. The period from 1926 to 1949 was its golden age (Jiang, 2011), during which it received significant recognition for the quality of its news reporting (Weiyi, 2016). Its Hong Kong edition was launched in 1938.

In 1948, it became pro-Communist (Cai, 2011). After the establishment of the People's Republic of China in 1949, it was taken over by the state. Currently, the newspaper is highly pro-Beijing. Its articles and commentaries criticise people from the pro-democratic camp and others who have anti-China views. News stories are also biased towards the Chinese government. According to a survey in 2013, *Ta Kung Pao* was ranked among the lowest of all major newspapers in Hong Kong in terms of credibility (Centre for Communication and Public Opinion Survey, 2014). While the majority of readers are from Mainland China (*Ta Kung Pao*, n.d.), the readership of the Hong Kong version is mostly the pro-Beijing older generation.

*Ta Kung Pao* set up its website in 1995 and was one of the first Chinese newspapers to do so (Dagongwang jianjie, n.d.). The online version of the newspaper can be read for free. In 2016, *Ta Kung Pao* and *Wen Wei Po* merged to form the Ta Kung Wen Wei Media Group (*Wen Wei Po, Ta Kung Pao* announce merger, 2016).

## Wen Wei Po

*Wen Wei Po* was established in Shanghai in January 1938. Its Hong Kong edition was launched in September 1948. Like *Ta Kung Pao*, it is one of the few newspapers authorised to publish the Hong Kong government's legal announcements and one of the few Hong Kong newspapers allowed to circulate freely in Mainland China. The online version of the newspaper can be read without payment.

Also like *Ta Kung Pao*, *Wen Wei Po* is state-owned. With the mission of "loving the country, loving Hong Kong", it is firmly pro-Beijing. Interestingly, back in 1989, its editorial board openly opposed and criticised the use of force by the People's Liberation Army in ending the Tiananmen Square protests in its editorial. Lee Tze-chung, the president for 38 years, was dismissed from duties afterwards, and Kam Yiu-yu, the then editor-in-chief, fled to the United States (*The Editor*, 2012). (Articles published by *Wen Wei Po* on the June Fourth Incident can be found at http://www.64memo.com/b5/7727.htm)

Again, just as in the case of *Ta Kung*, according to the 2013 survey mentioned above, *Wen Wei Po* was ranked among the lowest in credibility of all major newspapers in Hong Kong (Centre for Communication and Public Opinion Survey, 2014). While the majority of its readers are from China, its Hong Kong readership is mostly the older pro-Beijing generation. Many of its advertisements come from Mainland organisations.

As mentioned previously, in 2016, *Wen Wei Po* and *Ta Kung Pao* merged to form the Ta Kung Wen Wei Media Group (Wen Wei Po, Ta Kung Pao announce merger, 2016).

## Sing Pao Daily News

*Sing Pao Daily News* was founded in May 1939 by Ho Man-fat, a journalist who originally worked in Guangzhou. The newspaper reached its golden era in the 1950s, when it supplied almost half of the Hong Kong newspaper market (*Annual Report on Hong Kong*, 1955). However, the founding of the more up-to-date *Oriental Daily News* and *Apple Daily* in 1969 and 1995, respectively, caused sales of *Sing Pao* to decline.

In recent years, the ownership of *Sing Pao* has changed three times. It was first sold to Optima Media Holding for HK$150 million in 2000 (Jinnian wei shouguo zu, 2006), then passed to Sun Television Cybernetworks for HK$100 million ("Yangguang gou Chengbao", 2002), and in 2004 was acquired by businessman Qin Hui (Qin Hui, n.d.).

Unfortunately, these transfers of ownership did not revive the newspaper, and there have been frequent reports of financial difficulties. In 2006, it laid off thirty employees, amounting to 8% of its staff (Jiaodai qianxin, 2006). In 2008, *Sing Pao* was fined for failing to pay mandatory provident fund contributions for two staff members (Sing Pao fined, 2008). The same year, businessman Carson Yeung Ka-sing provided a loan of HK$60 million to *Sing Pao*'s parent company. Two years later Qin transferred his shares to Yeung, who took over the paper completely (Toh, 2010). In 2011, Tian Bingxing became the president of *Sing Pao*. In 2014, Chong Cha Hwa became the chairman of the board, but he resigned in the same year and was succeeded by Gu Zhuoheng.

In April 2015, creditor Korchina Culture filed a statutory demand notice on *Sing Pao*, which led the paper to seek a loan of HK$110 million. It stopped publication for several weeks beginning 17 July 2015 because it could not pay its printer, but the online version was unaffected during this period. On 12 August 2015, the High Court ruled that the paper's indebted parent company, Sing Pao Media Enterprises, should be liquidated. *Sing Pao* itself survived, however, and continued publishing (Chu, 2015).

*Sing Pao* is known for its pro-Beijing stance. However, it surprised Hong Kong people when it stepped out of character and criticised C. Y. Leung, the chief executive of Hong Kong, and Zhang Xiaoming, the director of the Liaison Office of the Central People's Government in Hong Kong, in consecutive front-page articles around 30 August 2016 (Chengbao touban hong Liang Zhenying, 2016; Chengbao touban zai hong Liang Zhenying, 2016).

## Oriental Daily News

*Oriental Daily News* was established in 1969 by two brothers: Ma Sik-chun and Ma Sik-yu. Since then, it has been owned and run by the Oriental Press Group. The group also published *The Sun*, another mainstream newspaper, which lasted 17 years until its closure in April 2016. Ricky Ma Ching-fat is the current chairperson. *Oriental Daily News* claims that it has been the most circulated newspaper in Hong Kong for 38 consecutive years. It was pro-Nationalist (Kuomintang) in its early years but since Hong Kong's handover in 1997, it has been pro-establishment.

*Oriental Daily News* is Hong Kong's most active newspaper when it comes to filing lawsuits against different people and organisations. It is very sensitive about perceived defamation by netizens and in online discussion forums (Duli Meiti, 2012; Dongfang Baoye kong Uwants, 2012). *Oriental Daily News* has been in keen competition with *Apple Daily* since the latter's establishment. *Oriental* has criticised *Apple Daily* for publishing sexually explicit material (Tanshedeng: Taibei yingqi yinmei, 2009) and infringing copyright (Dongfang rubing, 2008). Its news reports and commentaries regularly criticise Next Media (now Next Digital), its founder Jimmy Lai and people close to him.

## Sing Tao Daily

Founded in 1938 by Aw Boon-haw, a Burmese-Chinese entrepreneur, *Sing Tao Daily* had a pro-Nationalist (Kuomintang) stance and supported the government of the Republic of China, which moved to Taiwan in 1949 after its defeat by the Communists. Until 1992, the newspaper referred to the government of the People's Republic of China as "the Communist Party" and refused to recognise it.

Aw's successor, Sally Aw Sian, sold Sing Tao Holdings to the international investment bank, Lazard Asia because of losses that she suffered during the 1997 Asian financial crisis. The family of pro-Beijing businessman Charles Ho Tsu-kwok purchased the company (SYM Lab, n.d.) and since then the political stance of the newspaper has been pro-Beijing. The new stance became clear during the controversy over the proposed Article 23 legislation; while there was fear among the public that the proposed anti-subversion law would destroy freedom of speech in Hong Kong, *Sing Tao Daily* made it clear in its columns that it supported the proposed law (Dilu yue xi, 2003). Nonetheless, the paper has provided a platform for columnists from all political camps to air their views. It also has high credibility, according to the 2013 survey mentioned previously (Centre for Communication and Public Opinion Survey, 2014). Its major target audience consists of middle class people and students.

Lai Ting-yiu has been the editor-in-chief since 2013, following the appointment of his predecessor Siu Sai-wo as an executive director and chief executive officer of the company. On 1 April 2016, the group announced a pay cut of up to 20% for its senior news executives and the freezing of the salaries of other journalists owing to the economic downturn and the intense competition in the industry. In May that year, about twenty employees were sacked. These included staff members of *Sing Tao Daily* and of the two free newspapers that the Sing Tao News Corporation publishes, namely *Headline Daily* and *The Standard*, as well as the weekly *East Touch* (Mok, 2016).

*Sing Tao Daily* was the newspaper with the second largest amount of advertising in 2015 in terms of volume. The newspaper achieved growth in property advertising, and sizeable gains were also recorded in the automobile and home and living categories (Sing Tao News Corporation Limited, 2016). It is believed that the growth in advertising revenue was partly due to the boycotting of *Apple Daily* by several major corporations in Hong Kong.

## Ming Pao

*Ming Pao* was founded by the novelist Louis Cha Leung-Yung (Jin Yong) and his friend Shen Pao Sing in 1959. Cha promoted four major philosophies through *Ming Pao*: nationalism in greater China, Confucianism, opposition to war, and conservatism. In the 1960s, *Ming Pao* expressed different views on major issues in China from those of leftist newspapers, which caused a war of words (Bianle wei de Gang mei, 2010). *Ming Pao* was sold to Yu Pun Hoi in 1991 (Chushou Mingbao, n.d.), and was taken over in 1995 by Malaysian Chinese billionaire Tiong Hiew King.

*Ming Pao* itself has been in the headlines in recent years on account of several incidents. In 2014, Kevin Lau, a former chief editor of the newspaper, was attacked and badly injured by a hitman using a knife. Local journalists regarded the assault as an attack on press freedom. Some believe it was part of the so-called white terror campaign created by the Chinese government. The second incident was the pulling of a headline story in February 2015. Chief editor Chong Tien Siong replaced a lead story about details of the June Fourth massacre with a report about a fund for young Hong Kong entrepreneurs started by Jack Ma, founder of the Chinese internet giant Alibaba (Buckley, 2015). A similar incident occurred in 2014, when a lead story was changed to put a completely different emphasis on two events (Mingbao bianwu dongshi, 2014). The most recent major event was the termination of Keung Kwok-yuen, the executive chief editor of the paper, in April 2016 (Baodao Banama Wenjian, 2016; Mingbao chao Jiang Guoyuan, 2016). *Ming Pao* published the content of the Panama Papers on 20 April 2016, and Keung was dismissed on the same day. It is widely speculated that Keung was dismissed because of the sensitive nature of the report and his friction with chief editor Chong. Yet, *Ming Pao* explained the layoff of Keung was part of a cost-cutting move.

Though *Ming Pao* is regarded as one of the most credible news outlets in Hong Kong (Centre for Communication and Public Opinion Survey, 2014), its news reporting contains frequent errors, ranging from mistakes in names to inappropriate wording and translations. Nonetheless, it is still welcomed by a diverse audience, which includes the middle class, professionals and business people. Notably, *Ming Pao* was one of the earliest Chinese newspapers to set up its website, doing so in 1995.

## Hong Kong Economic Journal

The *Hong Kong Economic Journal* (*HKEJ*) was co-founded by Lam Shan-muk, more commonly known by his pen name Lam Hang Chi, and Law Chi-Ping. It published its first issue on 3 July 1973. Businessman Richard Li Tzar-kai acquired half the shares of the journal in 2006 and bought the rest in 2014 to become its sole owner.

The *HKEJ* specialises in economic and political news. Its political stance used to be centrist with pro-democracy tendencies, but it has recetly become ambiguous, publishing highly outspoken editorials criticising both the Hong Kong and Chinese governments. However, it is considered objective and fair in its reporting. It had a high credibility rating, rivalled only by *Ming Pao* among all Chinese newspapers according to a survey covering 2001 to 2006 (Centre for Communication and Public Opinion Survey, 2014). The Chinese government regards it as a reliable source of information about Hong Kong.

In 2013, Chief Executive C. Y. Leung demanded that the *HKEJ* apologize for and retract what he considered a defamatory column by commentator Joseph Lian (Lee, 2013). While Leung's action was deemed inappropriate, the *HKEJ* later cut Lian's column in 2016 in a move perceived by many to be self-censorship (Xinbao turan quxiao, 2016).

The main bulk of *HKEJ*'s readers are professionals. Its reporting style shows a preference for words over photographs, in contrast to many other newspapers. It has been in direct competition with the *Hong Kong Economic Times* since the latter's establishment in 1988. *HKEJ* came quite late to the online revolution, constructing its website in July 2008.

## Hong Kong Economic Times

The *Hong Kong Economic Times* was founded by Lawrence Fung Siu Por, Perry Mak, Arthur Shek and others in 1988. It is similar to the *HKEJ* in its news coverage, professional writing style, high quality columns and analysis. However, the *Hong Kong Economic Times* contains entertainment sections and employs a more visually appealing layout.

It has a centrist political stance that is not as critical of the Hong Kong and Chinese governments as its competitor. Its parent company has embarked on a variety of commercial opportunities from its main outlet, publishing also *Sky Post* (a free newspaper), *e-zone* (an IT magazine), *U Magazine* (a leisure magazine) and *iMoney* (a finance magazine).

## South China Morning Post

The *South China Morning Post* (*SCMP*) is an English-language newspaper founded by Tse Tsan-tai and Alfred Cunningham in 1903. After World War II, the Hong Kong and Shanghai Bank (HSBC) became its major shareholder. It was privatised when Rupert Murdoch's News Corporation bought it in 1987 but was relisted in 1990. Kerry Media, owned by the Malaysian tycoon Robert Kuok, acquired a controlling share of the paper in 1993. The political stance of Kuok was pro-Beijing. The Kuok years were noted for frequent internal turmoil. Within an eleven-year span at the start of the twenty-first century, the paper had ten chief editors (Li, 2012), and self-censorship was commonly noted (Tan, 2012). Wang Xiangwei was promoted to the position of chief editor in 2012 and Tammy Tam, previously senior editor of the China section, was elevated to deputy editor under Wang. In January 2016, Tam was promoted to succeed Wang (Tammy Tam, 2015). In December 2015, it was announced that Jack Ma's Alibaba Group would acquire the *SCMP* (Chow, 2015). The acquisition was completed in April 2016.

Although the *SCMP* generally takes a pro-Beijing stance, its website is blocked by the Chinese authorities and not accessible to Mainland netizens (*SCMP* website, 2016). The online version can be read for free.

## HK01

*HK01* is a weekly, published every Friday. It was founded by former *Ming Pao* owner Yu Pun Hoi in 2016, and its first issue came out on 11 March of that year. However, publication was suspended from 20 January to 13 February 2017 for major content revisions. Upon its resumption, the price of the weekly was reduced from HK$20 to HK$10 with a substantial reduction in content.

Since it is a periodical, its approach is different from that of daily newspapers. It features detailed and comprehensive news reports on selected topics. Furthermore, it has changed the game of traditional media by engaging the audience not only through social media, but also through sponsored activities. The initial staff of the newspaper were mostly headhunted from other newspapers and offered high salaries. Lung King-cheong, the chief editor of *HK01*, was a former chief editor of *Ming Pao Weekly*.

## Conclusion

According to a 2016 survey conducted, print papers are still the major source of news in Hong Kong, but the edge over other forms of digital media is small. While most papers have introduced digital platforms, paper readers are typically older and less educated. The News-in-Motion by *Apple Daily* is the only exception as it attracts many young users. All print papers provide online content to readers and some elite outlets, such as *Ming Pao* and *Hong Kong Economic Journal*, adopt a subscription model. *Apple Daily* has also been considering introducing a paywall for online content due to financial pressure.

In terms of their editorial policy, the major newspapers fall along a spectrum from pro-local (sometimes called pro-democracy) to pro-China (or pro-establishment). On the pro-local end stands *Apple Daily*, holding an anti-government stance and the largest readership. Nonetheless, its popularity does not generate correspondingly handsome advertising revenue as the paper has been boycotted by most major companies which have business in Mainland China. On the pro-China end of the spectrum, there are three papers: *Wen Wei Po*, *Ta Kung Pao* and *Hong Kong Commercial Daily*. Very few people surveyed reported reading these three papers.

The other papers taking a more centrist stance show more dynamics in the tension between local readership and political pressure. They are often criticised for self-censorship and for using strategic neutrality to avoid trouble. But from time to time, they shift towards a more critical stance in covering controversial issues, such as the proposed legislation of Article 23 in 2003 or the Panama Papers in 2016. In sum, Hong Kong-based print newspapers are pressured financially by people's changing media use habits and politically by Beijing's increasing influence.

## References

*Annual Report on Hong Kong for the Year 1954.* (1955). Hong Kong: Government Printer.

"Baodao Banama Wenjian rehuo? Xianggang Mingbao zhixing zongbianji bei jishi jiegu" [Retribution for reporting the Panama Papers? Executive chief editor of *Ming Pao* summarily dismissed]. (20 April 2016). Bowen Press. Retrieved from http://bowenpress.com/news/bowen_84109.html/.

"Bianle wei de Gang mei" [Hong Kong media as a shadow of their former selves] (22 July 2010). *New Epoch Weekly*. Retrieved from http://www.epochweekly.com/b5/184/8255p2.htm

Buckley, C. "Hong Kong Newspaper Staff Protests Editor's Shifting of Tiananmen Article". *New York Times* (5 February 2015). Retrieved from http://cn.nytimes.com/china/20150205/c05hongkong/en-us/.

Cai, X. *Zhongguo Baoren* [Chinese journalists]. (2011). Taipei: Showwe Information.

Centre for Communication and Public Opinion Survey. (2014). "Xianggang xinwen chuanmei gongxinli mingxian xiajiang" [Obvious decline in credibility ratings of Hong Kong news media]. Retrieved from http://www.com.cuhk.edu.hk/ccpos/images/news/PressRelease_140102_credibility.pdf.

Chan, J. M., & Lee, F. L. F. (2011). "The Primacy of Local Interests and Press Freedom in Hong Kong: A Survey Study of Professional Journalists". *Journalism*, 12(1), 89–105.

"Chen Jiankang zibao zuoyong-youbao fahua neimu, 'mou bao bi qian wo zuo sao'" [Chan Kin Hong reveals secrets of his libido. "A newspaper paid me for a show"]. (30 October 1998). *Oriental Daily News*, p. A01.

"Chengbao touban hong Liang Zhenying Zhonglianban, pan Zhongjiwei diaocha huan Gang shehui anning" [*Sing Pao* slams CY Leung and the Liaison Office on its front-page and wishes that the CCDI would investigate and restore peace in Hong Kong]. (30 August 2016). *Ming Pao*. Retrieved from http://news.mingpao.com/ins/instantnews/web_tc/article/20160830/s00001/1472517562888

"Chengbao touban zai hong Liang Zhenying Zhonglianban, cuting weihe xiebi. Dagong zhi Chengbao zhuxi yong duozhang weizheng" [*Sing Pao* again slams CY Leung and the Liaison Office and urges them to stop their strong-arm tactics. *Tao Kung Pao* claims that Chairman of *Sing Pao* had multiple forged ID cards]. (1 September 2016). *Ming Pao*. Retrieved from http://news.mingpao.com/ins/instantnews/web_tc/article/20160901/s00001/1472690412205.

Chow, C. "Alibaba buys *South China Morning Post* Group's media business, pledges to uphold editorial independence and remove paywall". (11 December 2015). *South China Morning Post*. Retrieved from http://www.scmp.com/business/companies/article/1890060/alibaba-buys-south-china-morning-post-groups-media-business.

Chu, J. "Hong Kong's Oldest Chinese-language Newspaper *Sing Pao* avoids closure after High Court orders Liquidation of Parent Company". (12 August 2015). *South China Morning Post*. Retrieved from http://www.scmp.com/news/hong-kong/economy/article/1848857/hong-kongs-oldest-chinese-language-newspaper-sing-pao-faces.

Chu Shou Ming Pao (n.d.) Retrieved from http://hk.chiculture.net/20404/html/b09/20404b09.html.

"Dagongwang jianjie" [About www.takungpao.com]. (n.d.). *Ta Kung Pao*. Retrieved from http://www.takungpao.com/corp/about.html.

"Dilu yue xi shengguo huanbingzhiji" [A resolute effort like the legendary horse Dilu leaping over the stream beats stalling]. (5 July 2003). *Sing Tao Daily*. Retrieved from http://std.stheadline.com/archive/fullstory.asp?andor=or&year1=2003&month1=7&day1=5&year2=2003&month2=7&day2=5&category=all&id=20030705j01&keyword1=&keyword2=.

"Dongfang Baoye kong Uwants taolunqu feibang, cu jiaochu 'TheOne88' yonghu geren ziliao" [*Oriental Daily News* sues the internet forum Uwants for libel and demands personal information of the user "TheOne88"]. (7 October 2007). *Ming Pao*. Retrieved from http://anti-oriental-censor.blogspot.hk/2012/04/uwants-theone88.html.

"Dongfang rubing jin Pingguo jizhe 'suoliao'" [*Oriental Daily News* files a lawsuit against *Apple Daily* and its reporters for obtaining information]. (6 December 2008). *Ming Pao*. Retrieved from http://web.archive.org/web/20081211200624/http://hk.news.yahoo.com/article/081205/4/9leg.html.

"Duli Meiti wu shan feibang Dongfang wenzhang pei shi wan" [inmediahk.net fined 100,000 dollars for not deleting an article which libeled *Oriental Daily News*]. (31 March 2012). *Ming Pao*. Retrieved from http://anti-oriental-censor.blogspot.hk/2012/04/10.html.

Guanyu Shangbao [About the *Hong Kong Commercial Daily*]. (n.d.). *Hong Kong Commercial Daily*. Retrieved from http://tp.hkcd.com/about/shangbao.html.

Kwok, D and Jim, C. (12 December 2014). "HK Media Tycoon Jimmy Lai Arrested over Democracy Protest, Quits Tabloid". Reuters. Retrieved from http://www.reuters.com/article/us-hongkong-china-idUSKBN0JP04H20141212.

"Hong Kong's *SCMP* Newspaper Website Blocked in China". (11 March 2016). Channel News Asia. Retrieved from http://www.channelnewsasia.com/news/asiapacific/hong-kong-s-scmp/2593510.html.

Hu Xian SYM Lab (n.d.). Retrieved from http://www.symedialab.org.hk/talk/%E8%83%A1%E4%BB%99/.

Jiang, H. "Xinji Dagongbao, baoye linian qianxi" [A new short account of the journalistic ideas of *Ta Kung Pao*]. (2011). *Wenxue jiaoyu*, 23. Retrieved from http://doc.qkzz.net/article/256e223e-a5ae-4b37-9cb7-3b5a22fa75ca.htm.

"Jiaodai qianxin qian Chengbao cai sanshi ren" [*Sing Pao* fires thirty people before clarifying about unpaid salaries]. (29 December 2006). *Apple Daily*. Retrieved from http://hk.apple.nextmedia.com/news/art/20061229/6665752.

"Jinnian wei shouguo zu, qiankuan yu sanbai wan, He Wenfa houren wuyi jiu Shengbao" [Sing Pao has not paid any rent this year. More than three million dollars in arrears. Children of Ho Man-fat don't intend to save the paper]. (29 April 2006). *The Sun*. Retrieved from http://the-sun.on.cc/channels/news/20060429/20060429022726_0000.html.

Kwok, B. "Meet *Apple Daily*'s new Female Editor-in-Chief". (10 March 2015). EJ Insight. Retrieved from http://www.ejinsight.com/20150310-meet-apple-daily-new-female-editor-in-chief/.

Lee, C. "Chief Executive CY Leung Demands Retraction of 'Defamatory' Article". (8 February 2013). *South China Morning Post*. Retrieved from http://www.scmp.com/news/hong-kong/article/1145631/chief-executive-cy-leung-demands-retraction-defamatory-article?page=all.

Lee, F. L. F. "Objectivity as Self-Censorship? Hong Kong Citizens' Beliefs in Media Neutrality and Perceptions of Press Freedom". (2007a). *Asian Survey*, 47(3), 434–54.

Lee, F. L. F. "Strategic Interaction, Cultural Co-orientation, and Press Freedom in Hong Kong". (2007b). *Asian Journal of Communication*, 17(2), 134–47.

Lee, F. L. F. & Lin, A. M. Y. "Newspaper Editorial Discourse and the Politics of Self-Censorship in Hong Kong". (2006). *Discourse & Society*, 17(3), 331–58.

Leung Mo-han. "Maybe I was a Reason for Lau's Brutal Attack!". *The Real Hong Kong News* (27 February 2014). Retrieved from https://therealnewshk.wordpress.com/2014/02/27/leung-mo-han-maybe-i-was-a-reason-for-laus-brutal-attack/.

Li, B. "Geqiangyouer: Nanzao chihua, Zhengxie zuo laozong" [The wall has ears: *South China Morning Post* turns red. A member of a Political Consultative Conference assumes chief editor role]. (1 February 2012). *Apple Daily*. Retrieved from http://hk.apple.nextmedia.com/news/art/20120201/16032020.

Li, Z. "Hong Kong Newspaper Punished for its Political Stance, says Publisher". (22 January 2014). *Epoch Times*. Retrieved from http://www.theepochtimes.com/n3/463714-hong-kong-newspaper-punished-for-its-political-stance-says-publisher/.

"Mingbao bianwu dongshi shan gai dati zao qianze" [*Ming Pao* editorial director slammed for arbitrarily changing a headline]. (3 July 2014). *Apple Daily*. Retrieved from http://hk.apple.nextmedia.com/news/art/20140703/18786450.

"Mingbao chao Jiang Guoyuan. Yuangong: ta shu linghun renwu, shi Zhong Tianxiang de dingxinshan" [*Ming Pao* fired Keung Kwok-yuen. Staff: He was the brains of the paper and the bane of Chong Tien Siong's life]. (21 April 2016). *HK01*. Retrieved from http://www.hk01.com/港聞/17470/-明報炒姜國元-員工-他屬靈魂人物-是鍾天祥的-頂心杉-.

Mok, D. "Hong Kong Newspaper Lays off Twenty Staff in Cost-Cutting Move". (25 May 2016). *South China Morning Post*. Retrieved from http://www.scmp.com/news/hong-kong/education-community/article/1954585/hong-kong-newspaper-lays-20-staff-cost-cutting.

"Pingguo zongbianji: wujihua daguimo caiyuan" [No major downsizing plan, according to editor-in-chief of *Apple Daily*]. (29 April 2016). *Hong Kong Economic Times*. Retrieved from http://topick.hket.com/article/1417709/.

Qin Hui gufen mianfei zeng Yang Jiacheng [Tan Hui's shares given free to Yang Jiacheng]. *Metro Daily* (n.d.). Retrieved from http://www.metrohk.com.hk/pda/pda_detail.php?section=daily&id=125235.

"*Sing Pao* Fined for Breaching MPF Law" (1 April 2008). Retrieved from http://archive.news.gov.hk/isd/ebulletin/en/category/lawandorder/html/02ddc835-96e7-4dc9-84d8-f5999734c854.htm.

Sing Tao News Corporation Limited. (2016). *Annual Report 2015*. Retrieved from http://www.singtaonewscorp.com/notice/annualReport/2_2016042116475906367.pdf.

"Tamed Hounds". (19 July 2014). *The Economist*. Retrieved from http://www.economist.com/news/china/21607879-press-hong-kong-though-still-free-has-lost-its-bite-tamed-hounds.

"Tammy Tam Named as *South China Morning Post* Editor-in-Chief". (6 November 2015). *South China Morning Post*. Retrieved from http://www.scmp.com/news/article/1876366/tammy-tam-named-south-china-morning-post-editor-chief.

Tan, K. "Veteran Reporter Paul Mooney Tells how he Got Sidelined by New *SCMP* Editor Wang Xiangwei." (2012). Shanghaiist. Retrieved from http://shanghaiist.com/2012/06/29/paul-mooney-wang-xiangwei-scmp.php.

"Tanshedeng: Taibei yingqi yinmei, Jiangfu ruanruo songrong" [Searchlight: Taipei cracks down on pimps but the Hong Kong government is weak and permissive]. (6 November 2015). *Oriental Daily News*. Retrieved from http://orientaldaily.on.cc/cnt/news/20091201/00176_099.html?pubdate=20091201.

"The Editor who Stood up to Beijing". (13 May 2012). *South China Morning Post*. Retrieved from http://www.scmp.com/article/1000790/editor-who-stood-beijing.

Toh, H. S. "Carson Yeung to Get Majority Ownership of SMI Publishing". (5 January 2010). *South China Morning Post*. Retrieved from http://www.scmp.com/article/702837/carson-yeung-get-majority-ownership-smi-publishing.

"Weiyi rongzhai Misuli Jiang huawen baozhang, bainian Dagong chiyu taxiang" [The only Chinese newspaper which won a Missouri Honor Medal. The century old *Ta Kung Pao* established its fame overseas]. (17 June 2016). *Ta Kung Pao*. Retrieved from http://news.takungpao.com.hk/mainland/focus/2016-06/3334366_print.html.

"Wen Wei Po, Ta Kung Pao announce merger to share resources". (3 February 2016). EJ Insights. Retrieved from http://www.ejinsight.com/20160203-wen-wei-po-ta-kung-pao-announce-merger-to-share-resources/.

"Xinbao turan quxiao Xianggang diyi jianbi Lian Yizheng zhuanlan, Cheng Xiang fengxi siyin" [The *HKEJ* sudden cuts the column of Joseph Lian, "writer of the most powerful prose in Hong Kong". Ching Cheong analyzes why]. (29 July 2016). *Apple Daily*. Retrieved from http://hk.apple.nextmedia.com/realtime/news/20160729/55427269.

"Yangguang gou Chengbao, mei gu 0.36 yuan" [Sun TV bought *Sing Pao* for $0.36 per share]. (10 December 2002). *Apple Daily*. Retrieved from http://hk.apple.nextmedia.com/financeestate/art/20021210/2993982.

# Chapter 2

# An Overview of Telecommunications, English Press and Magazines in Hong Kong

*C. K. LAU and Siu Wai CHEUNG*

## Introduction

This chapter will present the landscape of telecommunications, English-language media and magazines in Hong Kong. As the print sector is undergoing profound changes—given the decline in advertisement and the way the public consumes media—it is very important to discuss this sector within the broader landscape of telecommunications. Hong Kong has a robust telecommunications market. Its people are avid users of communication technology. At the end of 2017, the city had 7.4 million people (Census and Statistics Department) but 18.34 million mobile service subscribers, or a penetration rate of 247.8% (Office of the Communications Authority, 2017). The high mobile subscriber penetration rate was accounted for by the popularity of prepaid SIM cards for voice and data services, which are used by locals while travelling overseas and by visitors during their stay in Hong Kong. In 2017, visitors to the city numbered 58.5 million (Tourism Commission, 2017). Of the 18.34 million mobile subscribers, 16.89 million were 3G/4G mobile subscribers (Office of the Communications Authority, 2018). With more and more people acquiring smartphones and using them for longer periods of time and a wider range of purposes, mobile data use has surged (Office of the Communications Authority, 2018).

As of September 2017, fixed broadband companies had 2.64 million registered customers, and more than 92% of the city's households had fixed broadband connections. Wi-Fi access is also widespread. In November 2017, more than 48,594 public Wi-Fi hot spots and free public Wi-Fi services were available in 636 government premises (Office of the Communications Authority, 2017).

Even though more people have opted to dispense with a fixed line telephone connection at home, telephone density in Hong Kong is among the highest in the world. In September 2017, there were 4.2 million fixed lines, including 2.33 million residential connections; the latter number covered 92% of households (Office of the Communications Authority, 2017).

Hong Kong has a liberal telecommunications market with no controls on the number of service providers and no restrictions on foreign investment. Today, the market has four mobile network operators (Office of the Communications Authority, 2017), which engage in what industry analysts regard as healthy competition (BMI Research, 2016). The biggest operator is PCCW (formerly Pacific Century CyberWorks Limited), which has a 40.3% market share, followed by Hutchison (26.9%), SmarTone (17.4%) and China Mobile (15.5%) (BMI Research, 2016). They all provide a wide range of services, including telephone, broadband connection and mobile data. As of September 2017, there were 27 local fixed network operators, 258 external telecommunications services providers and 227 internet service providers (Office of the Communications Authority, 2017).

Hong Kong was ranked third in Asia and twelfth in the world in the Network Readiness Index, according to the Global Information Technology Report 2016 published by the World Economic Forum. (World Economic Forum, 2016) The index "measures the capacity of countries to leverage ICTs [information and communication technologies] for increased competitiveness and well-being."

## A Special Part of China

While censorship is a fact of life in Mainland China, where cyberspace is sealed by a "great firewall" to stop domestic users from accessing "undesirable" information, free flow of information remains the guiding principle in Hong Kong. Although media self-censorship may have become an issue in recent years, people can use their cell phones and other internet connections to freely "seek, receive and impart information and ideas" (Article 19 of the Universal Declaration of Human Rights). Government publicity materials make a point of noting that the free movement of information, along with that of capital, talent and goods, is a hallmark of Hong Kong's open business environment under "one country, two systems" (Invest HK, 2018).

The absence of governmental interference in telecommunications is also evident from the fact that buyers of prepaid SIM cards do not need any identification. A wide selection of SIM cards that can be activated in phones are readily available across the city. Some of them can also be used in Mainland China, Taiwan and Macau (see websites of leading telecom service providers).

## Overview of the Magazine Industry

The magazine industry in Hong Kong has witnessed tremendous changes since the beginning of the twenty-first century, with more speciality magazines in print than news magazines. Chinese magazines dominate the market. Besides the news, they cover a wide variety of genres, such as travel, leisure, entertainment, celebrity gossip, health and medicine, automobile, electronics, the arts, photography, home improvement, parenting and sports. People in Hong Kong usually buy magazines in the omnipresent convenience stores or from news stands on busy streets. Corporations and institutions may subscribe to magazines, partly for record keeping to facilitate relevant research in the future as some of them are not available on the internet.

Several news weeklies in Hong Kong carry in-depth stories on local politics, society or the daily lives of ordinary people, and they face a market that has been falling steadily for quite some time. Both the quality of the content and revenue from advertisements have declined. Most have far fewer pages than they did several years ago. The drop in popularity is due to the changing reading habits of Hong Kong people, who prefer to access information online rather than buying printed newspapers and magazines. Creativity in the media industry, technological improvements in telecommunications and a steady drop in monthly expenses for consumers have all contributed to the wide acceptance of online reading, and online revenues cannot match those once garnered in the print sector. This harsh reality has caused several publishers to shut down their magazines and lay off their employees, including *Sudden Weekly*, which was once very popular. More recently, as of 15 March 2018,

*Next Magazine*, which for many years was the most popular magazine with the largest circulation, halted its print edition to focus on the online edition. This event was seen as being extremely symbolic and is believed to be a new milestone in the history of Hong Kong's magazine industry.

The launch of *HK01* in 2016 gave the news magazine business a spark of hope. The selling point of the weekly is its in-depth reporting on political and social issues in Hong Kong, particularly controversial ones. *HK01* was founded by Yu Pun Hoi, a successful Hong Kong businessman with experience in running media institutions such as newspapers and television. The new magazine employs veteran journalists and focuses on one major issue every week, providing investigative reporting and in-depth analysis using traditional journalistic approaches. Every issue contains a full-fledged broadsheet newspaper and two magazines—*Being Global* and *Being HK*, which focus on global issues and local issues, respectively. The first issue of each month also contains a women's magazine, *Being Ms*. The broadsheet newspaper's colourful front page often carries a big photograph and a headline about the main issue to be discussed for the week.

*HK01* is widely considered to be a high-quality weekly and has won praise from media professionals. However, it is still in the stage of establishing itself and is burning cash to promote its brand name. It is hard to predict how long Mr Yu will finance such a costly business. Sooner or later, his determination to establish a good Chinese news magazine or even a media empire in Hong Kong may be pushed to the limit.

## Categories of News Magazines

The news magazines in Hong Kong can be divided into three categories. The first are local magazines, which cover Hong Kong politics, economy, finance, society and education as well as other current hot topics. The main publications in this group are *Next Magazine* (online edition since 15 March 2018), *East Week*, *HK01*, *Ming Pao Monthly*, *iMoney*, *Economic Digest*, *Capital Weekly* and *Hong Kong Economic Journal Monthly*. *Next Magazine* and *East Week*, which have the largest readership in this category, are archrivals. They share a similar style, and both focus on political exposés and investigative stories about the crimes or love affairs of local celebrities. Their main selling points are these sensational stories and the exclusive pictures accompanying them. Their covers are often filled with bold headlines and large photographs.

*Economic Digest*, *iMoney* and *Capital Weekly* are the main weekly financial/business magazines serving readers who are not financial professionals but who are interested in learning the latest developments in the financial and property markets. The three magazines are similar in form and content. They publish detailed statistics on different sectors of the Hong Kong economy, case studies of industries and companies, analyses and recommendations about individual stocks, and regular columns written by economists, stock analysts, foreign exchange experts and fund managers.

The second category is political gossip magazines, which specialise in political and social developments in Mainland China, with frequent stories about "factional infighting" within the Chinese leadership. About ten magazines of this nature are published every month. They are often available at news stands and convenience stores in areas with a steady flow of Mainland visitors. They provide truths, half-truths, pure speculation or even made-up stories about Chinese politics. Knowing most of their stories are unsubstantiated, few Hongkongers read these magazines, but the cover stories are often sensational enough to ignite the curiosity of people from Mainland China. With such publications forbidden on the Mainland, their producers avoid travelling there. In fact, Wang Jiamin and Guo Zhongxiao, who edited and published two magazines in this genre were arrested in Shenzhen in 2014 for distributing in the Mainland, a violation of Chinese law, and were held in jail until 2016, when they were tried in a Shenzhen court and sentenced to prison terms, though one was reportedly released later. This case shows the danger involved in publishing these magazines.

The third category of news magazines are based in Hong Kong but have an international focus, such as *Yazhou Zhoukan* (Asia Week), *Super Media* and the *Bloomberg Businessweek* (Chinese edition). They aim to inform readers about the world and provide news and analyses of local, regional and global politics, economics, social affairs and technology. They are respected in their niche markets but are not profitable because of their small readership.

## Loss of Advertising Revenues

The present state of Hong Kong's news magazine industry causes concern and anxiety because revenues from advertisements keep decreasing. Circulation numbers are top secret, but there are some visible signs of a magazine's financial health. One prime sign is the number of pages each issue contains.

Magazines now are much thinner than they were a few years ago. Some magazines used to publish a set of three separate magazines in one issue, each focusing on a major area, for example one on politics, another one on celebrity and entertainment news and a third on lifestyle and travel. Now most contain only two magazines. When launching a promotion campaign, they used to offer discounts of up to 75% off. Now the discount rate is much smaller because it cannot be offset against other revenues.

*Capital Weekly* is a typical example. It once published a set of three magazines (*Capital Weekly*, *Capital Money* and *Capital Commerce*) and offered, during a promotion in June 2013, a discounted price of $5 when its normal price was $20. Today it publishes a set of two magazines (*Capital Weekly* and *Capital Money*) and in October 2016 its promotional discounted price was $10 while the list price was still $20.

Some magazines organise events such as specialised seminars to which they invite as speakers investment bankers, mutual fund managers, foreign exchange specialists or education experts to provide analyses of certain financial products or tips on how to get young children enrolled in competitive primary schools or kindergartens. These activities help the magazines increase their visibility and improve their bottom lines, but are not enough to make up for the loss in advertising revenue.

## The Hong Kong English Press

A total of twelve English-language dailies are registered as newspapers in Hong Kong as of 31 August 2017 (Information Services Department, 2017). These include some that target local readers, the big names among which are the *South China Morning Post (SCMP)*, *The Standard* and the *China Daily Hong Kong Edition*. The rest are titles that appeal to select groups of readers or international titles that target a regional readership, such as the *Financial Times*, *The Wall Street Journal Asia*, *USA Today International* and *International New York Times*.

Founded in 1903, the *SCMP* is the city's oldest surviving newspaper. Its mission today is to provide comprehensive coverage of Hong Kong, China and the world. Retailing at HK$9 per copy on weekdays and HK$10 on Sundays (when it calls itself the *Sunday Morning Post, SMP*), it also offers student subscriptions at a discount during the school year. There is also an online edition, which used to be subscription only but has been free since the paywall was dropped in April 2016. At the end of 2016, the average net circulation (print and digital) of the *SCMP* was 105,347 and the *SMP* 82,117, and they had a combined readership of 335,000. In March 2017, the monthly page views of scmp.com amounted to 23 million (*SCMP*, 2017).

The *SCMP*'s main rival is *The Standard*, a free tabloid published by Sing Tao News Corporation Ltd. Launched in 1949 as a paid broadsheet, it was reduced to tabloid size in 2000 when it changed its name from *The Hong Kong Standard* to *Hong Kong iMail*. In 2002, it changed its name back to *The Standard*, and in 2007 became a free paper and is now distributed outside major subway stations during the morning rush hour and at selected residential estates, hotels and restaurants. No official circulation figures have been published. The Nielsen Report says *The Standard*'s combined average daily readership (hardcopy, web and app) was 54,000, with about 55% of its readers having university level education and 35% up to secondary level education (Nielsen Hong Kong Media Index Report, 2015).

*The China Daily Hong Kong Edition* was launched in 1997 and retails at HK$7 per copy. Besides carrying contents produced by its parent edition in Beijing, it has a city section that covers Hong Kong affairs. According to *China Daily*'s website, its eight domestic and foreign editions in several languages, including the Hong Kong edition, have a global circulation of 900,000 copies and 45 million print and web readers worldwide.

Apart from the English news website of Radio Television Hong Kong (RTHK) (see Chapter 4), the only digital news site in English dedicated to covering local news is the Hong Kong Free Press (HKFP). The non-profit news website was launched by a group of journalists headed by Tom Grundy and Evan Fowler in June 2015.

## Concerns over the *SCMP*

According to the Nielsen Report, the two most popular English-language dailies, the *SCMP* and *The Standard*, are regularly read by only 4.66% and 2.71% of its sampled readers respectively (Nielsen Hong Kong Media Index Report, 2015). However, the *SCMP* wields a clout far out of proportion to its relatively small readership. Back in the days when China was closed to the outside world and Hong Kong was a base for China-watchers, the paper built up an international reputation as a source of credible news on China. Before 1997, the *SCMP* was regarded as the establishment newspaper. Widely read by Hong Kong's small but powerful and affluent English-speaking elite, it was both highly influential and very profitable. Since 1997, the *SCMP*'s preeminent status has weakened, but it is still a paper to be reckoned with because it still has quality content and a strong following among the powerful. For local and international readers not literate in Chinese, the paper remains a useful source of information on Hong Kong and China.

On 11 December 2015, the Alibaba Group, China's e-commerce giant, announced that it would acquire the *SCMP* for HK$2.06 billion from Robert Kuok's Kerry Group, which had owned the paper since 1993. Alibaba, controlled by Jack Ma, formally took over the *SCMP* on 5 April 2016. The transaction has fuelled concerns over the future direction of editorial policy, as the new owner said the paper should offer readers a narrative of China that is different from that offered by Western media. In an interview following his new acquisition, Ma said, "The outside world's perception of China" has "all sorts of misunderstandings" due to the fact that the media do not give "the full picture". He hoped that "We [the Post] should let our readers see China from more angles and perspectives" (Chow, Apr 2016).

In a separate interview, Joseph Tsai, executive vice-chairman of the Alibaba Group, expressed his reservations about mainstream Western news organisations covering China through a "particular lens", saying it was his hope that the *SCMP* would "present facts, tell the truth" (Tsai, 2015). Tsai's view was criticised by the Hong Kong Journalists Association (HKJA), which expressed concern that Alibaba's control of the SCMP would "further compromise press freedom in Hong Kong" (Hong Kong Journalists Association, 2015). In reply, Tsai asserted that "the *SCMP* will be objective, accurate and fair" and that "day-to-day editorial decisions will be driven by editors in the newsroom, not in the corporate boardroom" (Tsai, 2015).

In fact, concern over self-censorship by the Hong Kong press has been growing, and the *SCMP*, along with a number of mainstream media outlets, has been a target of criticism (Reporters without borders, 2016). Under Kuok, a Malaysian Chinese businessman with extensive business interests in Southeast Asia and China, the *SCMP* was accused of allegedly practising political censorship to please Beijing (Asian Sentinel, 17 June 2014, 20 May 2015 and 13 July 2015). Despite these criticisms of the *SCMP*, *The New York Times*, while reporting critics' concerns over the *SCMP*'s future under Ma, pointed out that the *SCMP* (under Kuok) had a track record of reporting aggressively on political scandals and human rights cases in China that the country's state-run media were forbidden to cover (Barboza, 2015; Tsang, 2015). Under Ma, the *SCMP* has continued to carry stories on the plight of human rights activists on the Mainland (Lau, 2016; Gan, 2016; Associated Press, 2016), but its decisions to take part in a number of "stage-managed" interviews with people held in custody by the Chinese government has sparked controversies.

In July 2016, three months after Ma bought it, the *SCMP* came under criticism for conducting, apparently with the help of official Mainland sources, an interview with human rights activist Zhao Wei, who had just been released on bail after being detained for nearly a year. She and her employer, human rights lawyer Li Heping, were among hundreds of lawyers and activists arrested by the Mainland authorities in a crackdown in 2015. In her telephone interview with the *SCMP*, Zhao said she regretted her activism (*SCMP*, 11 July 2016). The paper's decision to conduct and publish the interview was seen as controversial because the admission seemed forced, making the *SCMP* look as if it had become a mouthpiece of the Mainland authorities. The Zhao controversy came after *Sing Tao Daily* had been criticised for becoming a propaganda tool by interviewing Lee Po, a Hong Kong publisher of sensitive books on Chinese politics who had been reported missing by his family. The interview, conducted with the help of Mainland authorities in an undisclosed location on the Mainland, came after public outcry that he might have been abducted by Mainland agents in Hong Kong and secretly ferried to the Mainland. Many people read in disbelief Lee's statement that he had "voluntarily" sneaked into the Mainland without going through immigration to assist with official investigations into his business affairs (Mok, 2016).

Unlike *Sing Tao*'s story, which offered no critical assessment of the circumstances in which the interview with Lee was conducted, the *SCMP* story on Zhao stated that "The Post [*SCMP*] could not verify Zhao's location or whether she was under surveillance during the interview." After the interview, the *SCMP* also called Zhao's husband, who said he had yet to see his wife despite her apparent release and suspected she had been forced to recant. The paper also quoted Zhao's lawyer as saying that he believed her freedoms were limited (*SCMP*, 11 July 2016). Pressed by *The Guardian* to reveal its sources, the *SCMP* said "Like *The Guardian* and other principled news organisations, the *SCMP* treats the protection of confidential sources as sacrosanct." It added "Our stand has not changed before or after we changed ownership and it is this: the SCMP's future will continue to depend on independent, critical journalism" (Phillips, 2016). Citing sources in the *SCMP*, the 2017 annual report of HKJA revealed that "Ms Zhao's contact number came from 'the top'" and that "frontline staff tried to handle the story in a more professional way." It also disclosed that a month after the incident, the *SCMP* was "chosen" by the Chinese government as one of the Hong Kong media outlets to interview another detained human rights lawyer Wang Yu. But even though the *SCMP* sent a reporter, the paper did not report on the interview as "the Post reporter did not think what Ms Wang said was truthful and the journalist was therefore told not to write anything" (HKJA, 2017).

In February 2018, the *SCMP* was criticised again for conducting an interview with Gui Minhai that was arranged by the Chinese government. A naturalised Swedish citizen, Gui was a business associate of Lee Po and had gone missing while travelling in Thailand in 2015 before surfacing in a Chinese jail. In the interview, Gui denounced the Swedish government, which had tried to secure his release, for trying to "sensationalise" what had happened to him. The *SCMP*'s report states that it "agreed to take part (in the interview), provided no conditions were put on the questions it could ask, after being approached by the ministry (of public security) on Wednesday" (Siu, 2018; Wade, 2018). In response to a complaint by Gui's daughter over the way the *SCMP* handled the interview, the paper's editor-in-chief, Tammy Tam, rejected accusations that it had collaborated with the Chinese authorities to portray Gui as speaking freely while in custody.

> We provided the facts and context, including a photograph showing him between two guards, and our reporter also talked to your father's friends so as to shed more light on the circumstances. All this allowed our readers to judge for themselves whether he was under duress. As journalists, we are often faced with difficult decisions. In this case, we were required to choose between interviewing your father in a stage-managed setting and having no access at all. We made the decision to go ahead on news merit, and stand by our professional judgment. (*SCMP*, 2018)

However, even amidst these criticisms, the *SCMP* does not seem to be beloved by Beijing because access to their websites as well as their Weibo and WeChat accounts is blocked on the Mainland from time to time.

It is important to note that even before this chain of events, the founders of the *HKFP* had cited the erosion of press freedom in Hong Kong as the reason for launching their venture. "We are not answerable to any corporate entity, business tycoon or Mainland Chinese conglomerate," the website says, and promises to provide an independent platform for critical voices to be heard. The website's crowdfunding appeal met with an enthusiastic reception, with members of the public contributing more than HK$500,000 even though it had hoped to raise only HK$150,000 (Baiocchi, 2015).

## Business Outlook

The first strategic move by the new owner of the *SCMP* was to expand the paper's global digital readership by removing the paywall. Tsai talked of his vision as being to attract users from all over the world who want to be informed about China. "It's a very internet company philosophy because we believe users should not pay for service or content—the people who end up paying are advertisers who want to reach out to these users," he said (Chow, 2015).

This strategy is contrary to that pursued by the *SCMP*'s previous owner, who had opted to maintain a paywall to prevent it cannibalising the print edition. This was because the print version, despite falling circulation in recent years, had provided a dependable revenue stream to underwrite the paper's profitability. With the removal of scmp.com's paywall under Ma, the *SCMP* was expected to find it challenging to balance its books. In 2015, when the paywall was still up, the paper had reported a 10% fall in net profit to HK$59.7 million and a 52% drop in revenue to HK$1,121.7 million (*SCMP* Group, 2015). Presumably, the dismantling of the paywall led more *SCMP* readers to cut their print subscriptions, further undermining its circulation and advertising base. The new *SCMP* management admitted that it was losing money, but pointed out that it was not in a hurry to achieve profitability. Tsai said he was putting the *SCMP* through a "10-year gestation period"—the first three years being devoted to creating a product that people like, the next three to five years being spent coming up with a revenue model and the final years of this period would focus on achieving profitability (Huang, 2017).

To reinvent itself, the *SCMP* has introduced a new corporate identity, moved its staff into new offices in a prime location and went on a hiring spree (*SCMP,* 6 February 2018). On the product front, Abacus, a news site that focuses on telling the story of China's tech industry, and Inkstone, a mobile application that reports on Chinese politics, business, technology and human interest with a light touch, were launched in early 2018 (Barclay, 2018; Inkstone, 2018). In May 2018, the *SCMP* announced that it would expand its coverage of U.S.-China relations by teaming up with Politico, an American news organisation known for its specialised coverage of U.S. politics and policy. Under the deal, "the newsrooms of the two media organisations will share content and collaborate on reporting opportunities and events in the United States and Asia." (*SCMP,* 22 May 2018).

While the *SCMP* has been able to tackle the digital challenge with the backing of Alibaba, its smaller rivals are not so lucky. As a small title in a large publishing group, *The Standard* has been able to stay in business only by running a lean operation and leveraging the shared resources of its sister publications. The *China Daily Hong Kong Edition* has never had a substantial circulation and its survival depends on state funding. The *HKFP* says on its website that it seeks to "become more sustainable over time with multiple revenue streams such as membership, crowdfunding, advertising, events, donations and content provision." So far, it has managed to publish a few scoops but has yet to gain sufficient traction to guarantee its future.

## Conclusion

Like most print media, news magazines and the English-language press face unprecedented challenges in today's digital world. More and more people choose to get news and other information from mobile apps on their smartphones, or to be informed from international media outlets that publish in English. This trend is universal and is unlikely to reverse. For Hong Kong's news magazines, there is an added difficulty: the pace of life in a metropolis. People in Hong Kong move fast, talk fast and get everything done fast. Fewer and fewer people have the leisure or the patience to read a fat magazine. Obviously, the challenges ahead will be much more severe than we have ever seen.

## Note

C. K. Lau is a former *SCMP* journalist. He left the paper in 2009.

# References

"Advertising and Marketing Solutions Media Kit 2017". (2017). *South China Morning Post*. Retrieved from http://advertising.scmp.com/sites/all/themes/scmpams/ratecard/South%20China%20Morning%20Post_Media%20Kit_HKD.pdf.

"An Exchange between Gui Minhai's Daughter and the Post's Editor-in-Chief". *South China Morning Post*. (18 April 2018). Retrieved from http://www.scmp.com/print/comment/letters/article/2142228/exchange-between-gui-minhais-daughter-and-posts-editor-chief.

Associated Press. (3 August 2016). "Most Prominent Cases in China by Lawyers Now in Custody". *South China Morning Post*. Retrieved from http://www.scmp.com/news/china/policies-politics/article/1998703/most-prominent-cases-china-lawyers-now-custody.

Baiocchi, F. (30 June 2015). "Activist Turned Editor Who Tried to Arrest Tony Blair Launches Crowdfunded Hong Kong News Website". *Press Gazette*. Retrieved from http://www.pressgazette.co.uk/activist-who-tried-arrest-tony-blair-launches-crowdfunded-news-website-hong-kong-free-press.

Barboza, D. (11 December 2015). "Alibaba Buying South China Morning Post, Aiming to Influence Media". *The New York Times*. Retrieved from http://www.nytimes.com/2015/12/12/business/dealbook/alibaba-scmp-south-china-morning-post.html.

Barclay, Andrew. (16 March 2018). "The Post Launches Abacus, a News Site that Focuses on Telling the Story of China's Tech Industry". *South China Morning Post*. Retrieved from http://www.scmp.com/print/tech/enterprises/article/2137586/post-launches-abacus-news-site-focuses-telling-story-chinas-tech.

BMI Research. (2016). Hong Kong Telecommunications Report Q4.

Census and Statistics Department. (2018). Retrieved on 22 May 2018 from https://www.censtatd.gov.hk/hkstat/sub/bbs.jsp.

Chow, C. Y. (11 December 2015). "Alibaba Buys South China Morning Post Group's Media Business, Pledges to Uphold Editorial Independence and Remove Paywall". *South China Morning Post*. Retrieved from http://www.scmp.com/business/companies/article/1890060/alibaba-buys-south-china-morning-post-groups-media-business.

Chow, C. Y. (21 April 2016). "Alibaba's Jack Ma On China's Economy, Hong Kong and The South China Morning Post: Full Q&A". *South China Morning Post*. Retrieved from http://www.scmp.com/news/china/economy/article/1937278/alibabas-jack-ma-chinas-economy-hong-kong-and-south-china-morning.

Fung, O. (22 March 2016). "Perception of Hong Kong Press Freedom Declines for Second Year, According to Journalists Association Survey". *South China Morning Post*. Retrieved from http://www.scmp.com/news/hong-kong/education-community/article/1929279/perception-hong-kong-press-freedom-declines.

Gan, N. (3 August 2016). "Brothers of Chinese Activist Barred From Trial and Forced to Return Home". *South China Morning Post*. Retrieved from http://www.scmp.com/news/china/policies-politics/article/1998850/brothers-jailed-activist-barred-trial-and-sent-forced.

"HK's *South China Morning Post* Softens China Arrests". (13 July 2015). *Asia Sentinel*. Retrieved from http://www.asiasentinel.com/politics/hongkong-south-china-morning-post-softens-china-arrests/.

HK Travel Blog. (2016). "Best 2016 Tourist HK Prepaid SIM Cards". Retrieved from http://hktravelblog.com/sim-cards/best-2016-tourist-hk-prepaid-sim-cards/.

Hong King Journalists Association. (11 December 2015). "HKJA's response to the control of South China Morning Post by Alibaba Group". Retrieved from https://www.hkja.org.hk/site/portal/Site.aspx?id=A1-1428&lang=en-US.

Hong Kong Journalists Association. (2016). "One Country, Two Nightmares: Hong Kong Media Caught in Ideological Battleground". Retrieved from http://www.hkja.org.hk/site/portal/main.htm.

Hong Kong Journalists Association. (2017). "Two Systems under Siege: Beijing Turns the Screws on Hong Kong Media". Retrieved from https://www.hkja.org.hk/site/Host/hkja/UserFiles/file/Annual_report_2017.pdf.

Hong Kong Tourism Commission. (2017). "Tourism Performance". Retrieved on 22 May 2018 from http://www.tourism.gov.hk/english/statistics/statistics_perform.html.

Huang, Zheping. (12 July 2017). "How Alibaba is Reinventing a 114-year-old Newspaper in Hong Kong". Quartz. Retrieved from https://qz.com/1027234/how-alibaba-baba-is-reinventing-the-south-china-morning-post-scmp-a-114-year-old-newspaper-in-hong-kong/.

Information Services Department. (2015). "Hong Kong Fact Sheet: The Media". Retrieved from http://www.gov.hk/en/about/abouthk/factsheets/docs/media.pdf.

Inkstone. (2018). "Introducing Inkstone". Retrieved from https://www.inkstonenews.com/introducing-inkstone/article/2128245.

InvestHK. (2018). "Open Business Environment". Retrieved on 22 May 2018 from https://www.investhk.gov.hk/en/why-hong-kong/open-business-environment.html.

Lau, M. (30 July 2016). "Conscience Conquers All: Wife of Detained Rights Lawyer Li Heping Says Her Respect Has Only Grown Deeper Despite Pain of Separation". *South China Morning Post*. Retrieved from http://www.scmp.com/news/china/society/article/1996642/conscience-conquers-all-wife-detained-rights-lawyer-li-heping.

"Leading Columnists Purged at Hong Kong's Paper of Record". (20 May 2015). *Asia Sentinel*. Retrieved from http://www.asiasentinel.com/politics/putsch-columnists-south-china-morning-post/.

Lhatoo, Y. (7 April 2016). "Censorship at the *South China Morning Post*: Fact, Fiction and Fallacy". *South China Morning Post*. Retrieved from http://www.scmp.com/comment/insight-opinion/article/1934542/censorship-south-china-morning-post-fact-fiction-and-fallacy.

Mai, J. & Gan, N. (4 August 2016). "Head of Beijing Law Firm Gets Seven Years as Crackdown on Rights Activists Continues". *South China Morning Post*. Retrieved from http://www.scmp.com/news/china/policies-politics/article/1999111/beijing-law-firm-director-jailed-seven-years-sweeping.

Mok, D. (1 March 2016). "I Sneaked into Mainland China Illegally to Help an Investigation and Gave Up My British Citizenship Too, Says Missing Hong Kong Bookseller Lee Po". *South China Morning Post*. Retrieved from http://www.scmp.com/news/hong-kong/law-crime/article/1918997/i-sneaked-mainland-china-illegally-help-investigation-and.

Nielsen Hong Kong. (2015). *Media Index Survey 2015 Year-End Report*.

Office of the Communications Authority. (2017). Hong Kong Fact Sheet: Telecommunications. Retrieved from https://www.ofca.gov.hk/filemanager/ofca/en/content_113/telecommunications.pdf.

Office of the Communications Authority. (2018). Key Statistics for Telecommunications in Hong Kong: Wireless Services. Retrieved on 22 May 2018 from https://www.ofca.gov.hk/filemanager/ofca/en/content_108/wireless_en.pdf.

Phillips, T. (25 July 2016). "Mysterious Confession Fuels Fears of Beijing's Influence on Hong Kong's Top Newspaper". *The Guardian*. Retrieved from https://www.theguardian.com/world/2016/jul/25/south-china-morning-post-china-influence-hong-kong-newspaper-confession:

"Post, Politico Announce Groundbreaking Partnership to Expand Expert Coverage of US-China Ties". (22 May 2018). *South China Morning Post*. Retrieved from http://www.scmp.com/print/news/hong-kong/article/2147279/post-politico-announce-groundbreaking-partnership-expand-expert.

Reporters without Borders. (29 April 2016). "Beijing's Invisible Hand Reaches Ever Deeper into Hong Kong Media". Retrieved from https://rsf.org/en/reports/beijings-invisible-hand-reaches-ever-deeper-hong-kong-media.

SCMP Group Limited. (2015). *Annual Report 2015*.

Siu, Phila. (10 February 2018). "Transcript of Gui Minhai's Government-Arranged Interview: 'Swedish Government Used Me'". *South China Morning Post*. Retrieved from http://www.scmp.com/news/hong-kong/politics/article/2132813/transcript-gui-minhais-interview-swedish-government-used-me.

"*South China Morning Post* Turns to The Mainland". (17 June 2014). *Asia Sentinel South*. Retrieved from http://www.asiasentinel.com/politics/south-china-morning-post-china-coverage/.

"*South China Morning Post* Introduces New Identity". (6 February 2018). *South China Morning Post*. Retrieved from https://corp.scmp.com/2079-2/ and http://www.scmp.com/news/article/2132136/south-china-morning-post-moves-times.

Tsai, J. C. (11 December 2015). "Letter to Readers of the *South China Morning Post*, From Alibaba's Executive Vice Chairman". *South China Morning Post*. Retrieved from http://www.scmp.com/news/hong-kong/article/1890058/letter-readers-south-china-morning-post-alibabas-executive-vice.

Tsang, A. (11 December 2015). "When *The South China Morning Post* Waded Into Controversy". *The New York Times*. Retrieved from http://www.nytimes.com/interactive/2015/12/10/business/international/south-china-morning-post-history.html?version=meter+at+0&module=meter-Links&pgtype=article&contentId=&mediaId=&referrer=&priority=true&action=click&contentCollection=meter-links-click&_r=1.

Wade, Samuel. (2018). "SCMP Confronted Over Forced Confession Coverage" *China Digital Times*. Retrieved from https://chinadigitaltimes.net/2018/04/daughter-confronts-scmp-editor-over-forced-confession-coverage/.

World Economic Forum. (2016). "Networked Readiness Index". Retrieved from http://reports.weforum.org/global-information-technology-report-2016/networked-readiness-index/.

World Economic Forum. (2016). "Global Information Technology Report 2016". Retrieved from http://reports.weforum.org/global-information-technology-report-2016/.

"Young Chinese Legal Activist 'Regrets' Civil Rights Activism". (11 July 2016). *South China Morning Post*. Retrieved from http://www.scmp.com/news/china/policies-politics/article/1988501/young-chinese-legal-activist-regrets-civil-rights.

# Chapter 3

## Allies and Foes:
## The Impact of Technological Convergence and Public Participation on Television Journalism in HK

*Florin C. SERBAN*

## Introduction

This chapter explores the effects of technological convergence and public participation on television news production practices. No longer defined solely by linear content provided by its professional journalists and broadcast with a one-way communication model, news television channels are nowadays subject to technological convergence and the emergence of user-generated content (UGC). An array of user contributions ranging from amateur videos uploaded on various video platforms, posts on social networking sites, blogs and alternative media platforms are now challenging the production practices of traditional news broadcasters. These challenges are redefining the production practices of journalistic institutions and their means of distribution as well as causing them to re-evaluate their business model. This chapter aims to discuss the growing presence of media convergence practices, understood in its technological and organisational aspects. It is based on a case-study that took place in the newsroom of Cable News, a media outlet perceived to be credible and trustworthy by other local journalists (Chan, 2017).

In Hong Kong, the presence of amateur videos in local media has witnessed a surge in recent years (Lee, 2012). In a region where technology is extremely pervasive, many "random acts of journalism" (Holt and Karlsson, 2015) are provided by citizens who are equipped with smart devices capable of capturing and uploading video footage. I will closely analyse the role played by technological convergence in this process, since hi-tech advancements enable the audience to create and distribute their own content (Robinson, 2011; Bivens, 2014). From an organisational perspective, this process is repositioning the audience as a source of information, rather than as only a consumer of information.

## Hong Kong's Television Market and Cable News

There are three main cable companies that operate in Hong Kong: Television Broadcasts Limited (TVB) Pay Vision, PCCW (formerly Pacific Century CyberWorks Limited) Media and Hong Kong Cable Television. All of them have also developed their own channels, which are competing with free-to-air broadcasters. These three companies reach approximately 60% of the households in Hong Kong and collectively offer up to 170 channels (van der Haak, 2011).

i-Cable Communications Limited is one of the largest media organisations in Hong Kong, and it provides paid television, broadband and telephone services (i-Cable, 2015), thus fitting in what Anthony Fung describes as "non-organisational concentration" (2008). Over its broadcasting and telephone services, television operations had the highest turnover, which in 2011 increased by more than 12% over 2010 (i-Cable, 2012). Original programming is provided for sports, entertainment, movies and for the flagship news division. There are currently four news-channels offered to its subscribers: i-Cable Weather Channel, i-Cable Finance Info Channel, i-Cable News Channel and i-Cable Live News Channel. The content made available by these television channels can also be accessed by subscribers through any media platforms of their choice, such as the application C-online which allows subscribers to watch programmes on their mobile devices at no additional fee. The programmes produced in-house by i-Cable take into consideration the digital synergies available and strive to achieve a higher standard of production compared to free-to-air channels. It is also worth mentioning that most of the audience have the financial means to acquire up-to-date new media devices through which they can access programmes produced by the cable company. This aspect needs to be considered, as the production of various programmes has to satisfy the mobility and the consumption behaviour of the audience.

As stated in their internal reports, one of the major threats for i-Cable Communications Limited is the growing mobile device usage in Hong Kong and the lack of financial means to capitalise on them (i-Cable, 2015). Although the group is successful in its paid-television operations, it is also aware that other platforms can achieve a broader reach on mobile devices. However, by being a content provider as well as a platform operator, the company aims to extend its cross-platform reach during special events, such as the Olympic games (i-Cable, 2012).

i-Cable Communications Limited is heavily reliant on the paid-television operations and is, at present, losing financially as a consequence of not providing services in the wireless telecommunication sector. Although mobile applications have been developed for both cable company subscribers and the public at large, the group does not provide an infrastructure for the wireless transfer of media content. The daily production practices of i-Cable journalists are not directly affected by this situation, but some of the senior managers are afraid their editorial independence will be affected by the inherent convergence with the new media department (NMD). The main concern comes from the fact that news will have to be written not only for television programmes but also for online platforms, such as the website and social media channels. Presently, news reports are structured under the supervision of experienced television journalists and are designed to meet the demands of broadcast television. However, not long from now journalists will have to produce news reports which are more appealing for those who are accessing them via a computer or through mobile devices. Unlike the current situation, manufacturing and broadcasting the news report on television will have to be done simultaneously on other media platforms.

Devastating news for the journalists working for i-Cable News came in March 2017 when it was announced that Wharf Holdings would end funding for paid-television operators in an effort to focus on property development. Discussions on the sale of i-Cable Communications were previously on the table, but the company announced that it had not found a suitable buyer. In addition, previous loans would not be extended upon expiry. i-Cable also suffered a net loss of HK$313 million in 2016 due to a plunge in advertising revenue (Chan, 2017). i-Cable News has a license that was due to expire at the end of May 2017, but has recently received an extension for 12 more years from the Hong Kong government. In the weeks that followed the announcement that Wharf Holdings would end its funding of the television, minority stakeholders stepped up and announced they would rescue the station (Siu, 2017). Although stable at the time of writing this chapter, the situation endured by television journalists highlight the professional difficulties faced by all journalists. Dependent on the public through the nature of their profession, journalists are struggling to capture the attention of an audience prone to consume news from a myriad of other sources than legacy media. The aim of this study is to understand how legacy journalists from i-Cable News deal with technological convergence and public participation and how these two processes are affecting their everyday routines.

## Assessing Operations and Production Practices

The data for this study comes from participant observation in the newsroom of i-Cable News and in-depth interviews with eleven journalists, ranging from junior editors to the station's news controller, as Table 3.1 shows. Although the majority of details for this analysis come from the News Channels' editorial

### Table 3.1
### Respondents

| ID | Position inside i-Cable | Years of Working Experience | Years of Working for I-Cable |
|---|---|---|---|
| R1 | News writer for China desk | 1 | 1 |
| R2 | News writer for foreign desk | 2 | 2 |
| R3 | Managing editor for foreign news | 10 | 1 |
| R4 | Principal sub-editor | 21 | 17 |
| R5 | News controller/Head of newsroom | 25 | 19 |
| R6 | Senior reporter | 8 | 6 |
| R7 | Planning editor | 28 | 19 |
| R8 | Managing editor | 28 | 18 |
| R9 | News writer for China Desk | 14 | 7 |
| R10 | Reporter | 5 | 3 |
| R11 | Reporter | 4 | 4 |

staff, connections between the integrated operations among the channels were also made possible through observation and were facilitated by interviews and informal discussions with the journalists.

In order to have "a holistic description of cultural membership" (Lindlof and Taylor, 2002) most of the analysis will rely on what Cottle distinguished in the ethnographic studies as "focused production-based study" (2009). This method aims to reach a deep understanding of the working practices inside the newsroom, by making use of two dimensions: observation of the operations and production practices and discussions with the actors involved. I will analyse the institutionalised production practices and the journalists' relationships with news producers and their audience, perceived to be both content consumers and content distributors in the converged realm. Participant observation provides a proper understanding of media convergence levels inside the newsroom through informal talks, observations and interviews with the journalists and with some of the senior managers. I find one of the strengths of this method to be the triangulation of data which results from the research. The observation, the interviews and the study of archival documents leave little room for important considerations to be overlooked.

## Daily Practices and the Fast Pace of Production

There is constant pressure for journalists to report on events as they are developing. This pressure is both self-imposed and generated by competition with other local news stations. With the means to broadcast events on the Live News Channel available, journalists feel obliged to present their viewers with the most newsworthy and relevant events as they unfold. The mediascape of Hong Kong is subject to harsh competition. This prompts journalists to pay constant attention to what their local news television competitors are doing, with the help of television screens which are spread all around the newsroom. Chinese news stations, such as CCTV, and international news stations, such as CNN, BBC and Sky News, are constantly monitored, preventing journalists from losing sight of what needs to be broadcast on i-Cable channels. Television programmes are running in the background while journalists perform their daily tasks. Since new media platforms facilitate the use of videos, they are regarded as both a complementary source of information and as rivals in the battle to attract viewers, as note by one of the interviewees:

I perceive news aggregators as competition. Particularly since we are a twenty-four-hour news station, speed is very important. It is quite often that I go to a press conference and my story will be broadcast and then featured on our website two or three hours later. But before that, you can see already that some reporters have instant coverage from that press conference through live text. It is kind of disappointing since they can cover the events before me. We're in a kind of competition, but in two different ways because they have speed, but they may omit [details] and not be as accurate as we are. Accuracy is very important. My main competitors are other broadcasters, not newspapers or magazines. We are also making use of their initial coverage because since they are faster we find them to be a good resource for us, we may refer to their information. (R1)

Journalists are also concerned about the fact that online competitors can spread incorrect information. This is becoming a challenging aspect of their daily routine as sometimes they do not know how to react. If they do not report on a false story that is buzzing everywhere else in the media, they might be regarded as lagging behind their competitors. If they decide not to ignore the false story, then they have to try and find some newsworthy truth to report on. Commenting on this situation, a senior journalist said: "In terms of disseminating the information, no matter if it is true or rumours, no television or radio are stronger than the internet." (R8)

The competition with other media outlets is not a new experience for television journalists. An old practice which still exists today is the morning review of the newspapers. One of the main responsibilities of the night reporters is to read the newspapers and alert the morning editors if there are any notable events or stories covered by other newspapers that are missing from the editorial plan. This gives journalists an opportunity to initiate their own coverage. Permanently monitoring the activity of competitors adds to the fast pace of news production, but is also puts pressure on decision-makers:

The challenge of new media is every day present. We still have to monitor and see what our competitors broadcast, if they have some scoops or if they collected news items from other sources faster than us. We feel there is a pressure growing, but still we have to stand firm on some guidelines and principles because we have to see whether it is newsworthy, true, comprehensive, balanced or biased. We have to do all the calculation, but yes, there is a growing pressure. And sometimes, this may affect our judgement; I am scared this will happen. (R8)

Regardless of the high level of digitisation inside its physical newsroom, i-Cable is structured and functions as a news television programme of the broadcast era (Lotz, 2007). All operations are put in order according to the structure and the logic of a broadcasting television station in which the most important aspect is what is being aired. In the past decade, an NMD has been established, but it has not been integrated into the newsroom's daily practices yet. This leads to a clear division of tasks between television journalists and new media journalists, with the former being responsible for the news content that is provided by the three television channels, while the latter have the task of repurposing the journalistic content for distribution on other media platforms. By having access to the editorial system with read-only rights, the NMD provides content for the website and for the mobile applications developed by the station. Since this study is concerned with the effects of convergence and UGC on the production methods of frontline journalists, I have found it more suitable to carry out the research inside the newsroom and to focus less on the practices of the NMD.

The most important live coverage provided by the Live News Channel is also broadcast by the News Channel. In the eventuality of breaking news, all the journalistic and technological efforts are prioritised in order to provide an immediate live report from the scene. These are challenging events for the journalistic daily routines, which were previously discussed in newsroom meetings. Also, the emergence of unpredictable events leads to the reallocation of resources, including live broadcasting equipment and the placement of reporters and editorial staff. After discussing some of the daily practices inside the i-Cable newsroom, the following section will attempt to map the technological convergence and its effect on the production practices inside i-Cable through participant observation.

## Effects of Technological Convergence on Daily Production Practices

This section will look at the use and impact of technological convergence inside the newsroom. The production of news is fully digitised, meaning that the daily production operations of filming, putting together the montage and broadcasting are done with the help of non-linear digital networked equipment. Technological convergence not only allows for journalists to fill in their stories remotely, but also to add a voice track remotely for news reports. In recent years, it has often been the case that reporters in the field have less information than the journalists in the newsroom. By having access to more sources (i.e., other news television stations or online newspapers), newsroom editors have the means to compile a more coherent picture of the events than the journalists who are in the field broadcasting live and collecting interviews from witnesses. Therefore, it comes as no surprise that from time to time the script is edited in the newsroom and sent to the journalist who is in the field via email or through social media platforms, such as Facebook Messenger or WhatsApp. Once the reporter has recorded the voice track, the audio file will be sent via email to the video editors. This normative description of one of the many production practices inside i-Cable demonstrates how journalists are making use of convergent technologies to achieve their duties faster. Thus, journalists do not only use convergent technologies that were exclusively developed for media professionals, they are also users of commonly available technologies that enable a smoother workflow.

All of the News Channel programmes are broadcast live from a studio in the newsroom, with the exception of the evening news bulletins which are pre-recorded. In fact, all three of the major news channels rely greatly or exclusively on live broadcasts. This has led to heavy investing in broadcasting capability ever since the news station first aired in 1993. The rampant pace of technological development has been noticed especially by the experienced journalists who have witnessed the transition from analogue production practices to digitisation:

> When I joined the television business in the 80's, the environment was old. We used the paper to write the script and the play-out system was extremely difficult, making us work with use a lot of tapes. In the mid-90's when I arrived [in i-Cable] the environment was changing. There was already an automatic system and we were using the computer ... (R8)

Today, technology that allows wireless transmission from the camera to a microwave collecting point and from there to the station's headquarters is already in use. The newest technology the television station has at its disposal is the TVuPack. This mobile broadcasting device can transmit a live HDTV signal over 4G or other Wi-Fi networks, allowing for a camera operator to broadcast from any place in Hong Kong with the help of a transmission kit that fits inside a backpack. In addition to this technology, journalists rely on Inmarsat phones, video phones or phones with 4G capacity to broadcast from around the city. However, given that the TVuPack is running at a low cost and allows for high mobility and HDTV quality, it remains the main choice, especially when breaking news unfolds. In light of this, the previous scarcity of live broadcasting has turned into an abundance of live options, as long as events allow for it. 4G technology, which is a popular means of live communication, is already an obsolete broadcasting technology for news television. Whilst the audience is mastering the techniques of producing its own media content, journalists are also schooled in making the best use of technological convergence. For the newsroom, the process of appropriation is not only being done with UGC but also with technology.

Journalists who had to work with analogue technology when they were reporting from China still remember the limitations of that technology and how it was subjected to state control: "In my older days we used to transmit the tape by coming back to Hong Kong by plane or train. Later, we had the satellite, but it was also subjected to the censorship, since you were not allowed to broadcast it [from China]". Technological developments have not only helped journalists to disseminate their messages faster but also help manoeuvre around censorship. The same journalist continues:

> Then the low speed broadcasting came into place. You would have to wait for almost one hour to send back two minutes of [filmed] material. Now everything can be transmitted back to our studio through TVU and other wireless broadcast technologies. From this perspective, I would say the technology helps us very much. (R9)

Another journalist underlines the benefits gained from technological convergence in terms of live transmissions:

> The most striking thing is that in the late 80s, when you wanted to do a live transmission outside of Hong Kong, you had to find a third party service provider. It was the only way to go live, but now, it is self-contained. We can go live anywhere in the world; there is a telecommunication network that can allow us to do anything we can. Back in 2003, a few days before George W. Bush decided to invade Iraq, we made some thirty live satellite

bookings per a day, but if another war will come now, we'll just have video phones or TVUs. (R7)

From an editorial standpoint, the constant use of live reports is being questioned by some of the journalists in terms of value:

We have live signals all the time as breaking news unfolding, we are there before it even happens, we go live as it happens and at times we have multi-camera options. I would from time to time ask myself ...are we running a newscast? Does our audience expect to watch such a newscast? What are the impacts? Are we doing good or evil? (R7)

Regular live broadcasts are encouraged by the use of the most up-to-date technology and by the high level of competition with other local media outlets. By admitting that live reports can get out of hand and escape editorial logic, journalists acknowledge they have a problem with handling what is being broadcast. The most important events which interrupt the daily workflow of journalists are the public statements given by politicians. While these public appearances are expected, the exact time when politicians will come out to talk to the press is never known in advance, and these events are often not only confined to press conferences. These public comments by politicians mostly happen in the first part of the day and overlap with the first couple of minutes of the hourly newscasts. This caused one journalist to comment:

[The politicians] have very good counselling and know when to carry out their speeches. They definitely know when they will benefit for maximum exposure and that we will broadcast them live as long as they don't overlap with commercial breaks. (R7)

Whilst journalists are aware of their programmes consisting of too many live reports, it is hard for them to stop. The pressures coming from the other local stations that will also be broadcasting the statements are constraining the journalists to go live no matter what, as noted during one interview:

In Hong Kong you have to go live before your competitors. Everything is changing fast, you have to go fast to the scene, switch from single camera operation to multi-camera operation. You don't have a tradition of liaising with the interviewer in advance and then you have to prepare for the worst. You have to assign more than one crew to the scene, switch on the camera and be prepared. The first thing to do is to catch the eyeballs, while in other markets perhaps the emphasis is on the content of the broadcast. (R7)

In this case, the control over programme production is shared with forces outside the newsroom. Notably, in this case, is the tacit understanding between politicians and journalists. They both rely upon each other, as the former need live coverage to address their opinions when and how they want to with the audience, while the latter use live coverage of politicians to show the audience that they provide the latest updates. It is also important in this equation not to miss something which has been seized by competitors.

## Convergence as a Production Practice

Tons of stories are produced and broadcast everyday by i-Cable journalists. To facilitate this fast pace, technological improvements have been implemented inside the newsroom. Furthermore, to offer context and background for daily reports, a huge digitised archive can be accessed from the computers available on reporters' desks. This archive allows access to all the news bulletins that have been broadcast by i-Cable in the last four years and by its main competitors in the past two years. The news material is stored in digital format on computer servers. In the eventuality that a journalist would like to have a look at previous political statements or to learn how a news subject was previously treated, the reporter can search for it with keywords on the database. This facility can save valuable time in the production process, as there is no need for the reporter to go into the analogue archive and search for a certain video fragment through older videocassettes. Given that the older recording can be accessed in its digital format, the archive can be directly used in both the input and the output process of production.

There are also aspects of technological convergence that are not fully embedded in daily operations. This is mostly visible on the China desk where the news writers are highly dependent on videos posted on Chinese social networks. Although there are i-Cable offices in China, the sheer size of the country makes it impossible for correspondents to cover all newsworthy events. Hence, journalists based in Hong Kong constantly check the websites of local Chinese television stations and browse social media platforms to look for video support for their stories. As the accuracy of incoming information is always regarded with strong skepticism due to censorship, the journalists prefer to rely on the coverage provided by trusted wires, such as Reuters.

Even so, the problem of video footage still remains. No matter how accurate the information may be, footage from the event will only be provided by news agencies at a later stage. In most of these situations, the footage is provided by local Chinese television stations and then used to illustrate a story, while the information on the event will be taken from other sources. Since the video quality provided by local television websites is usually low, journalists are left to employ hybrid forms of production. The most prominent technique used to improve the quality of a video coming from a secondary source is for a camera operator to film the computer monitor while the video is being played. From there, the video footage will be processed and the end result will have significantly better resolution than the original clip. There have been situations when this process was repeated five times in a single day prompting the camera operator to ironically say "I am a web camera man, not a camera man". Apart from this hybrid form of analogue and digital production, most output operations make use of technological convergence. There are times when the television screen resembles a computer screen due to the heavy use of 3D graphics or other graphic elements, such as the clock, weather symbols, voice-over, the crawl (news ticker) and photos when video footage is unavailable.

## Journalists and their Technologies

After scrutinising the role of institutionalised technologies in the production process, I will now turn my attention to the relationship between journalists and their personal technologies. I refer here to their mobile phones, tablets or laptops and the applications they are accessing through these devices. During my presence in the newsroom, I noticed the constant use of these devices and the effect they had on staff activity. When asked about the impact of technology outside of their office hours, most of the journalists had positive remarks:

> Technology makes it easier for me as a person because when I come to work I spend one hour on the train and I can check up what had happened during the night. In that hour I get to make myself an image about what happened in Hong Kong, China and the rest of the world. (R1)

At the same time, there is also a prevalent opinion that the growing presence of these devices and their applications are also affecting their daily work. The same journalist pointed out the downside:

> I am highly influenced by what my friends are reading and sharing on social networks. It's kind of an *information bombardment* and as a reporter I have to know what subjects I should choose and what would be the main point of a story among all the available reports. (R1, my emphasis)

This opinion resonates with the conceptualisation of networked societies offered by Castells (2007) in which all the domains of social life are affected by the ongoing communication transformations.

The analysis shows that technological convergence does not present a disruptive factor in the newsroom's daily production. Journalists have come to master new ways of embedding technological convergence into their work processes. Notably, technological convergence did not appear out of nowhere. It was slowly implemented as a way to enhance production practices. Journalists have a positive opinion on the technology that allows them to better perform their tasks while they remain doubtful regarding the role technological convergence will play in the future. Based on my observations and interviews, journalists are not worried about adopting new technology as long as they are able to control it.

## Conclusion

The study presented in this chapter explores how the process of technological convergence has transformed production practices inside Hong Kong's 24-hour news television stations. The findings of this case study suggest that convergence has a meaningful impact on this field, one that is not exclusively negative. Unlike some previous studies conducted in television newsrooms, such as that provided by Williams et. al, who concluded that it was "business as usual" at the BBC (2011), my research shows that the process of technological convergence has seriously transformed journalistic production practices. In this case study, the process of technological convergence does not appear to have a disruptive effect on the news production process, but it is instead embedded in daily practices. This process has helped journalists secure their relevance against their competitors and in front of their audience.

The most obvious change is in the faster pace of news production. From collecting and editing to broadcasting the news, convergence has added a constant state of immediacy in the process of news production. Inside i-Cable's newsroom, technological convergence is a process that journalists embrace and put to good use. Although it has brought about a reconsideration of their daily practices, it is not a disruptive factor since it has been implemented in stages. This research indicates that journalists have learned to use technological convergence to their benefit, rather than viewing it as something against them. This state of immediacy that convergence has led to is regarded by journalists as beneficial to their work.

Although it is hard to tell what the future of Cable News will be, it would be unfair to blame the journalists for not being able to adapt to a technologically converged environment. Instead, there is a need for further studies to investigate the effects of political and economic pressure on the media system in Hong Kong.

# References

Bivens, R. (2014). *Digital Currents: How Technology and the Public Are Shaping TV News*. Toronto: University of Toronto Press.

Castells, M. (2007). "Communication, Power and Counter-Power in Network Society", *International Journal of Communication*, 1(1), 238-66.

Chan, Y. (13 March 2017). "Likely End of Cable News a Blow to Independent, Quality Reporting in Hong Kong." *Hong Kong Free Press*. Retrieved from https://www.hongkongfp.com/2017/03/13/likely-end-cable-news-blow-independent-quality-reporting-hong-kong/.

Fung, A.Y.H. (2008). "Political Economy of Hong Kong Media: Producing a Hegemonic Voice" in *Media Politics in Post-Handover Hong Kong*, edited by Chan, J.M. and Lee, L.F.F. p. 26-38. London and New York.

Holt, K. & Karlsson, M. (2015). "Random Acts of Journalism?: How Citizen Journalists Tell the News in Sweden." *New Media & Society* 17(11), 1795–1810. doi:10.1177/1461444814535189.

i-Cable. (2011). "2011 Final Results". Retrieved from http://www.i-cablecomm.com/ir/presentation/2011/2011Final.pdf.

i-Cable. (2012). *Annual Report*. Retrieved from http://www.i-cablecomm.com/ir/annual/2012/e01097_Annual%20Report.pdf.

i-Cable. (2015). *Annual Report*. Retrieved from http://www.i-cablecomm.com/ir/annual/2016/e01097%20Annual%20Report.pdf.

Lee, F. L. F. (2012). "News from YouTube: Professional Incorporation in Hong Kong Newspaper Coverage of Online Videos." *Asian Journal of Communication* 22(1), 1–18.

Lindlof, R.T. & Taylor, B. (2002). *Qualitative Communication Research Methods* (2nd edition). Thousand Oaks, CA: Sage.

Lotz, A. D. (2007). *The Television Will Be Revolutionized*. New York and London: New York University Press.

Robinson, S. (2011). "Convergence Crisis: News Work and News Space in the Digitally Transforming Newsroom." *Journal of Communication* 61, 1122–41. doi:10.1111/j.1460-2466.2011.01603.

Siu, P. (13 March 2017). "i-Cable Rescued for Now, but Hong Kong Broadcaster Must Rebrand and Embrace Internet Age to Survive, Experts Say." *South China Morning Post*. Retrieved from http://www.scmp.com/news/hong-kong/education-community/article/2096134/i-cable-rescued-now-hong-kong-broadcaster-must.

van der Haak, B. (2011). *Creative Future Television: Ideas for a New Curriculum*. City University of Hong Kong: Hong Kong.

Williams, A., Wardle, C., & Wahl-Jorgensen, K. (2011). "Have They Got News for Us? Audience Revolution or Business as Usual at the BBC?" *Journalism Practice* 5(1), 85–99. doi:10.1080/17512781003670031.

# Chapter 4

# The State of the Radio Sector in Hong Kong

*Jenny LAM*

## Introduction

There are three commercial sound broadcasting licensees in Hong Kong: Commercial Radio Hong Kong (CRHK), Digital Broadcasting Corporation (DBC) and Metro. Radio Television Hong Kong (RTHK) is the government-run public broadcaster. Between them, they provide thirteen analogue radio channels: three are broadcast by CRHK, three by Metro and seven by RTHK. In addition, DBC and Metro are licensed to provide Digital Audio Broadcasting (DAB) services (Hong Kong Communications Authority, 2014–15). RTHK also operates seven DAB channels.

## Programme Production and Broadcasting Hours

With the exception of RTHK's relay of BBC World Service on Radio 6 and programmes transmitted by Beijing's China National Radio on its digital radio service, nearly all programmes aired in Hong Kong are produced by the broadcasters themselves (Table 4.1).

According to the Communication Authority's 2014–15 annual report, in March 2015 sound broadcasting in Hong Kong amounted to 5,040 hours per week. The thirteen analogue channels accounted for 2,184 hours per week and the seventeen digital channels provided 2,856 broadcast hours per week.

CRHK, Metro and RTHK provide their services in both FM and AM modes. Seven of the FM channels transmit their signals via seven hilltop sites supplemented by two low-power FM gap-fillers. Six of the AM channels are broadcast from two island and hilltop sites, with six low-power AM/FM gap-fillers. The signals reach the whole of Hong Kong.

The analogue sound broadcasting licences of CRHK and Metro expired on 25 August 2016. Following a two-month public consultation exercise, the Communications Authority agreed to renew both licenses for a period of twelve years. Both will be subject to a mid-term review in 2022. Over the new licence period, CRHK is committed to investing HK$908.6 million between 2016 and 2022. Of this, $25 million will be capital investment and $883.6 million programming investment. Metro meanwhile proposed to invest $685

**Table 4.1**

**Analogue Audio Broadcasting Channels in Hong Kong**

| Operator | Channel | Programme Type |
|---|---|---|
| CRHK | CR 1 (FM) | Cantonese: news, current affairs, finance, talk shows |
| CRHK | CR 2 (FM) | Cantonese: entertainment and pop culture targeting young listeners |
| CRHK | AM 864 | English: mainly music |
| Metro | Metro Finance (FM) | Cantonese: real time financial market information |
|  | Metro Info (FM) | Cantonese: music, entertainment, lifestyle |
|  | Metro Plus (AM) | English, Tagalog, Hindi, Bahasa and Urdu: programmes targeting Filipino, Indian, Indonesian and Pakistani communities |
| RTHK | Radio 1 | Cantonese: news, information and general programming |
|  | Radio 2 | Cantonese: youth, entertainment and pop music |
|  | Radio 3 | English: news, information and general programming |
|  | Radio 4 | Bilingual English and Cantonese, classical music |
|  | Radio 5 | Cantonese: programmes targeting the elderly |
|  | Radio 6 | English: BBC World Service relay |
|  | Radio 7 | Putonghua: general programming |

Source: Communications Authority Annual Report 2014–15.

million over six years, $22.3 million in capital investment and $662.7 million in programming (*The Standard*, 2016)

Licensed broadcast services, both television and radio, produced $7.9 billion in 2014, which was 0.35% of Hong Kong's gross domestic product that year. Most of that came from the sale of advertising spots. Moreover, the majority came from television, and according to admanGo Limited, radio accounted for only 4% of the sum (Statista, 2016).

## Public Broadcasting

Since 1997, RTHK has consistently been rated as the most trusted electronic media in Hong Kong, according to the Centre for Communication and Public Opinion Survey at the Chinese University of Hong Kong. The operation of RTHK, a department of the government, is bound by a charter published on 13 August 2010 (Charter of Radio Television, Hong Kong 2010). It gives details of the broadcaster's public purposes and mission, its editorial independence, its key programme areas and mode of delivery, and it provides for performance evaluation and the maintenance of transparency. The aim of RTHK, as stated in the 2016 government budget, is to "inform, educate and entertain the public through high quality programmes that are not adequately provided by commercial broadcasters" (HKSAR government, 2016). To that end, the purposes and mission of RTHK include promoting understanding of the community and of the "one country, two systems" principle and its implementation in Hong Kong. It also seeks to engender a sense of citizenship and national identity in addition to providing a platform for the free exchange of views and opinions and to stimulate creativity to encourage multicultural growth in the community.

### Appointment of the Director of Broadcasting

In August 2015, the government announced the appointment of Leung Ka-wing as the new director of broadcasting. Leung is a veteran journalist who had previously served as a news controller, first at Television Broadcasts Limited (TVB) and then at Asia Television (ATV). Staff at RTHK and the Hong Kong Journalists Association (HKJA) welcomed Leung's appointment, relieved that the government station would no longer be headed by a bureaucrat as it had been previously. However, they also expressed reservations that Leung might bow to political pressure (Lau & Lam, 2015).

## RTHK's Budget

RTHK's budget for the 2016–17 financial year was estimated to be HK$385.5 million, a 6.6% increase from the previous year (Table 4.2). The cost per hour was highest for Radio 2 at $6,840 and lowest for the BBC World Service relay channel Radio 6, which was only $88.

### Table 4.2
### RTHK's Budget in 2016–17

| Channels | Budget Estimate (million HKD) |
|:---:|:---:|
| 1 | 8,760 |
| 2 | 7,640 |
| 3 | 8,760 |
| 4 | 6,570 |
| 5 | 8,100 |
| 6 | 8,760 |
| 7 | 6,935 |
| TOTAL | 55,525 |
| Hours of news programming output | 7,140 |

Source: Hong Kong Government Budget 2016–17.

## Transfer of ATV's Spectrum to RTHK

When ATV finally folded in March 2016 after years of effort to keep it going, the government asked RTHK to take over the vacated free-to-air television spectrum. It increased the public broadcaster's budget by 6.6% for the 2016–17 financial year, an additional 2.5% points over the previous year. RTHK staff were very upset about the increased pressure caused by this change. According to the Hong Kong Journalists Association's 2015 annual report, their union said it could not set up a twenty-four-hour news operation so quickly, and "called the decision hasty and irresponsible and one made without prior consultation and detailed planning."

## Application to Build a New Broadcasting House

In 2013, RTHK applied for just over HK$6 billion to build a New Broadcasting House at the Tseung Kwan O Industrial Estate. The 27,660 square-metre space was supposed to provide studios for the broadcaster's analogue services as well as room for expansion into digital audio broadcasting. There would also be five new television studios and a news centre plus engineering and archive storage facilities. RTHK said its existing premises on Broadcast Drive, Kowloon Tong, opened in the 1960s, had become "extremely crowded". It also needed to upgrade its facilities to fulfil the mission set out for it by the government under its charter. In January 2014, the Legislative Council turned down the application, with lawmakers pointing out that the amount was four times the estimate of the HK$1.6 billion given in an earlier application in 2009 (Hong Kong Legislative Council, 2013).

## Digital Audio Broadcasting (DAB)

The DAB broadcasters—DBC, Metro and RTHK—adopted the DAB+ standard for transmission of their programmes. The network is made up of seven principle transmission stations that were launched in 2012. In 2015, a DAB gap-filler was added to improve the area covered. In May 2016, DAB services reached more than 80% of Hong Kong.

The Hong Kong government invited applications for DAB operations in February 2010, and in March 2011, granted licences valid for twelve years to Wave Media Limited (which subsequently became DBC), Metro Broadcast Corporation Limited (Metro) and Phoenix U Radio Limited (Phoenix U Radio). The three licensees were to provide thirteen channels: three each from Metro and Phoenix U and seven from DBC. They were required to launch their services within eighteen months of being granted the licences. However, Phoenix U Radio later opted to return its licence. Meanwhile, RTHK was to provide five DAB programming channels, so that in March 2016 there were altogether fifteen DAB channels (Table 4.3).

**Table 4.3**

**Digital Audio Broadcasting Channels (March 2016)**

| Operators | Channels | Types of Programme |
|---|---|---|
| Metro | Metro Finance Digital | Cantonese: financial information |
|  | Metro Music Digital | Cantonese: music and entertainment |
|  | Metro Life Digital | Cantonese: lifestyle and information |
| RTHK | DAB 31 | Putonghua: general programming, news and finance |
|  | DAB 32 | Cantonese: China National Radio Hong Kong edition relay |
|  | DAB 33 | English: news, information and general programming |
|  | DAB 34 | English: BBC World Service relay |
|  | DAB 35 | Cantonese: programmes targeting the elderly |
| Digital Broadcasting Corporation Hong Kong Limited (DBC) | DBC 1 | General programming |
|  | DBC 2 | General programming |
|  | DBC 3 | General programming |
|  | DBC 4 | General programming |
|  | DBC 5 | General programming |
|  | DBC 6 | General programming |
|  | DBC 7 | General programming |

Source: List of Digital Audio Broadcasting Services in Hong Kong
http://www.ofca.gov.hk/en/home/index.html

## Radio Listeners Survey

In June 2016, Hong Kong Baptist University commissioned a telephone survey about news consumption and use of social media in Hong Kong. Researchers interviewed 1,012 respondents, of whom 47.7% were male. Only 4.7% of the respondents said they listened to radio news regularly, making it by far the least popular of all the platforms for getting news. About 30% got their news from newspapers, another 30% from television, 7.5% from websites and 14.5% from social media. More than half the respondents (56.2%) said they did not listen to radio news at all.

**Figure 4.1**

**Share of News Listeners of Different Radio Stations in Hong Kong**

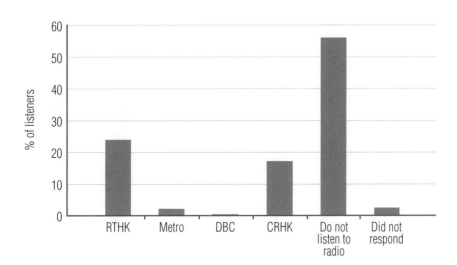

Of those who did get their news from radio, nearly 25% said they listened to RTHK, while 17.3% listened to CRHK, 2.3% to Metro and 0.6% to DBC (Figure 4.1). Of the two most popular stations, RTHK had the bigger share of listeners aged fifty and above while CRHK had a bigger share of younger listeners, mainly forty or below (Figure 4.2). The most common means of listening, cited by more than half of the respondents, was via radio sets, while 23% used mobile phones, 15.8% car radios and 6.4% computers. Those who used radio sets were mostly over 40 years of age, while younger listeners tended to listen via their mobile phones (Figure 4.3). The higher the listeners' education level, the less likely they were to listen to the news on a radio set (Figure 4.4). About a third of the listeners said they listened to the news for between one and fifteen minutes, while another third said they listened for more than an hour. People with lower incomes were likely to spend longer listening to radio news (Figure 4.5). Indeed, respondents who earned HK$9,999 or less a month were more likely to listen in for an hour or longer. Unemployed respondents were likely to spend the longest time listening, followed by labourers, housewives and retirees.

**Figure 4.2**

**Age of Listeners and Percentage Share of Audience for RTHK and CRHK**

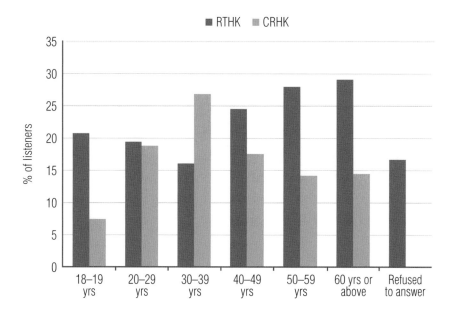

**Figure 4.3**

**Age of Listeners and Devices Used to Listen to Radio News**

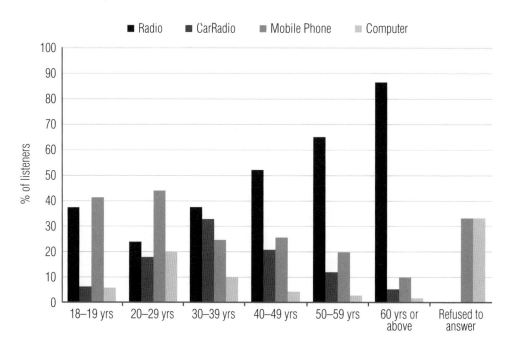

**Figure 4.4**

**Education Levels of Listeners and Devices Used for Listening to Radio News**

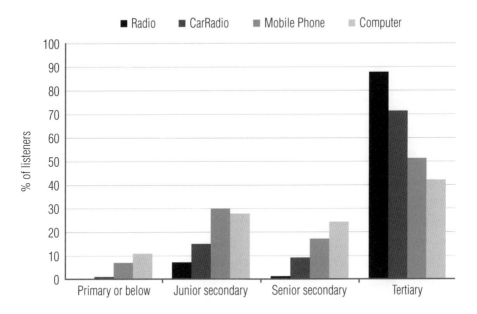

**Figure 4.5**

**Income Levels of Listeners and Time Spent Listening to Radio News**

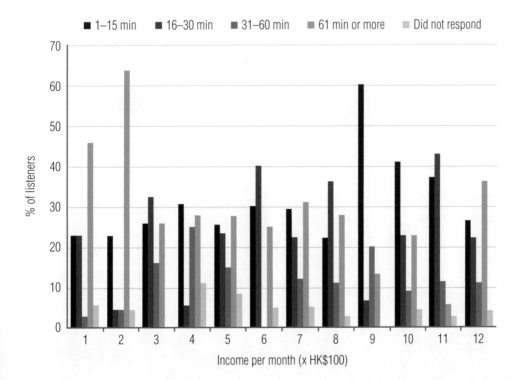

## Public Complaints about Radio Programmes

Between January 2014 and May 2016, the Communication Authority dealt with a variety of complaints (Table 4.4). Of these, twenty-four were public complaints against audio broadcasting services—fifteen about CRHK, one about Metro Radio and the rest were about RTHK. Eleven of the complaints against CRHK concerned *The Summit* (光明頂), a late-night talk show on global affairs, the majority of these referenced inaccuracies or unfairness. However, most were found to be unsubstantiated. The complaints against RTHK were all against news or news-related programmes, most significantly against the current affairs talk show *Talkabout* (千禧年代). Most cited partiality, inaccuracies or unfairness. Again, most were found to be unsubstantiated or unjustified. Complaints about crude language on radio mostly involved their coverage of Legislative Council proceedings. The only exception was a complaint against the programme *On A Clear Day* (在晴朗的一天出發) where foul language was uttered briefly. Only two of the twenty-five complaints warranted warnings by the Communications Authority. Both were against CRHK: one for the bad language used briefly during the programme *On A Clear Day* (在晴朗的一天出發), and the other was for an inappropriate religious reference on *The Summit* (Table 4.5).

### Table 4.4
**Distribution of Complaint Cases Processed by the Communications Authority (2014–15)**

| Operator | Number of Complaint Cases | Number of Complaints Involved |
|---|---|---|
| CRHK | 211 | 730 |
| Metro | 48 | 50 |
| DBC | 10 | 12 |
| RTHK | 270 | 342 |

Source: https://www.legco.gov.hk/yr16-17/english/counmtg/papers/cm20161214-sp047-e.pdf

**Table 4.5**

**Public Complaints against Radio Programmes (January 2014–May 2016)**

| Dates | Broadcaster | Programme | Complaint |
|---|---|---|---|
| Apr 2015 | CRHK | *The Fun Box* (大玩派) | Promotion of car hailing app |
| Aug 2015 | CRHK | *On A Clear Day* (在晴朗的一天出發) | Foul language<br>Indirect advertising |
| Oct 2014 | CRHK | *Circles* (圈圈) | Advertising |
| 20 Nov 2014 | RHTK Radio 4 | News report | Partiality |
| 3 Dec 2014 | RTHK Radio 1 | *Talkabout* (千禧年代) | Partiality |
| 25 Sep 2014 | RTHK Radio 4 | News report | Inaccuracy |
| 28 Nov 2014 | CRHK | *On A Clear Day* (在晴朗的一天出發) | Partiality |
| 8 Jul 2014 | CRHK | *The Summit* (光明頂) | Inappropriate religious reference |
| 31 Jul 2014 | CRHK | *The Summit* (光明頂) | Inaccuracy |
| 15 May 2014 | CRHK | *The Summit* (光明頂) | Crude language and sexual connotation |
| 24 Jun 2014 | RTHK Radio 4 | Hourly news summaries | Inaccuracy and unfairness |
| 2 Jul 2014 | RTHK Radio 5 | Legco meeting | Crude language |
| 18 Aug 2014 | RTHK Radio 1 | *Talkabout* (千禧年代) | Inaccuracy |
| 20 Aug 2014 | CRHK | *The Summit* (光明頂) | Inaccuracy and unfairness |
| 4 Aug 2014 | CRHK | *The Summit* (光明頂) | Inaccurate pronunciation |
| 14 Aug 2014 | CRHK | *The Summit* (光明頂) | Inaccuracy |
| 31 Jul 2014 | CRHK | *The Summit* (光明頂) | Inaccuracy |
| 15 May 2014 | CRHK | *The Summit* (光明頂) | Crude language and sexual connotation |
| 24 Jun 2014 | RTHK | Hourly news summaries | Inaccuracy and unfairness |
| 2 Jul 2014 | RTHK 5 | Legco meeting | Crude language |
| 18 Aug 2014 | RTHK 1 | *Talkabout* (千禧年代) | Inaccuracy |
| 20 Aug 2014 | CRHK | *The Summit* (光明頂) | Inaccuracy and unfairness |
| 4 Aug 2014 | CRHK | *The Summit* (光明頂) | Inaccurate pronunciation |
| 14 Aug 2014 | CRHK | *The Summit* (光明頂) | Inaccurate pronunciation |

Source: Communications Authority.

It is difficult to draw any conclusions about why *The Summit* in particular drew more complaints than any other programme. The data provided by the Communications Authority does not state who the complainants were. It is possible that the programme genuinely has more inaccuracies than most other radio shows, but it is also possible that complaints came from certain individuals (or a single individual) who disliked the programme's format or the way it was presented or even its host, Chip Tsao. It is also possible that *The Summit* is simply a popular programme with a wide audience and, therefore, gets a bigger share of complaints. But what the data does suggest is that complaints tend to be about comments on current or political affairs, suggesting that the listening public may be particularly sensitive toward these topics.

## The Radio Licensing Controversy

### The Return of Phoenix U Radio's DAB License

At the end of 2012, the pro-Beijing Phoenix U Radio was operating two channels: a comprehensive new/entertainment channel and a music channel. However, its third channel never materialised. In September 2015, Phoenix U applied to return its licence and cease programming by the end of the month. The company told the government that the potential audience was not large enough to attract advertisers and that there was no way of making the operation commercially viable. The Chief Executive in Council approved the termination, and Phoenix stopped broadcasting in November 2015 (HKSAR government, 2015).

Within weeks of Phoenix U Radio returning its licence, the government said it needed time to review the development of DAB and would, therefore, not be inviting any more licence applications for the time being. This sparked a barrage of criticism against the government for what some perceived as the administration's lack of commitment to DAB. Rival station DBC's chief executive officer, Law Chan, said the government had a lot to answer for in the failure of Phoenix U Radio. Law said the government did not enable drivers to install digital audio receivers in their vehicles, facilities in the tunnels were not good enough for DAB signal reception, and public housing estates were not equipped with DAB receivers. Legislator Wong Yuk-man, in a letter addressed to the Legislative Council (Wong 2015), asked why in-car installation for DAB had not been improved in the four years since licences were granted. In response (Administration's written response to the letter from Hon Wong Yuk-man on issues relating to the policy on digital audio broadcasting, 2015), a spokesman for the secretary for Commerce and Economic Development explained that, while there was no statutory prohibition against the installation of DAB radios in cars, visual display units that might be visible to the driver are banned by law.

## DBC Returns its DAB License

DBC was founded in 2008 by veteran broadcaster and commentator Albert Cheng King-hon. It launched its services in 2012, but it ran into financial problems within a month when some of its pro-Beijing backers refused to invest any further. One shareholder even revealed that the Central Government's Liaison Office in Hong Kong did not like one of the programme hosts DBC was trying to recruit. Cheng eventually sold his stake in DBC and moved on to start an online radio station called D10 (Yeung, 2015). DBC chief executive officer, Loh Chan complained that DAB operators faced unfair competition because the government had not come up with a timetable for DAB to replace analogue FM radio (*Apple Daily*, 2015). There was much speculation that the administration was dragging its feet on the development of DAB for political reasons. In its defence, the government said it had injected HK$46 million into the installation of re-broadcasting facilities in eleven government-operated tunnels, which was supposed to boost transmission power and co-ordinate frequencies with Mainland Chinese authorities.

In August 2016, DBC applied to the government to return its DAB license. The chief executive officer, Loh Chan, cited the lack of digital audio reception in car radios as the main problem. "Even if the government requires all 50,000 imported cars every year to be equipped with both FM and DAB radio players, it would still take us twelve years to compete on the same footing with FM radio broadcasters," he said in a press conference. In September 2016, DAB ceased broadcasting new programmes.

## Delay in the Renewal of Licences for CRHK and Metro

In April 2016, lawmaker Chan Chi-chuen asked why no decision had been made on whether to renew the analogue radio licences of CRHK and

Metro only four months before they were due to expire. He asked if the development of DAB would be an added requirement for analogue radio licensees. He noted that Albert Cheng, the controversial owner of online station D10, intended to apply for one of the new set of DAB licences on offer and asked if there was any reason why parties other than CRHK or Metro would be barred from doing so (Chan Chi-chuen's question on the analogue radio licences of Commercial Radio Hong Kong and Metro Broadcast Corp. Ltd., 2015). The government announced that CRHK and Metro would have their licences renewed for twelve years but said that, due to the difficulties encountered by DAB broadcasters, it was reviewing the development of the platform. In November 2016, Metro Radio's application to give up its DAB licence was approved by the Executive Council. That left RTHK as the only digital radio provider.

## RTHK's Attempts to Develop Digital Broadcasting

The Legislative Council's vote to reject the HK$6 billion funding request for RTHK's proposed new headquarters was a major setback to plans for the public broadcaster to develop DAB. Indeed, it had already planned to launch digital terrestrial broadcasts in 2018, and the funding setback meant that RTHK remains an antiquated broadcaster. Some of its audio recording equipment, studios and even computers are outdated, some being more than twenty years old. The station has developed some new services, however. Its news section, for example, launched a video desk to provide content for its website, a common practice in modern-day DAB worldwide. However, the video team is small and consists of experienced freelancers and inexperienced interns that use basic software. As a result, content updates are often slow and not comprehensive. While the hard-working staff at RTHK should be commended for their efforts to operate on a shoestring, the development of RTHK into a fully digital public broadcaster is impossible without funding.

## Media Freedom

According to the HKJA's Press Freedom Index of March 2015, journalists felt that the government had become more manipulative towards the media, with their assessment on a scale of one (low) to ten (high) rising from 5.6 in 2013 to 6.2 in 2014. The question of freedom of speech on radio has come under scrutiny over the years, but has spiked following the many controversies in the sector. CRHK's refusal to renew the contract of Albert Cheng in 2004 sparked speculation that it had to do with the radio host's criticism of the government. Six years earlier, in 1998, Cheng had been the victim of a brutal knife attack outside the CRHK building, and later told the *South China Morning Post* (*SCMP*) (Lee and Lee, 2004) that he believed he was targeted because of the pro-political reform comments he made on his radio show. Ten years later, in February 2014, CRHK sacked Li Wei-ling (Chiu, 2014), another outspoken critic of the government. She hosted the morning talk show *On A Clear Day*. CRHK wanted to move her to a less prominent programme. When that didn't work out, Li was fired.

At RTHK, the station's refusal to offer civil service terms to its long-term employees has been a bone of contention since 2010, when the government broadcaster decided to recruit new blood to fill certain senior posts instead of allowing internal promotion in 2010. Staff reacted by staging protests (Wan 2011). Today, most of the newsroom staff at RTHK are on contract terms, which are much less generous than civil service terms. In December 2015, RTHK's decision to axe two programmes hosted by presenters who were linked to the 2014 Occupy Central movement caused complaints from staff of political motivation. Chan Ka-ming, host of the phone-in entertainment talk show *Sik Si Fung*, one of the cancelled programmes, told the *SCMP* (Tsang, 2016) that staff had been told to downplay certain topics, including the Occupy movement. He said he did not know who was giving instructions but "we all felt the pressure". *Sik Si Fung* ended after eight years in early January 2015. *Cultural Renaissance* was also cancelled. RTHK's programme staff union issued a statement expressing concern that the public broadcaster may cut back on political discussions and infringe on freedom of expression, which is guaranteed under Hong Kong's Basic Law. RTHK denied there was any political motive behind the cancellation of *Sik Si Fung* and *Cultural Renaissance*. A spokeswoman for RTHK's management said the changes were made for the benefit of listeners.

Audio broadcasters along with the rest of the media in Hong Kong have been accused of self-censorship. In February 2016, the British Government's six-monthly report (*The Six-monthly Report on Hong Kong 1 July to 31 December 2015–2016*) on Hong Kong expressed concern over the erosion of freedom in the region. It cited the HKJA's Press Freedom Index's to highlight increasing self-censorship in the pres. There was no direct reference to any particular audio broadcasters or stations. Furthermore, according to the annual Press Freedom Index published by Reporters Without Borders (*World Press Freedom Ranking*, 2016), Hong Kong ranked sixty-ninth in 2016, a drop of nine places from the previous year. In 2002, Hong Kong came sixteenth.

## Conclusion

Data from the survey presented in this chapter shows that the preference for radio channels is significantly associated with age and education. CRHK is more popular with younger listeners and lower income earners, whereas RTHK is more popular with older listeners. Respondents who were likely to have more spare time (i.e., the unemployed, housewives and retirees) listened to the radio longer. Most of them listened using a radio set. The survey did not distinguish between those who listened to traditional analogue broadcasts and those who used digital channels. But DBC, which only broadcasts digitally, had the smallest audience share among the channels.

Notably, the findings also show that radio is the least popular means of getting news and is, therefore, the least effective way of broadcasting news to the masses. Radio broadcasters should take note of the fact that listeners tend to be older, with lower incomes and education levels. they should, therefore, cater to these groups' interests and reflect on why they are not attracting younger and more highly educated listeners. The BBC in the United Kingdom, for example, found that changing programming schedules and presenters helped to boost the number of listeners ("Radio 1 gains 750,000 listeners after schedule changes", 2015). The decline in the popularity of radio is not unique to Hong Kong. Research published by Nielsen showed that the audience size of National Public Radio (NPR) in the United States dropped by 11% from 2010 to 2015 (Farhi, 2015). Jeff Hansen, programme director at Seattle's public radio station KUOW, suggested the following reason: "Public radio was invented by people in their 20s in the 1970s, largely at stations funded by colleges and universities. What they didn't realise at the time was that what they were inventing was programming for people like themselves—baby boomers with college degrees." Here in Hong Kong, RTHK was set up on the model of the BBC in the United Kingdom, but while the BBC has updated and reinvented itself many times in the past few decades, RTHK has seen little change. The station's attempts to bring itself into the digital age have been thwarted by funding problems and bureaucratic road blocks.

The delay in the renewal of licences for CRHK and Metro and the halt in the development of DAB came within a year of the government's refusal to grant a free-to-air television licence to Hong Kong Television, a controversial broadcaster headed by a prominent critic of the government. These events fuelled suspicion in the pro-democracy camp and the press that the government wanted to tighten control on the media by excluding parties that might be deemed politically incorrect in the government's view.

Regardless of whether accusations of self-censorship are based on substantiated evidence, what broadcasters need to be aware of is the public's heightened sensitivity to freedom of the press and of expression in Hong Kong in recent years. Mere statements of denial every time new accusations crop up are not convincing and only fuel unhealthy speculation. There need to be open discussions on air to address these concerns, and policies should be implemented to prove to listeners that the broadcasters, be they public or private, have Hong Kong's best interest at heart.

## References

Administration's written response to the Hon Wong Yuk-man on issues relating to the policy on digital audio broadcasting. (6 November 2015). Retrieved from http://library.legco.gov.hk:1080/articles/1183343.270971/1.PDF.

Application by Phoenix U Radio for Termination of Sound Broadcasting License. (3 November 2015). Retrieved from http://www.digitalradio.gov.hk/en/doc/LegCo_Brief_Phoenix_Eng.pdf.

Center for Communication and Public Opinion Survey. "Evaluation of Media Credibility". Retrieved from http://www.com.cuhk.edu.hk/ccpos/en/research/Credibility_Survey%20Results_2013_ENG.pdf

Charter of Radio Television Hong Kong. Retrieved from http://rthk.hk/about/pdf/charter_eng.pdf

"Chan Chi-chuen's Question on Licensing for CRHK and Metro". Retrieved from http://www.legco.gov.hk/yr15-16/english/fc/fc/w_q/cedb-cci-e.pdf

Chiu, J. (14 February 2014). "Protestors Demand Answers after Commercial Radio Host Li Wei ling is Sacked". South China Morning Post. Retrieved from http://www.scmp.com/news/hong-kong/article/1426971/protesters-demand-answers-after-commercial-radio-host-li-wei-ling

"Commercial Radio and Metro Licenses Renewed". (22 March 2016). The Standard. Retrieved From http://www.thestandard.com.hk/breaking-news.php?id=72796.

Farhi, P. (22 November 2015). "NPR Is Graying And Public Radio Is Worried About It". Retrieved from https://www.washingtonpost.com/lifestyle/style/npr-is-graying-and-public-radio-is-worried-about-it/2015/11/22/0615447e-8e48-11e5-baf4-bdf37355da0c_story.html.

Hong Kong Communications Authority. (2015). Annual Report 2014–15. Retrieved form http://www.legco.gov.hk/yr15-16/chinese/counmtg/papers/cm20151216-sp051-ec.pdf.

Hong Kong Government Budget 2016-17. (2016). Retrieved from http://www.budget.gov.hk/2016/eng/pdf/head160.pdf

Kwok, B. (6 August 2015). "RTHK Has a new Chief and It's the Same Man We Know". *EJ Insight*. Retrieved from http://www.ejinsight.com/20150806-rthk-has-a-new-chief-and-its-the-same-man-we-knowi-know/

Lau, S., & Lam, J. (6 August 2015). "Veteran Journalist Leung Ka-wing Named New Head of RTHK at Critical Time for Hong Kong's Public Broadcaster". *South China Morning Post*. Retrieved from http://www.scmp.com/news/hong-kong/education-community/article/1847085/hong-kong-names-ex-atv-news-chief-head.

Lee, E. & Lee, S. (2 April 2004). "Albert Cheng Says Death Threats may Force Him off Air". *South China Morning Post*. Retrieved from http://www.scmp.com/article/450720/albert-cheng-says-death-threats-may-force-him-air.

"Most Popular Radio Stations in Hong Kong". Retrieved from http://www.radioguide.fm/internet-radio-hong-kong.

"New Broadcasting House for Radio Television Hong Kong". (18 December 2013). Retrieved from http://www.legco.gov.hk/yr13-14/english/fc/pwsc/papers/p13-28e.

"New RTHK Boss Confident of Withstanding Pressure". (7 August 2015). Retrieved from http://news.rthk.hk/rthk/en/component/k2/1203566-20150807.htm.

Statista. (2015). "Distribution of Advertising Revenue in Hong Kong in 3rd Quarter 2015". Retrieved from http://www.statista.com/statistics/481899/ad-spend-medium-hong-kong/.

*The Six-monthly Report on Hong Kong by the UK Government*. (31 December 2015). Retrieved from https://www.gov.uk/government/uploads/system/uploads/attachment_data/file/500119/Six_Monthly_Report_on_Hong_Kong_-_1_July_to_31_December_2015.pdf (accessed May 28, 2016).

Tsang, E. (7 January 2016). "Occupy-linked DJs Dumped as Hong Kong Broadcaster RTHK Accusations". *South China Morning Post*. Retrieved from http://www.scmp.com/news/hong-kong/politics/article/1898961/occupy-linked-djs-dumped-hong-kong-broadcaster-rthk-rejects.

Wan, A. (22 March 2011). "RTHK Contract Staff in Job Protest". *South China Morning Post*. Retrieved from http://www.scmp.com/article/740687/rthk-contract-staff-job-protest.

Wong, Y. (21 September 2015). "Letter from Hon Wong Yuk-man on Issues Relating to Digital Audio Broadcasting". Retrieved from http://library.legco.gov.hk:1080/articles/1182738.269904/1.PDF.

"World Press Freedom Ranking 2016". (2016). Retrieved from https://rsf.org/en/ranking.

Yeung, S.C. (22 September 2015). "Why is the Government So Worried about Issuing Radio Licenses?" *EJ Insight*. Retrieved from http://www.ejinsight.com/20150922-why-is-the-government-so-worried-about-issuing-radio-licenses/.

鳳凰撤牌經營難？DBC歸咎政府懶懶閒令營商環境不公. (19 September 2015). Retrieved from http://hk.apple.nextmedia.com/realtime/news/20150919/54223294 (accessed May 28, 2016).

# Part II

New Media

# Chapter 5

## The Emergence of Internet Media in Hong Kong

*Alice Y. L. LEE*

## Introduction

The rapid development of digital technologies has brought a sea of change to the media environment. The widespread use of the internet and mobile phones has changed people's news consumption habits. With print media in Hong Kong in decline, internet media have mushroomed and hugely diversified the market. This chapter explores this paradigm shift of news media in Hong Kong.

In 2015, a number of long-established print media outlets in Hong Kong shut down. *Hong Kong Daily News*, one of the oldest newspapers in the city, closed after 56 years. *Sudden Magazine*, once the top-circulating magazine, ceased publication. The Next Media group also cut costs by combining the publication of its flagship *Next Magazine* with *me!* and *Eat* and *Travel Weekly* (Kwok, 2015). There is intense discussion about whether print media are facing a countdown to oblivion and whether internet media will dominate the news sector in the near future. Scholars and media practitioners are also studying how traditional media can survive in the digital era and how internet media can contribute to the public sphere.

Internet media are called *"wang mei"* in Chinese. In this chapter, the term is used to refer to online-only sites that focus on current affairs and excludes the online sites of the traditional print newspapers and broadcast stations. Focusing on these new internet media, this chapter has the following objectives: to describe the emergence of internet media in Hong Kong and explore their common characteristics; to examine the unique positioning of popular internet media in Hong Kong; to set out the criticisms of internet media; and to discuss the challenges internet media are facing.

## The Development of Internet Media

As a technologically advanced city, Hong Kong has seen internet technology and digital devices spread extremely quickly. By June 2016, household broadband penetration reached 84.6% of the population and mobile subscriber penetration was 227.9% (Office of the Communications Authority, 2016). Out of the city's 7.3 million people, 4.4 million are Facebook users, and more than 3.1 million of these log on to Facebook every day, spending an average of 30 minutes on each visit (Go-Globe, 2015). Many people, particularly the young, have shifted to online and mobile platforms for news and information, giving internet media a large potential audience. At the same time, internet technology has enabled start-up media to set up and operate at a comparatively low cost. This has provided investors with more opportunities in the media market.

Several big social and political events have also contributed to the rapid development of internet media in Hong Kong. Some scholars suggest that the history of internet media in the city can be traced to the social movements of the 2000s. On 1 July 2003, for example, half a million Hong Kong people took to the streets to express their objections to a proposed anti-subversion law designed to implement Article 23 of the Basic Law. Just over a year after these protests, in October 2004, a group of public intellectuals, media workers and social activists launched the site InMediaHK (Leung, Tsui & Ma, 2011). Around the same time, internet radio stations such as Openradio and People's Radio Hong Kong appeared. These new online outlets have been described as "activists performing civil disobedience" (Leung et al., 2011).

The internet offered the groups that emerged after 2003 a cost-effective and logistically feasible means to express their opinions (Leung, 2015a). Subsequent protests, such as the Anti-Express Rail Link Movement (2009–10), the Anti-Moral and National Education Movement (2012) and the Umbrella Movement (2014), contributed to the rapid growth of various internet media outlets, including Dash, SocREC, VJMedia, Passion Times and Local Press. These new online alternative media differ from mainstream media in the nature of their organization, the character of their content, their production processes, and the features of their distribution (Yung & Leung, 2014).

Some commentators have pointed out that the quick rise of internet media is likely due to their special strengths in these areas (Liu & Liang, 2015; Yeung, 2015). Most notably, they can reach a large audience without being limited by geographical boundaries. They also provide speedy breaking news and live reporting. In addition to the sites being interactive, readers can select what they want to read, thus participating in the experience. They can give comments and share the stories on social media. Most of the sites and stories can be accessed free of charge and are multimedia-oriented. For the post-90s generation, internet media are particularly appealing. As digital natives, these young people search for news on internet media through apps or websites. Traditional print and broadcast are unable to match their navigation needs.

Apart from the general advantages mentioned above, internet media in Hong Kong have many other unique characteristics:

1.  They provide content not usually found in mainstream media, such as the citizen journalists' stories that appear on the site of InMediaHK.
2.  Most have a clear political stance. According to a local mini-survey among university students, there is a perception that many internet media have a tendency to endorse local consciousness (So, 2016).
3.  Hong Kong values are often emphasised.
4.  Although these media can reach greater China, most of their readers are from the local community (Table 5.1).
5.  Many have a format similar to The Huffington Post, focusing on blogs, news story curation, commentary on current affairs and analytical features.
6.  They depend heavily on social media (e.g., Facebook) for distribution (Table 5.2).

## The Position of Internet Media in Hong Kong

To survive in an information-saturated environment, internet media have to have a unique selling point. In particular, providing special content is very important for their competitiveness; "content is king" is still the rule (Tang, 2015). Table 5.1 shows the ranking of the popular internet media sites in Hong Kong. The top sites heavily target local netizens and all try to provide distinctive content which is not easily available elsewhere.

**Table 5.1**

**Ranking of the Hong Kong Internet Media**

| Internet Media | Website | Year of Launch | Rank | Visitors by Country (Top Four) | |
|---|---|---|---|---|---|
| Bastille Post (巴士的報) | www.bastillepost.com | 2013 | 13 | HK 83.3% Taiwan 1.9% | China 7.4% USA 1.7% |
| Stand News (立場新聞) | www.thestandnews.com | 2014 | 35 | HK 75.1% USA 4.2% | China 8.0% Taiwan 2.6% |
| HK01 (香港01) | www.hk01.com | 2016 | 50 | China 42.1% Taiwan 9.2% | HK 39.1% USA 2.4% |
| Passion Times (熱血時報) | www.passiontimes.hk | 2012 | 128 | HK 84.8% USA 2.8% | Taiwan 3.3% Canada 2.2% |
| MemeHK (謎米香港) | www.memehk.com | 2013 | 190 | HK 63.5% USA 8.4% | China 14.8% Canada 5.1% |
| Post 852 (852郵報) | www.post852.com | 2013 | 340 | HK 78.9% USA 4.0% | China 8.9% Belgium 2.1% |
| Initium Media (端傳媒) | https://theinitium.com | 2015 | 414 | Taiwan 40.1% HK 18.2% | China 26.5% USA 7.9% |
| VJMedia (輔仁媒體) | www.vjmedia.com.hk | 2012 | 587 | HK 76.7% Canada 4.2% | S.Korea 5.0% USA 3.3% |
| InMediaHK (香港獨立媒體) | www.inmediahk.net | 2004 | 614 | HK 64.5% Taiwan 3.3% | China 22.2% USA 2.8% |
| Orange News (橙新聞) | www.orangenews.hk | 2014 | 812 | HK 67.2% USA 1.7% | Taiwan 22.0% |
| Hong Kong Free Press | www.hongkongfp.com | 2015 | 981 | HK 43.0% UK 5.6% | USA 23.0% Canada 4.0% |
| HKGpao (HKG報) | www.hkgpao.com | 2015 | 2133 | HK 66.6% Canada 4.5% | USA 6.1% |
| Local Press (本土新聞) | www.localpresshk.com | 2014 | 3101 | HK 60.9% | Taiwan 5.9% |

Source of Ranking and Visitors by Country: Alexa (http://www.alexa.com). Information retrieved on 8 October 2016.

**Table 5.2**

**Facebook Page Likes of Internet Media in Hong Kong**

| Internet Media | Total Facebook Page Likes |
|----------------|---------------------------|
| Bastille Post | 826,650 |
| InMediaHK | 484,315 |
| Passion Times | 415,462 |
| Orange News | 189,877 |
| Stand News | 168,768 |
| HK01 | 164,840 |
| Initium Media | 157,339 |
| MemeHK | 127,451 |
| VJMedia | 105,890 |
| Post 852 | 56,951 |
| Local Press | 55,172 |
| HKGpao | 53,851 |
| Hong Kong Free Press | 53,255 |

Information retrieved from individual internet media's Facebook pages on 6 October 2016.

Bastille Post, one of the top ranked internet outlets, puts great emphasis on providing immediate information in the form of both hard news and soft news. Its editorial strategy is to break exclusive stories, but its large amount of soft news is also attractive to its readers. The site curates appealing human interest stories and viral video clips from all over the world and also provides many entertainment stories.

A few months after the popular online site House News closed down in 2014, after just two years of operation, some of its members launched a new web outlet, Stand News, which is independent and not-for-profit. Its stated aims are to safeguard Hong Kong's core values of democracy, human rights, freedom, rule of law and social justice. Its stated principles are to report the truth and voice the opinions of the powerless. It says that Hong Kong is the "home court" of its people, and defending this home court is its committed task (Stand News, 2014). It is well known as a news site that emphasises local Hong Kong local awareness.

Passion Times integrates news reporting with social collective action. It regards the mainstream media in Hong Kong as unable to play the important journalistic role of the fourth estate. It claims that a "passionate sword" is needed to break the "net of lies" in the current media environment (Passion Times Facebook, 2016). Passion Times is closely linked with Civic Passion, an anti-communist, nativist political group that holds strong localist views and advocates autonomy for Hong Kong.

Local Press is another outlet that covers news and offers commentaries from a local perspective. It also criticises the mainstream media in Hong Kong for ignoring public opinion and failing to speak for the general public. VJMedia too was launched out of dissatisfaction with the mainstream media and positions itself as striving for equal rights for all citizens and disadvantaged groups.

InMediaHK also has strong roots in Hong Kong. It promotes various political movements in the city with the stated aim of developing a public sphere free from manipulation by the government, business corporations or political parties. The site is built as an open platform for citizen journalists to speak for disadvantaged groups. InMediaHK has been engaged in several important movements, including the Anti-Express Rail Link Movement and the Umbrella Movement.

MemeHK, launched by media personality Stephen Shiu in 2013, also emphasises the Hong Kong spirit. Here the term "meme" refers to the transfer of ideas. MemeHK has produced a series of infotainment programmes and current affairs commentary programmes with the stated aim that through the discussion and analysis of its content, Hong Kong values and independent thinking can be spread and inherited (The Encyclopedia of Virtual Communities in Hong Kong, 2016).

Post 852 provides "breaking views" (Chung, 2015). It combines curation of news with commentary. Set up in 2013 by veteran editor Yau Ching Yuen, who left the *Hong Kong Economic Journal* to launch it, Post 852 specialises in "instant commentary", and its political gossip has raised some eyebrows. It states that one of its major tasks is to safeguard press freedom in Hong Kong.

Initium Media, meanwhile, is the first Hong Kong-based internet outlet that aims to serve Chinese readers all over the world. Table 5.1 shows that 40.1% of its readers are in Taiwan, 26.5% are in Mainland China and 18.2% are in Hong Kong. Political neutrality and freedom of speech are its two main principles, and it specialises in in-depth reporting and data journalism (Initium

Media, 2015). Its news articles are relatively long and contain in-depth and comprehensive analysis.

The newly established (2016) HK01 is a bigger organisation than most other Hong Kong online outlets, with over 200 staff members. HK01's aim is to advocate social and media reform in Hong Kong. Although it primarily covers Hong Kong issues, more than 40% of its readers are in Mainland China. HK01 is mainly web-based but also publishes a weekly print magazine.

While most of these new online media are in Chinese, an English internet news website has joined their ranks: Hong Kong Free Press (HKFP) was launched in 2015 by an enthusiastic young English blogger. According to its website, HKFP "strives to bridge the gap between Chinese and English reporting while providing a platform to raise global understanding of Hong Kong and China issues." In particular, it pays attention to the defence of press freedom in Hong Kong (HKFP, 2015). The site focuses on local breaking news as reported by its own staff while also featuring translated and viral content.

In 2017, a group of veteran journalists set up a news website called the Hong Kong Citizen News. This site emphasises professionalism in news reporting, upholding press freedom and maintaining editorial independence. It aims to provide high-quality news stories which are objective, accurate and fair and to safeguard the core values of Hong Kong. It also offers in-depth news analysis (Hong Kong Citizen News Facebook, 2017).

As stated above, many of these newly established internet media sites espouse a clear political stance that advocates the democratic development of Hong Kong. However, there are also online pro-establishment internet media sites, such as Orange News and HKGpao, which report and analyse current affairs from the perspective of the establishment and say it is important to promote the betterment of Hong Kong (Lok Siu, 2016). Orange News says it sets out to offer balanced and high-quality news stories for online readers and stimulate new ideas (Orange News, 2016), while HKGpao advocates positive energy and the "Lion Rock Spirit" (named after a famous local peak) of Hong Kong people (HKGpao, 2016).

## Criticism of Internet Media

While the mushrooming internet media usage in Hong Kong in recent years has greatly enhanced the diversity of the sector, it has also attracted criticism from academics and commentators. One complaint is that most *wang mei* are

**Table 5.3**

**A Survey of Media Credibility in Hong Kong**

| Internet Media | Response Rate (%) | Credibility Score* |
|---|---|---|
| Stand News | 35.6 | 5.24 |
| InMediaHK | 37.3 | 5.11 |
| Bastille Post | 38.9 | 4.93 |
| HK01 | 38.3 | 4.87 |
| Post 852 | 29.0 | 4.84 |
| Initium Media | 27.9 | 4.51 |
| Passion Times | 43.1 | 4.20 |
| Internet media (average) | 35.7 | 4.81 |
| Social media (average) | 88.8 | 4.59 |
| Free newspapers (average) | 71.9 | 5.83 |
| Paid newspapers (average) | 75.9 | 5.58 |
| Broadcast media (average) | 82.8 | 6.36 |
| All media (average) | 66.9 | 5.60 |

Source of information: So, C. Y. K. (2016, September 8). Hong Kong media credibility hit a new low. Ming Pao Daily News, 8 September 2016. P. A28.

* Credibility score: on a scale of 1 to 10, with 10 being the highest

short of resources and use curation to collect news and information rather than providing the rich original content and in-depth special features found in traditional media. Moreover, many of them are algorithm-driven. Click rates often dictate the importance of news stories on digital platforms. Some have sensational headlines and do not have enough real substance. As these outlets rely heavily on social media, in particular their Facebook pages, to deliver their products, they employ desperate tactics to grab "likes." It has been said that the online news world is full of information with high click rates but low quality (Liu & Liang, 2015).

This leads to the main criticism of internet media: their credibility. Hong Kong's online outlets in general have lower credibility than other media, except social media (Table 5.3). Unlike traditional media, many lack a team of professional journalists and employ staff members with little media training.

Some rely on contributions from bloggers and citizen journalists of variable quality. Speed and timeliness are the strengths of these media, but they are also their weaknesses. They often do not have enough time to verify breaking news stories and may use reports without sufficient support. They may also use the unverified breaking news to provide hasty, and sometimes incorrect, stories (Leung, 2015b).

Online media have difficulty ensuring a stable income and have to depend on donations and sponsorship. This leads to concerns that their editorial stance can be easily manipulated by their financial supporters and the possibility that some may be political tools of certain groups.

## The Challenges Ahead

The internet media in Hong Kong are facing a number of challenges besides their credibility crisis. Their lack of sustainable business models is a big issue. Another is the lack of recognition by the government, preventing some of them from covering official events.

### Refusal of Reporting Rights

Internet media and citizen journalists were barred from attending government events and press conferences and did not receive notices and press releases from the Information Services Department for many years. Five internet media sites—namely, Stand News, InMediaHK, MemeHK, HKFP and Initium Media—released a statement in 2016 criticising the government for being "archaic" in their refusal to open up to internet media, saying "press freedom and the right to report does not belong to any media outlets, but to every civilian" (Yuen, 2016).

According to the government, internet outlets are denied entry to media centres during elections and government press conferences for two reasons: there is not enough room in the venues for all media, and internet media are not registered publications. The government requires all print and broadcast media distributed in Hong Kong to register, a process that is one of record rather than control, but registration also confers the right to government information. Tsang Tak-sing, the former secretary for Home Affairs, commented that limiting the right to report of internet outlets was necessarybecause "any person can set up an online media website" (Yuen,

2016). The Hong Kong Journalists Association (HKJA) called the ban "ridiculous" (Stand News, 2016a). Media scholars have also suggested that it should be lifted (Lee, 2016). Tom Grundy, founder of HKFP, applied for legal aid to challenge the policy of barring online media outlets from government press conferences and press releases (Stand News, 2016b).

In September 2017, the government changed its policy and introduced a new arrangement. Eligible internet media can apply to cover government press conferences and media events if they meet the following criteria: the outlets must be staffed by at least an editor and a reporter, they are registered under the Registration of Local Newspapers Ordinance, their news platform must be updated at least five days a week, and they must provide proof of regular online news reports published in the previous three months (Information Services Department, 2017).

## Searching For a Sustainable Business Model

The internet media in Hong Kong have diverse funding sources: online advertising, donations, sponsorship, crowdfunding and investment. However, it seems that most are still searching for a sustainable business model.

InMediaHK, operating for more than ten years, insists on being a non-profit entity. Refusing sponsorship and corporate donations, it mainly depends on readers' monthly or one-off payments. Stand News and Post 852 accept online advertising, but they also eagerly seek sponsorship from readers. Both have an established membership scheme.

HKFP is funded differently. It tries to combine online advertisements, a paid membership scheme, crowdfunding, sponsored events and merchandising to generate revenue (Baiocchi, 2015). It has launched crowdfunding campaigns via FringeBacker, and its first campaign raised HK$588,000. A second campaign was launched in late 2015 for its 2016 operations.

Some internet media are supported by investors and donors. Bastille Post is partly supported by the Sing Tao News Corporation, a long-time newspaper publisher. Initium Media and HK01 have their own investors for funding. Since doubts exist about the political background and agenda of internet media investors, the editorial stance of many outlets is constantly under scrutiny. For example, in April 2017, Initium Media restructured the company and laid off a substantial number of staff due to cash flow difficulties. It was said that a potential investor backed out (HKFP, 2017). It then changed to adopt a reader-subscription model.

## Conclusion

Internet media outlets contribute significantly to the diversity of public opinion but represent a tremendous challenge to traditional media. Interestingly, a survey carried out by Hong Kong Baptist University in the summer of 2016 indicated that most Hong Kong people still get news mainly from newspapers and television. The consumption of internet media is at a comparatively low level at this stage.

As noted above, internet media sites have comparatively low credibility. They need time to improve and grow. For now, it is unlikely that they can best print media. According to media critics and communication scholars, traditional media still remain in the mainstream (So, 2015; Tang, 2015). However, as more traditional media sources in Hong Kong have become conservative in their editorial stance, internet media outlets may be more attractive in the future due to their free reporting styles and critical approaches to news analysis.

## References

"About Orange News." (2016). Retrieved from http://www.orangenews.hk/siteinfo/about.shtml.

"About Us". (2014) Stand News. Received from https://www.thestandnews.com/about_us.

"About Us." (2016). Hkgpao. Retrieved from http://hkgpao.com/about-us.

Baiocchi, F. (30 June 2015). "Activist Turned Editor Who Tried To Arrest Tony Blair Launches Crowdfunded Hong Kong News Website." *Press Gazette*. Retrieved from http://www.pressgazette.co.uk/activist-who-tried-arrest-tony-blair-launches-crowdfunded-news-website-hong-kong-free-press.

Chung, M. (30 January 2015). "Why Does Post 852 Exist?" VJmedia. Retrieved from http://www.vjmedia.com.hk/articles/2015/01/30/97786.

"Digital Hong Kong News Outlet Initium Media to Lay Off Substantial Number of Staff amid Funding Fears." (6 April 2017). *Hong Kong Free Press*. Retrieved from https://www.hongkongfp.com/2017/04/06/digital-hong-kong-news-outlet-initium-media-lay-off-substantial-no-staff-amid-funding-fears/.

"HKFP Founder Successfully Applied for Legal Aid for Challenging the Government's Ban on Reporting Rights of Internet Media". (4 May 2016b). *Stand News*. Retrieved from https://thestandnews.com/media/hkfp%E5%89%B5%E8%BE%A6%E4%BA%BA%E6%88%90%E5%8A%9F%E7%94%B3%E6%B3%95%E6%8F%B4-%E6%8C%91%E6%88%B0%E6%94%BF%E5%BA%9C%E7%A6%81%E7%B6%B2%E5%AA%92%E6%8E%A1%E8%A8%AA%E5%AE%89%E6%8E%92/.

"HKJA Made Complaints about the Limit on Information Rights Regarding the Refusal to Recognize Internet Media". (13 June 2016a). *Stand News*. Retrieved from https://www. thestandnews.com/media/%E8%A8%98%E5%8D%94%E5%90%91%E7%94%B3%E8%A8 %B4%E5%B0%88%E5%93%A1%E6%8A%95%E8%A8%B4-%E6%94%BF%E5%BA%9C%E6% 8B%92%E8%AA%8D%E5%8F%AF%E7%B6%B2%E5%AA%92-%E9%99%90%E5%88%B6%E

Hong Kong Citizen News Facebook. (2017). "Story. Hong Kong Citizen News Facebook." Retrieved from https://www.facebook.com/pg/hkcnews/about/?ref=page_internal.

Hong Kong Free Press. (2015). "About Hong Kong Free Press." Hongkongfp. Retrieved from August 20, 2016 from https://www.hongkongfp.com/about.

Information Services Department. (19 September 2017). "Online Media Granted Access." News.gov.hk. Retrieved from http://www.news.gov.hk/en/categories/health/ html/2017/09/20170919_10485 7.shtml.

Initium Media. (2015). "Initium Media Technology Limited." Hk.jobsdb.com. Retrieved from http://hk.jobsdb.com/HK/en/Search/FindJobs?JSRV=1&Key=%22Initium+Medi a+Techn ology+Limited%22&KeyOpt=COMPLEX&SearchFields=Companies&    JSSRC=SRLSC.

Kwok, C. L. (2015). "The Ice Age of the Print Media and the Hot Season of the Internet News Websites." *Candlelight Network, Society of True and Light*. Volume 104, 22.

Lee, F. (17 March 2016). "Who Are The Media? Who Are Reporters? On The Reporting Rights of Internet Media and Other Things." *Ming Pao*. Retrieved from http://news.mingpao. com/pns/dailynews/web_tc/article/20160317/s00012/1458150477121.

Leung, D. K. K., Tsui, C. Y. S., & Ma, M. L. Y. (2011). "Internet Social Movement Media." In *Encyclopaedia of Social Movement Media*, edited by Downing, J. D. H. 282–5. Thousand Oaks, CA: Sage.

Leung, D. K. K. (2015a), "The Rise of Alternative Net Radio in Hong Kong: The Historic Case of One Pioneering Station." *Journal of Radio & Audio Media*, 22(1) 42–59.

Leung, Y. Y. (9 September 2015b). "Wu Jun: Irreplaceable, Print Media are Much More Credible than Internet Media." *China Press*. Retrieved from http://www.chinapress.com. my/20150909/%E5%90%B3%E9%A7%BF%E7%84%A1%E6%B3%95%E8%A2%AB%E5%8F %96%E4%BB%A3%E5%A0%B1%E7%AB%A0%E5%85%AC%E4%BF%A1%E5%8A%9B%E9% 81%A0%E8%B6%85%E7%B6%B2%E5%AA%92.

Liu, Q., & Liang, Y. D. (2015). "A Cold Winter for Print Media and an Early Spring for Internet Media". Jumbo, 48.2, 30–33. Retrieved from https://issuu.com/_hkbusueb/docs/ jumbo48.2

Lok, S. (2016). "Dot, Orange, Light, G, Kin...attention to the rise of pro-establishment Internet news websites". Stand News. Retrieved from https://thestandnews.com/ politics/%E9%BB%9E-%E6%A9%99-%E8%BC%95-g-%E5%A0%85-%E5%BB%BA%E5%88% B6%E7%B6%B2%E5%AA%92%E5%87%BA%E6%B2%92%E6%B3%A8%E6%84%8F.

"MemeHK." (2016). The Encyclopaedia of Virtual Communities in Hong Kong. Retrieved from http://evchk.wikia.com/wiki/%E8%AC%8E%E7%B1%B3%E9%A6%99%E6%B8%AF.

Office of the Communications Authority. (2016). "Key Communications Statistics." Retrieved from http://www.ofca.gov.hk/en/media_focus/data_statistics/key_stat/.

So, C. Y. K. (13 August 2015). "Traditional Media Are Still Dominant." *Ming Pao*. Retrieved from http://news.mingpao.com/pns/%E8%98%87%E9%91%B0%E6%A9%9F%EF%B9%95%E5%82%B3%E7%B5%B1%E6%96%B0%E8%81%9E%E5%AA%92%E9%AB%94%E4%BB%8D%E7%84%B6%E4%B8%BB%E5%A0%B4/web_tc/article/20150813/s00012/1439403055808.

So, C. Y. K. (5 October 2016). "Political Parties and the Media in the Eyes of University Students." Initium Media. Retrieved from https://theinitium.com/article/20161005-opinion-clementso-umbrellamovement.

"Social Media Usage in Hong Kong – Statistics and Trends." (2016). Go-globe. Retrieved from http://www.go-globe.hk/blog/social-media-hong-kong.

"Story." (9 October 2016). Passion Time Facebook Page. Retrieved from https://www.facebook.com/passiontimes.

Tang, S. M. (9 October 2015). "Print Media Live On." Start Up Beat. Retrieved from http://startupbeat.hkej.com/?p=22319.

Yeung, C. F. (20 August 2015). "Internet Media Dominate as the Print Media Environment Was Reshaped." *Education Post*. Retrieved from http://www.educationpost.com.hk/zh-hk/resources/education/150820-expert-says-new-media-vs-traditional-media.

Yuen, C. (12 March 2016). "Online Media Outlets Slam HK Gov't's 'Backward' Refusal of Reporting Rights." *Hong Kong Free Press*. Retrieved from https://www.hongkongfp.com/2016/03/12/online-media-outlets-slam-hk-govts-backward-refusal-of-reporting-rights/.

Yung, B., & Leung, L. Y. M. (2014). "Diverse Roles of Alternative Media in Hong Kong Civil Society: From Public Discourse Initiation to Social Activism." *Journal of Asian Public Policy*, 7(1), 83–101.

# Chapter 6

## Social Media in Hong Kong's Changing Ecology of News Production and Consumption

*Roselyn DU and Alex TANG*

## Introduction

Worldwide, the rapid development of social media has brought profound changes to people's lives in every possible way, especially to their news consumption habits. Nowadays news consumption is "unfettered by wires and cables", freed from its previously restricted space-time constraints (Hemment, 2005). News is constantly consumed throughout the course of the day while people access their devices (most smartphones come with many social media applications automatically on them now) to fill the gaps in their schedules (Dimmick, Feaster & Hoplamazian, 2010).

News consumption on social media has been a significant topic for both practical and scholarly research. In the United States, the birthplace of the world's most popular social networking sites, studies have found that a large portion of the public receives news via social media platforms such as Facebook. Indeed, social recommendation has become increasingly important in attracting online traffic to many top U.S. news websites, with Facebook emerging as the major source of traffic for the top five most visited sites (Purcell, Rainie, Mitchell, Rosenstiel & Olmstead, 2010; Olmstead, Mitchell & Rosenstiel, 2011). Studies based on the uses and gratifications theory have also found that a higher level of socialising and information seeking is associated with a higher level of intention to share news online through social media (Lee & Ma, 2012). As Olmstead et al. (2011) suggest, if searching for news was the most important development in the first decade of the twenty-first century, sharing and forwarding news may be the most important of the current decade. It is made possible by the phenomenal popularity of social media among the general public.

Hong Kong has an internet penetration of 79% of the population, with 66% being active social media users and 59% being active mobile social users (We Are Social, 2016—We Are Social is a UK-based global agency specialising in social media research). This is of great potential for news consumption on social media. According to the *2016 Digital Yearbook* (We Are Social, 2016), the average daily time spent on social media (via any device) in Hong Kong is 1.5 hours, exceeding that of most of the other 232 countries/regions studied around the world. The most used social network in Hong Kong is Facebook, which has 4.4 million active local users (more than half of the total population). According to Lam (2014), 44% of Facebook users used Facebook as their first point of contact when reading breaking news.

The nearly saturated penetration rate of mobile phones in Hong Kong certainly plays a role in this phenomenon. According to Computerworld Hong Kong (2016), Hong Kong's mobile subscriber base has a population penetration of 95%. One previous study demonstrated that the mobile phone has taken a prominent position as a source of news in Hong Kong, becoming the second most used medium for the 18–34 age cohort and the fourth most used medium for the 35–54 age cohort (Chan, 2015).

Getting news from social media is associated with a high level of immediacy and mobility, which may create the expectation that news will come to us whether we seek it or not, whether we share/forward it or not. What are the defining characteristics of these social media news consumers? Are gender, age, occupation, family income and education shaping Hongkongers' appetite for and attitudes toward getting news on social media, and if yes, how?

A survey in Hong Kong (n=1012) conducted in early 2016, a joint effort by Hong Kong Baptist University School of Communication colleagues, reveals a Hong Kong public that is actively consuming news on social media on a greater scale than in the U.S. In fact, compared to the 62% of U.S. adults who get news on social media (and the 18% who do so often, according to a 2016 survey by Pew Research Center and the Knight Foundation), 77% of Hong Kong adults aged eighteen and above indicated that they get their news from social media, and 22% said they did so often.

To better understand news consumption on social media in Hong Kong, and to answer the research questions we raised, this study further focused on the 77% of respondents (based on valid cases) who are news consumers on social media. All the following analysis and findings are based on this sub-sample (n=633).

## The Appetite for News

The top three categories of news that Hongkongers get from social media are local news, international news and health and medical news (Table 6.1). Sharing/forwarding news stories on social media is not so popular, with less than 10% of the respondents saying they do so often, with the majority saying they do it seldom or only occasionally (Table 6.2). This is not surprising because Hongkongers have a reputation for being some of the busiest people in the world. As for the reasons for sharing or forwarding news, the top three are relevance to oneself or one's relatives/friends, importance in public affairs and being interesting (Table 6.3).

When asked whether they perceive news on social media to be more relevant to their lives, more interesting and more comprehensive, nearly half of the respondents were neutral. Regarding whether social media sites

**Table 6.1**

**Type of News that Hongkongers Get from Social Media by Rank**

|  | N | % |
|---|---|---|
| 1. Local news | 456 | 72.0 |
| 2. International news | 283 | 44.7 |
| 3. Health and medical news | 157 | 24.7 |
| 4. Entertainment news | 148 | 23.3 |
| 5. Mainland news | 117 | 18.5 |
| 6. Sports news | 95 | 15.0 |
| 7. Information and technology news | 58 | 9.2 |
| 8. Community news | 49 | 7.7 |
| 9. Other news | 13 | 2.0 |
| Total | 633 | 100.0 |

and applications are the most effective way of learning about local news and events, nearly half agreed or strongly agreed, while when it came to international news fewer agreed or strongly agreed (Table 6.4).

As for sharing/forwarding news on social media, about 30% of people agreed or strongly agreed that it is a way of expressing oneself, 12% agreed or strongly agreed that it can provide gratification and 22% agreed or strongly agreed that it can enhance their relationships with others (Table 6.5).

**Table 6.2**

**How Often Hongkongers Share or Forward News
to Relatives or Friends on Social Media**

|  | N | % |
|---|---|---|
| Never | 188 | 29.6 |
| Seldom | 233 | 36.7 |
| Occasionally | 156 | 24.7 |
| Often | 57 | 8.9 |
| Total | 633 | 100.0 |

**Table 6.3**

**Reasons for Hongkongers to Share or Forward News
on Social Media by Rank**

|  | N | % |
|---|---|---|
| 1. Relevance to oneself or relatives/friends | 201 | 31.7 |
| 2. Important public affairs | 176 | 27.7 |
| 3. Interesting | 173 | 27.3 |
| 4. Indignant | 109 | 17.2 |
| 5. Breaking news | 91 | 14.4 |
| 6. Entertaining and gossip | 33 | 5.2 |
| Total | 633 | 100.0 |

**Table 6.4**

**Perceptions of News on Social Media**

|  | Strongly disagree | Disagree | Neutral | Agree | Strongly Agree |
|---|---|---|---|---|---|
| News on social media is more relevant to your life | 10 (1.5%) | 46 (7.3%) | 289 (45.7%) | 203 (32.1%) | 79 (12.4%) |
| News on social media is more interesting | 7 (1.2%) | 42 (6.6%) | 300 (47.4%) | 234 (37.0%) | 42 (6.6%) |
| News on social media is more comprehensive | 32 (5.0%) | 126 (20.0%) | 307 (48.5%) | 118 (18.7%) | 43 (6.8%) |
| Social media are the most effective way of learning about local news and events | 22 (3.5%) | 73 (11.5%) | 245 (38.8%) | 216 (34.0%) | 67 (10.6%) |
| Social media are the most effective way of learning about international news and events | 27 (4.3%) | 79 (12.5%) | 268 (42.3%) | 189 (29.9%) | 59 (9.4%) |

**Table 6.5**

**Gratification Obtained by Sharing or Forwarding News on Social Media**

|  | Strongly disagree | Disagree | Neutral | Agree | Strongly Agree |
|---|---|---|---|---|---|
| Sharing/forwarding news on social media is a way to express yourself | 11 (1.7%) | 54 (8.5%) | 187 (29.6%) | 147 (23.2%) | 39 (6.1%) |
| Sharing/forwarding news on social media can provide you with gratification | 34 (5.3%) | 93 (14.7%) | 235 (37.2%) | 64 (10.1%) | 14 (2.2%) |
| Sharing/forwarding news on social media can enhance your relationship with others | 16 (2.5%) | 67 (10.6%) | 222 (35.1%) | 108 (17.1%) | 30 (4.7%) |

## Factors Affecting News Consumption on Social Media

To examine the possible influences of gender, age, occupation, family income and education on news consumption on social media, we conducted a series of statistical tests, including correlation and chi-square (cross tabulation) tests. Overall, as Table 6.6 and Table 6.7 indicate, age, education and occupation have a more significant impact on news consumption habits and attitudes than gender and family income.

It seems that gender matters only when it comes to how often people share or forward news on social media (women are more likely to do so than

### Table 6.6

**Relationships between Social Media Use and Age, Education and Family Income Based on Pearson's Correlations (r)**

|  | Age | Education | Family Income |
|---|---|---|---|
| How often Hongkongers share or forward news to relatives or friends on social media | – | – | – |
| News on social media is more relevant to your life | –.16** | – | – |
| News on social media is more interesting | –.21** | .08* | – |
| News on social media is more comprehensive | –.16** | – | – |
| Social media is the most effective way of learning about local news and events | –.08* | –.13** | – |
| Social media is the most effective way of learning about international news and events | –.14** | – | – |
| Sharing/forwarding news on social media is a way to express yourself | –.13** | – | – |
| Sharing/forwarding news on social media can provide you with gratification | .09* | –.24** | –.15** |
| Sharing/forwarding news on social media can enhance your relationship with others | .22** | –.24** | –.22** |

** significant at the 0.01 level.
* significance at the 0.05 level.

men) and to what extent they think the news on social media is more relevant (women are more likely to think so than men). Age, however, appears to play a role in almost all aspects, and our results suggest that older people are, in general, more cautious and reserved in using and distributing news on social media. Education also comes into play in many aspects. Indeed, a higher level

**Table 6.7**

**Statistical Differences by Gender, Age, Education, Occupation and Family Income Based on Pearson Chi-Squared Tests ($\chi^2$)**

|  | Gender | Age | Education | Occupation | Family Income |
|---|---|---|---|---|---|
| How often Hongkongers get news from social media | – | 80.03** | 54.44** | 91.53** | – |
| How often Hongkongers share or forward news to relatives or friends on social media | 8.49* | – | 32.18** | – | 56.38** |
| News on social media is more relevant to your life | 16.10** | 49.67* | 57.72** | 74.00* | – |
| News on social media is more interesting | – | 61.49** | 36.76* | 86.00** | – |
| News on social media is more comprehensive | – | 44.23* | 37.82** | 87.24** | 103.15** |
| Social media is the most effective way of learning about local news and events | – | 53.57** | – | 85.30** | – |
| Social media is the most effective way of learning about international news and events | – | 58.87** | 34.16* | – | – |
| Sharing/forwarding news on social media is a way to express yourself | – | – | 83.21** | – | – |
| Sharing/forwarding news on social media can provide you with gratification | – | – | 55.50** | – | – |
| Sharing/forwarding news on social media can enhance your relationship with others | – | 62.63** | 74.61** | 91.36** | 84.84** |

** significant at the 0.01 level.
* significance at the 0.05 level.

**Table 6.8**

**Influence of Occupation on How Often Hongkongers Get News from Social Media**

| Occupation / Frequency | Managers/ senior administrative staff | Specialists | Assistants | Clerks | Service/ sales |
|---|---|---|---|---|---|
| Rarely | 26 | 11 | 16 | 24 | 20 |
| Occasionally | 25 | 15 | 15 | 23 | 19 |
| Often | 27 | 23 | 24 | 14 | 18 |
| Total | 78 | 49 | 55 | 61 | 57 |

| Occupation / Frequency | Labourers | Students | Housewives | Retirees | Unemployed |
|---|---|---|---|---|---|
| Rarely | 36 | 4 | 39 | 34 | 9 |
| Occasionally | 19 | 31 | 23 | 11 | 5 |
| Often | 7 | 55 | 21 | 18 | 5 |
| Total | 62 | 90 | 83 | 63 | 19 |

of education appears to be related to a more critical attitude towards news on social media. Occupation seems to matter in many aspects as well. For example, students are the most likely to get news from social media, while labourers and retirees are the least likely to do so (Table 6.8).

In contrast, family income does not appear to be an influential factor. It is only associated with the level of gratification people get from sharing or forwarding news on social media and whether they think sharing or forwarding news on social media can help enhance relationships with others. The negative correlations found here mean that people with higher family incomes care less about these issues.

As the use of digital media has become more widespread among the general public in Hong Kong, mainstream media outlets have also jumped on board, using mobile and social media in various ways. The following section

**Table 6.9**

**Use of Digital and Social Media by Major Hong Kong TV Broadcasters in June 2016**

| Media | TVB | Cable TV | Now TV | ViuTV |
|---|---|---|---|---|
| Website | ✔ | ✔ | ✔ | ✔ |
| Apps | ✔ | ✔ | ✔ | ✔ |
| Facebook likes | 925,000+ | 14,000+ | 91,000+ | 273,000+ |
| Twitter followers | 43,000+ | <100 | ✔ | ✔ |
| Instagram followers | 79,000+ | <500 | ✔ | 8,000+ |
| Weibo fans | 1,460,000+ | 1,500+ | <100 | <500 |
| YouTube subscribers | 252,000+ | 6,000+ | 72,000+ | 17,000+ |

For likes/subscribers/fans fewer than 1,000, only a range is provided: <100 or <500.

provides an overview of the patterns and trends in this relationship. The types of mainstream media studied in this section include major television stations, radio stations, paid newspapers and free newspapers. Digital media platforms include websites and mobile apps as well as social media platforms, including Facebook, Twitter, Instagram, Weibo and YouTube.

## Use of Digital and Social Media by Television Broadcasters

Today television broadcasters in Hong Kong provide much of their content online (Table 6.9), primarily through mobile apps and websites whose viewership can be easily monitored and tallied. Online platforms and mobile apps provide a choice of content and have none of the broadcasting schedule restrictions of traditional television. Mainstream media sources often operate multiple social media accounts, platforms and apps that offer different kinds of content for different audiences. For instance, Television Broadcasts Limited (TVB) has one Facebook page for its Cantonese speaking channel, another for its English channel TVB Pearl and yet another for its Entertainment News. Most online platforms are free because social media sites, such as Facebook, Instagram, and YouTube, do not charge, but payment is required for those using paid mobile apps or set-up boxes (e.g., TVB's MyTV Super) that provide extra content. Apps also allow producer-consumer and consumer-consumer interaction via discussion forums, voting, games and lucky draws.

Social media platforms are not hosted by the broadcasters themselves and, therefore, are used mostly for promotions and public relations, with Facebook being the most frequently used by television broadcasters. TVB is the only television station that operates in all the platforms analysed here. Of all the outlets it has, by far the highest number of fans is on Weibo, indicating a connection with audiences in Mainland China.

Many television stations have accounts on multiple social media sites, but most have little engagement with users. Some of the accounts are even idle. All broadcasters do better on Facebook than on other platforms. ViuTV has the highest number of Facebook subscribers (273,000+), followed by Now TV (91,000+) and Cable TV (14,000+). YouTube is also often used to share video content online. The popularity of YouTube channels of these stations vary. NowTV (72,000+) performs better than CableTV (6,000+) and ViuTV (17,000+) in terms of the number of subscribers.

## Use of Digital and Social Media by Radio Stations

All major radio stations in Hong Kong have apps and websites for digital broadcasting (Table 6.10). Multiple apps exist for different channels of the

**Table 6.10**

**Use of Digital and Social Media by Major Hong Kong Radio Broadcasters in June 2016**

| Media | RTHK | Commercial Radio Hong Kong | Metro Broadcast Corporation |
|---|---|---|---|
| Website | ✔ | ✔ | ✔ |
| Apps | ✔ | ✔ | ✔ |
| Facebook likes | 73,000+ | 56,000+ | 119,000+ |
| Twitter followers | 1,000+ | <100 | <500 |
| Instagram followers | ✔ | 12,000+ | ✔ |
| Weibo fans | ✔ | 14,000+ | 10,000+ |
| YouTube subscribers | 131,000+ | 66,000+ | ✔ |

For likes/subscribers/fans fewer than 1,000, only a range is provided: <100 or <500.

same station or for specific purposes, such as a news app independent of the general radio station app.

With radio being audio in nature, radio broadcasters are much less interested in using multimedia social media platforms compared to television stations, with the exception of Facebook. Facebook generally serves the purpose of promoting programmes and news content for all news broadcasters. Of the three radio broadcasters in Hong Kong, only Commercial Radio has an Instagram account, which offers visual content, possibly because of its close connection with celebrities in the entertainment business. Both Radio Television Hong Kong (RTHK) and Commercial Radio have YouTube channels. RTHK has more subscribers on YouTube, which is not surprising as they also produce television programmes.

## Use of Digital and Social Media by Newspapers

### Paid newspapers

All paid newspapers in Hong Kong have their own websites providing readers with online content that is constantly updated (Table 6.11). Most newspapers also have mobile news apps, with the exception of Hong Kong Commercial Daily, whose readership is relatively small.

The popularity of social media platforms varies widely among newspapers. As with television and radio, Facebook is an important platform. The Facebook pages of pro-Beijing newspapers, such as *Ta Kung Pao* and *Wen Wei Po,* have fewer than one thousand likes. In contrast, *Apple Daily*'s Facebook page has 1.8 million likes, about five times as many as the *South China Morning Post* (*SCMP*), the newspaper with the second highest number of likes.

The *SCMP*, an English newspaper, has the highest number of followers on Twitter, probably because of its expatriate and international readership and the relative unpopularity of Twitter among local readers. By contrast, *Sing Pao Daily*'s Twitter account has fewer than ten followers and *Hong Kong Commercial Daily* does not have a Twitter account.

All of the newspapers have a Weibo account, except *Apple Daily* and the *SCMP* (whose account was deleted in early 2016), and their continued absence is likely because of political reasons. *Ta Kung Pao* has the highest number of Weibo fans, with more than 3.6 million, over twelve times as many as *Hong*

**Table 6.11**

**Use of Digital and Social Media by Paid Hong Kong Newspapers in June 2016**

| | Apple Daily | Hong Kong Commercial Daily | Hong Kong Economic Journal | Hong Kong Economic Times | Ming Pao |
|---|---|---|---|---|---|
| Website | ✔ | ✔ | ✔ | ✔ | ✔ |
| Apps | ✔ | ✔ | ✔ | ✔ | ✔ |
| Facebook likes | 1,894,000+ | <500 | 167,000+ | 148,000+ | 262,000+ |
| Twitter followers | 112,000+ | <50 | 13,000+ | <500 | 44,000+ |
| Instagram followers | 119,000+ | ✔ | <500 | ✔ | <500 |
| Weibo fans | ✔ | 286,000+ | 1,000+ | 221,000+ | 1,000+ |
| YouTube subscribers | 998,000+ | ✔ | <10 | 14,000+ | 31,000+ |

| | Oriental Daily News | Sing Pao Daily News | Sing Tao Daily | South China Morning Post | Ta Kung Pao | Wen Wei Po |
|---|---|---|---|---|---|---|
| Website | ✔ | ✔ | ✔ | ✔ | ✔ | ✔ |
| Apps | ✔ | ✔ | ✔ | ✔ | ✔ | ✔ |
| Facebook likes | 169,000+ | <1,000 | 7,000+ | 349,000+ | <500 | <1,000 |
| Twitter followers | 6,000+ | <10 | <1,000 | 285,000+ | 19,000+* | 19,000+* |
| Instagram followers | 1,000+ | ✔ | ✔ | 19,000+ | ✔ | ✔ |
| Weibo fans | 49,000+ | 206,000+ | 7,000+ | ✔ | 3,645,000+ | 196,000+ |
| YouTube subscribers | 9,000+ | 1,000+ | ✔ | 19,000+ | ✔ | ✔ |

For likes/subscriptions/fans fewer than 1,000, only a range is provided: <10, <50, <500, or <1,000.

*Ta Kung Pao* and *Wen Wei Po* share a Twitter account. Hence, the number of followers is the same.

Table 6.12

**Use of Digital and Social Media by Free Hong Kong Newspapers in June 2016**

| Newspaper | AM730 | Headline Daily | Sky Post | Metro Daily | The Standard |
|---|---|---|---|---|---|
| Website | ✔ | ✔ | ✔ | ✔ | ✔ |
| Apps | ✔ | ✔ | ✔ | ✔ | ✔ |
| Facebook likes | 116,000+ | 91,000+ | 138,000+ | 80,000+ | 4,000+ |
| Twitter followers | ✔ | 15,000+ | <500 | ✔ | ✔ |
| Instagram followers | ✔ | <1,000 | <500 | <500 | ✔ |
| Weibo fans | ✔ | 7,000+ | 10,000+ | ✔ | ✔ |
| YouTube subscribers | <100 | 14,000+ | <500 | Did not disclose | ✔ |

For likes/subscriptions/fans fewer than 1,000, only a range is provided: <100, <500 or <1,000.

*Kong Commercial Daily*, the newspaper with the second highest number of fans. It is worth noting that *Ta Kung Pao* and *Hong Kong Commercial Daily* are far less active and less popular on other social media. As Weibo is closely connected with Mainland China, the difference in the use of Weibo in contrast with other social media platforms illustrates that the use of social media to a certain extent parallels political leanings in the general mainstream media landscape of Hong Kong.

Finally, YouTube is used only by newspapers that also produce videos. *Apple Daily* again has the highest number of subscribers (over 998,000), while *Ming Pao* comes a distant second with over 31,000. Of course, even if a newspaper produces videos, it may choose not to post them on YouTube but to embed them in its website (for example, *Oriental Daily News'* news website) or put them on apps. As hosting videos on their own channels gives them sole rights to advertising revenue, newspapers tend not to run a YouTube channel with which they would have to split revenue.

## Free Newspapers

Online and social media platforms are important for free newspapers which rely on circulation and viewership to provide advertising revenue. All free newspapers have websites and mobile apps providing content (Table 6.12), and they also all have Facebook pages. With the exception of *The Standard*, which is the only free English newspaper in Hong Kong and has lower circulation and less than 15,000 Facebook likes, all other free newspapers have around 100,000 Facebook likes, similar to the average number of Facebook likes of a paid newspaper. *The Standard*, as a subsidiary of *Sing Tao* daily, does not serve the majority of the local population. At the same time, as a free newspaper, it has a weaker competitive position for international audiences compared to the *SCMP* which also provides free news content via Facebook.

Free newspapers use other social media less frequently, possibly because of the relatively low extra benefits compared to the costs required to operate and generate content for multiple platforms. *Headline Daily* is more active in generating and providing videos on YouTube, which is also the only social media platform used by AM730 apart from Facebook, but the latter's YouTube channel has very few subscribers. *The Standard* does not use any social media other than Facebook.

## Conclusion

The adoption and use of digital and social media by mainstream media sources is growing, and the level of engagement these platforms have with audiences is also changing quickly. While this chapter provides only a cross-sectional snapshot of the situation, some general patterns can be summarised. Generally speaking, digital and social media are widely used by Hong Kong mainstream media broadcasters for content provision. Mobile apps provide the means for content differentiation (using different apps for different content) and revenue generation (from paid content). Content providers use other social media platforms mainly for promotion. The kind and level of use depends on multiple factors, including the target audience (e.g., Facebook for local audiences, Twitter and Weibo for non-local audiences), political orientation, the costs and benefits of multimedia content production (e.g., YouTube videos) and the maintenance of social media accounts. The general patterns of social media use by audiences and of spending by advertisers are likely to be guiding forces in the future development of social media platforms by mainstream media sources in Hong Kong.

# References

Chan, M. (2015). "Examining the Influences of News Use Patterns, Motivations, and Age Cohort on Mobile News Use: The Case of Hong Kong." *Mobile Media & Communication*, 3(2), 179–95.

Computerworld Hong Kong. (2016). "Hong Kong's Mobile Penetration Grows to 95%." Retrieved from http://www.telecomasia.net/content/hong-kongs-mobile-penetration-grows-95.

Dimmick, J., Feaster, J. C., & Hoplamazian, G. J. (2010). "News in the Interstices: The Niches of Mobile Media in Space and Time." *New Media & Society*, 20(10), 1–17.

Hemment, D. (2005). "The Mobile Effect." *Convergence: The International Journal of Research into New Media Technologies*, 11(2), 32–40.

Lam, L. (2014). "Facebook is Hong Kong's Top Digital Platform in Survey Commissioned by Company". *South China Morning Post*. Retrieved from http://www.scmp.com/news/hong-kong/article/1578755/facebook-citys-top-digital-platform-survey-commissioned-company.

Lee, C. S., & Ma, L. (2012). "News Sharing in Social Media: The Effect of Gratifications and Prior Experience." *Computers in Human Behavior*, 28(2), 331–9.

Olmstead, K., Mitchell, A., & Rosenstiel, T. (2011). "Navigating News Online: Where People Go, How They Get There and What Lures Them Away." *Pew Research Center's Project for Excellence in Journalism*. Retrieved from http://www.journalism.org/2011/05/09/navigating-news-online/.

Pew Research Center. (2016). "News Use across Social Media Platforms 2016." http://www.journalism.org/2016/05/26/news-use-across-social-media-platforms-2016/.

Purcell, K., Rainie, L., Mitchell, A., Rosenstiel, T., & Olmstead, K. (2010). "Understanding The Participatory News Consumer". Pew Internet and American Life Project. Retrieved from http://www.pewinternet.org/2010/03/01/acknowledgements-13/.

We Are Social. (2016). *2016 Digital Yearbook*. Retrieved from http://www.slideshare.net/wearesocialsg/2016-digital-yearbook.

# Chapter 7

# Social Media Use in Hong Kong

*Ke ZHANG and Yunya SONG*

## Introduction

In recent years, Hong Kong has witnessed the rapid development of digital media, online communities and social applications amid a worldwide boom in information and communication technology. As with other developed Asian cities, Hong Kong has high internet penetration rates and also has a mobile phone penetration rate among the highest in the world (Chan, 2015; Lin, Cheong, Kim & Jung, 2010). Today, social media are often the first destination in a search for information on a range of topics, including education, health management, shopping and entertainment. Social media not only influence individuals' lifestyles but also influence their attitudes toward social and political issues. Facing the new trend of 5G networks and smart cities, Hutchison Telecommunications Hong Kong has partnered with Huawei Technologies Co. Ltd. to complete the construction of the end-to-end narrowband Internet of Things by September 2017. This will assist Hong Kong's transition into a technological savvy city as it enters the era of 5G networks (Zhuo, 2017).

With these major developments over the past decade, there has been a growing body of research on social media in Hong Kong. This chapter reviews existing studies focused on social media use in Hong Kong to provide an overview of the directions of current research. A series of keywords (e.g., social media, digital media, online community, Hong Kong) were used to retrieve relevant academic articles from Sage Journals, Springer Link, Taylor & Francis and Wiley Online Library. In addition to academic sources, this review also extends its scope to newspapers and periodicals as well as industry reports and blogs to provide a variety of practical evidence along with an in-depth theoretical analysis. It begins with an introduction to the usage and demographics of social media platforms in Hong Kong. Then, it provides a review of articles from academic and popular sources that examine social media use in a variety of fields, ranging from business and politics to health and education. The results of this review are then used to provide a critical diagnosis of current research and to identify general tendencies in the development of social media in Hong Kong.

## Social Media Platform Usage and User Demographics

According to the article "The State of Social Media Usage in Hong Kong" published on the Business 2 Community website in 2015 (Rudolph, 2015), the top five active social media platforms in terms of the percentage of the Hong Kong population that uses them were WhatsApp (41%), Facebook (33%), Facebook Messenger (23%), WeChat (23%) and Line (14%). In the fourth quarter of 2016, among active social media users in Hong Kong, Facebook occupied a leading position with 72% of the total users, followed by YouTube (69%), WhatsApp (64%), Facebook Messenger (42%), Instagram (40%) and WeChat (33%) (GlobalWebIndex, 2017).

In June 2016, there were 5.75 million internet users in Hong Kong, amounting to 80.2% of the population (Internet World Stats, 2016). Of these internet users, 88.7% (i.e., 5.1 million) used Facebook. From May to August 2017, the average number of Facebook fans kept up a steady pace of growth. Users have shown a preference for liking published content (70% of users in August 2017) and posting photos on their virtual walls (44% of users in August 2017; Socialbakers, 2017). In addition to accessing and sharing news and information, users utilized Facebook to express individual opinions and to organise collective action in social movements (Tang & Lee, 2013; Leung & Lee, 2014; Lee & Chan, 2016).

WhatsApp has more than one billion users in over 180 countries (WhatsApp, 2017) and has become the preferred messaging medium for Hong Kong's young people (Ma, Wong & Hou, 2016). It is owned by Facebook, having been bought in 2014 for US$22 billion. Research conducted by the Online Communication Research Centre of Hong Kong at Shue Yan University has revealed that WhatsApp is the most frequently used means of instant messaging between people in Hong Kong. WhatsApp also has more users for general functions such as communicating with friends and sharing pictures and videos than Facebook. However, Facebook is more prominent in delivering news to users (Ma, Ng, Chow & Hui, 2015).

WeChat, launched by Tencent, is the first Chinese social media application with the potential to go global (Wong & Huang, 2012). As of June 2017, a total of 877 million global users log into their WeChat accounts every day (China Channel, 2017). WeChat has, thus, become embedded in Chinese people's daily activities and interactions. As trade and exchange between Hong Kong and Mainland China have expanded, so has the penetration of WeChat in Hong Kong (Tmtpost, 2015). Its functions include both one-on-one and group conversations, picture and video sharing, WeChat payments linked to bank cards, Moments (where users can post on-the-spot captioned pictures and other content) and several Bluetooth-enabled social networking tools. The WeChat app is now the most popular social media platform in Mainland China. In addition, WeChat has several interactive features such as Shake, Drift Bottle and Look Around that allow users to search for new friends nearby by shaking their phone (Wong & Huang, 2012). To promote WeChat in Hong Kong, marketers have partnered with various corporations such as McDonald's and Starbucks to support online payments. Nonetheless, WeChat use and penetration into the Hong Kong market remains limited (Tmtpost, 2015).

Line was launched by NHN Japan in June 2011 and launched in the Hong Kong market after WhatsApp, but before WeChat. Line's designers emphasise both its technology and the cute "Line friends" characters used to promote the platform. With the same functionality as WeChat, Line allows users to make free voice calls or send messages with whimsical maps attached. Users can also play games in Line's games centre (Hysan, 2017).

It has been shown that each internet user in Hong Kong watches an average of 147 online videos per month (Rudolph, 2015). YouTube, which allows users to upload and broadcast their own video products for free, is one of the most popular video sites in Hong Kong (Chu, 2009). People can also like or leave comments below videos, and by tracking user activity, YouTube recommends videos related to users' interests as well as popular videos with high view counts. Using these capabilities, YouTube provides a space for spreading popular culture and nurturing grassroots celebrities who represent this culture. It has also become a public sphere for local people to produce collective action (Chu, 2009).

In terms of their social media usage habits, Hongkongers are the most active in the evening. Thus, it is easier for organisations and individuals to reach audiences through these platforms during this time. Notably, Western-origin social media platforms (e.g., Facebook and WhatsApp) are more popular among Hongkongers than China's homegrown social media platforms (e.g., Weibo and WeChat; Hoebarth, 2013). Hong Kong is known for its high mobile internet usage rate, which creates a considerable demand for mobile applications. Survey findings indicate that the smartphone users in Hong Kong are particularly interested in news apps, and most of the respondents use the apps while commuting (Chua, 2011). In fact, a study of mobile news use patterns and motivations (Chan, 2015) chose Hong Kong as the study context based on the popularity of mobile news among citizens. Mobile devices have become a prominent platform for accessing the news in Hong Kong, especially for the 18–34-year-old cohort and the 35–54-year-old cohort. In addition, the usage rate of public transport services in Hong Kong is the highest in the world, which helps create the conditions in which mobile news platforms thrive. When commuting by public transport, people often pass the time using smart phones to access daily news and timely information.

Hongkongers' social media usage habits reflect not only a modernised way of life, but also their East Asian cultural roots. Song et al. (2016) explored cross-cultural differences in how social media is used as a source of health information among users in the United States, Hong Kong and South Korea. Hongkongers—who are part of a holistic culture in which the mode of thinking tends to regard the context as a whole with a focus on the relationship between a focal object and the context, and who prefer to explain and predict situations based on such a relationship—tend to place more trust on experience-based health information shared on social media. In comparison, Americans make more frequent use of expertise-based health information sites. The latter are part of a culture in which the mode of thinking tends to focus on the attributes of an object, rather than the whole context. They prefer to explain and predict a situation by utilising rules about categories. The findings of this study point toward cross-cultural variability in the use of intuitive versus analytic reasoning when it comes to health information. East Asians prefer to use intuitive, experience-based reasoning to inform their judgment, whereas Westerners prefer a rule-based, analytic cognitive mode.

## Social Media and Business

### The Use of Social Media in Marketing

According to the Asia Pacific Institute for Strategy, over 90% of enterprises use social media such as Facebook, WeChat, WhatsApp or LinkedIn to expand their business (APIS, 2017). Social media have also become increasingly popular platforms for enterprises to promote their products. For example, Facebook's massive user base provides enterprises with instant access to a large potential customer base. Meanwhile, Facebook's various functions, such as tracking customers' preferences by analysing their profiles, allows potential advertisers to locate their target customers and promote their products to them (Huang, 2015). Therefore, advertising on social media can both realise peer-to-peer promotion patterns and achieve the effects of large-scale promotions.

One practical application of social media-driven promotions is highlighted by the first social media campaign in China, which was launched by Hong Kong Express Airlines in March 2016. The campaign aimed to provide customers with all the information needed to choose company products. Consumers could see all the menu details from the social media platform and had enough time to compare the prices and functions of various products. As many passengers in southern China often fly out of Hong Kong due to its geographical proximity and convenient transportation, Hong Kong Express Airlines hoped to attract Chinese consumers through social media promotions, focusing on those in the Pearl River Delta region (Zhiniuer Media, 2016). This kind of social media campaign is a new means for local enterprises in Hong Kong to expand their influence among Mainlanders, and it indicates that there is no social media boundary between Hong Kong and the Mainland.

Hong Kong Express Airlines' social media campaign was not unique. Hong Kong insurance companies have also begun to use WeChat to promote insurance policies to Mainlanders. Fearing inspections from Chinese regulators, Hong Kong insurers no longer organise public promotion conferences in Mainland China as they did before but have instead turned to a more subtle way of selling insurance—posting on social media (Ding, 2016). This example shows that businesses recognise the potential of expanding into the Mainland market via social media.

As business communication between Hong Kong and Mainland China through social media has increased, the government has begun to improve social media functionality in order expedite travel from the Mainland into Hong Kong. For example, Guangdong residents can now integrate their electronic Hong Kong and Macao Travel Permit into their WeChat accounts. As of September 2017, they can have their documents both checked and renewed online (Ithomenews, 2017).

Although WeChat is the most popular social media platform in Mainland China, and has become increasingly accepted by Hongkongers for personal communication, WeChat Pay is still not widely used in Hong Kong (Jie Media, 2017). However, as of 2017, WeChat Pay has gradually become accepted in some large shopping malls and brand-name stores in Hong Kong, including Ocean Park, Sasa, Colourmix, Aesop, Max Mara and TSI. Nine hundred 7-Eleven stores in Hong Kong also started accepting WeChat Pay in August 2017 and have special offers and promotions for those who use it (Li & Wan, 2017). This adoption reflects the increased popularity of Chinese social media by both enterprises and citizens in Hong Kong.

According to Lee and Huang (2016), there is no significant relationship between the kinds of social media used and the implementation of media strategies by businesses when they use social media to enhance public relations. However, considering the potential consumption levels of Mainlanders, as well as differences in user activity between the Mainland and Hong Kong, the choice of social media regarding functionality should not be ignored by enterprises running promotions geared toward meeting the demands of various consumer groups.

## The Use of Social Media in Enterprise Development

Facebook is the main social media platform used by enterprises for business, while cultural industries such as advertising, public organisations, media and the arts tend to use WhatsApp. LinkedIn is frequently used by enterprises to recruit employees (APIS, 2017).

Employees primarily use social media to communicate with colleagues and partners at work (Lee & Huang, 2016). For example, WhatsApp's role in social interaction among colleagues has grown (Chen, Yang, Jin, Hung-Baesecke & Li, 2016). Creating and joining WhatsApp groups provides users with a platform for discussing work-related issues and for interpersonal interaction. When individuals discuss matters with colleagues in WhatsApp groups at work, they naturally internalise the external rules of communication manners, thus creating bonds between group members. Although WhatsApp has been indispensable in uniting individuals and organisations, both in private and in the work environment, research elucidating how this app constructs these networks through individual and group interactions is still lacking.

In addition to communication within organisations, social media enables organisations to communicate with society. Hoebarth (2013) points out that non-profit art organisations in Hong Kong can gain visibility, recognition and quick feedback by using social media, which provide an exchange platform for organisations, audiences, fans and supporters. For example, the Development Bank of Singapore (Hong Kong) launched the DBC Business Class social digital platform in order to help small and medium-sized enterprises and start-ups contact industry experts and investors. The industry experts and investors can then inform the enterprises about the latest market trends and also provide expert advice. This has enabled enterprises to exchange practical information and collect business intelligence by referring to the views and cases of other enterprises (Zhang, 2016). Opinion-makers have stated that this could assist small- and medium-sized enterprises in both their short- and long-term development.

Social media can also provide a means of monitoring and disseminating information as well as a platform for organisations to communicate with stakeholders during a crisis (Mei, Bansal & Pang, 2010). However, social media may also have negative effects on organisations by escalating crises. Mei, Bansal, and Pang (2010) have put forward a new media crisis communication model suggesting a new categorisation of new media based on different platforms. To solve these negative effects, enterprises should be able to protect their private data and enhance their capacities to deal with public relations crises.

## Social Media and Politics

With the increased interest in Hong Kong's democratic development over the past few decades, the Hong Kong public, especially pro-democracy politicians, have discussed the openness in the policy-making process in matters such as elections (Lee, 2016). It is undeniable that political context influences how the public use social media as a channel to express their political opinions. A number of articles related to social media in Hong Kong have focused on public political participation: Lin, Cheong, Kim & Jung (2010); Leung, Lam,

Yau & Chu, (2010); Tang & Lee (2013); Leung & Lee (2014); Lee (2014, 2015a, 2015b, 2016); Lee, So & Leung (2015); Adorjan & Yau (2015); and Lee & Chan (2015, 2016). They show that groups in Hong Kong, especially students, participate in protests against the authorities due to a lack of democratic communication channels. Facebook's head of Public Policy, George Chen, claims that although we cannot conclude if digital media will transcend traditional media as a form of political discussion and become the first choice for voters looking to interact with political candidates, social networks have become a broad platform for carrying out political dialogue (PRView, 2017). Indeed, social media have filled the vacuum and provided a platform for citizens to express their political opinions, including their negative impressions of the government.

## Social Media and the Polarisation of Opinion

The fragmentation and obfuscation of information transferred through social media means users can only fully understand reality by integrating each piece. When information is disseminated in this manner, it is difficult for public opinion to remain rational and balanced. In a period of growing political conflict, social media tend to polarise opinions and promote extreme attitudes because of people's selective exposure to unbalanced information (Lee, 2016). For example, during the Umbrella Movement in 2014, social media was regarded as an insurgent public sphere that intensified public support for the political campaign and the populace's disaffection (Lee, So & Leung, 2015). The movement produced polarised attitudes towards both the Hong Kong government and the Chinese government (Lee, 2016). The internet, social media and online alternative media have, thus, played an important role in shaping political attitudes in Hong Kong, and they are often used to voice negative evaluations of the government (Leung & Lee, 2014; Lee, 2015a).

Lee and Chan (2015) have found that protesters in the Umbrella Movement were the most active in activities involving online expression, online debates, online explanatory activities and mobile communication. Both connection with public political actors and exposure to shared political information played significant roles in influencing the impact of social media use on political participation (Tang & Lee, 2013). Moreover, Lee (2014) examined the way young people understand politicians and the government through online political communication during the 2012 election of the territory's chief executive. He concluded that a high degree of exposure to online user-generated satire caused younger voters to regard the candidates and the electoral system itself in a negative light. However, those who were more knowledgeable were less influenced by exposure to candidate-centred satire.

Lee (2016) also found that people with clear political orientations tend to have more extreme attitudes than those without clear political orientations in terms of their political communication activities, such as expressing opinions that attack the government. He also found that many activities related to political discourse, such as criticising government regulations, on social media are also related to more extreme political attitudes. Ong (2014) suggests that there should be monitors to take responsibility for removing offensive content from social media websites but at the same time has also said that individual participants should be aware of their liabilities when posting on social websites and should control their use of potentially libellous words.

## Social Media and Collective Action

In addition to providing a channel for the public to express political opinions and participate in political movements, the internet also helps ordinary citizens mobilise and organise for collective action. In Hong Kong, the government advocates an active e-society and information industry (Lin, Cheong, Kim & Jung, 2010). This, along with Hong Kong's small area and dense population, has paved the way for the online mobilisation of offline movements (Lee, 2015b).

In collective action, internet-supported self-mobilisation and the mobilisation of social movement organisations are complementary. Their dynamic combination drives the progress of protest movements as the online environment substantially facilitates the mobilisation and spread of awareness among the public. Public opinion formed on social media provides the emotional, psychological and cognitive basis for people to organise collective action. Anyone on social media can be a journalist and publish news through his or her own information gathering devices, and such unedited content can stimulate emotions and result in psychological resonance among the public. Meanwhile, social media bring a social organisation mode to communities formed on the basis of group identity, enabling people with similar views to gather and organise new participants (Lee, 2015b).

In addition to the influence of social media activities on public willingness to participate in protests, online opinion leaders may also replace the role of participant leaders in physical protest movements. This phenomenon has been discussed by Lee and Chan (2016), who found that only young participants are influenced by social media leadership. The reasons for this may lie in the fact that younger people with less experience in collective action rely on social media to gather political information.

Collective action driven by the interactions between internet-based self-mobilisation and social movement organisations occur not only in the political context but also in environmental protection movements (Lee, 2015b). However, although new social media outlets have been used extensively in political campaigns, their use in social issues such as environmental protection has not gained traction in Hong Kong.

## Social Media and Health in Hong Kong

In recent years, many online health communities based on Health 2.0 technology have emerged. These include communities such as Patientslikeme, Medhelp and WebMD in the West and Haodf, Fh21 and HC3i in Mainland China. All of these communities are accessible to users in Hong Kong. Using them, patients from different locations gather in online health communities to discuss issues of common interest and to help one other. In addition to exchanging information, online health communities also enable users to make friends and receive feedback to help improve health self-management.

It has been shown that online health communities can provide users with social support and that they have a positive effect on users' health (Yan & Tan, 2014). For example, Facebook, along with Hong Kong University, the Hong Kong Federation of Youth Groups and the Samaritan Befriends, released an instruction manual detailing skills for dealing with emotional crises and suicidal behaviour (CSRP, 2016). Social media can also support those in need, based on its far-reaching impact on young people.

The community-based approach is especially suitable for the healthcare field (Fichman, Kohli & Krishnan, 2011). The high level of specialised medical knowledge and the complexity of diseases, especially chronic diseases, require patients to constantly access treatment information. However, there are no convenient and flexible means of communication between doctors and patients in current healthcare systems, and doctors often lack the time to listen to patients' descriptions of trivial aspects of their symptoms (Sbaih, 1995). This is where online health communities come in, providing new channels for patients to access health information at any time and from any location. Song et al. (2016) found that Asian users prefer online health information presented on social sites, such as blogs and social support groups, while American users prefer online health information presented on professional sites. This might be due to the fact that experience-based information is more valued in Asian culture, while expertise and rule-based information is more valued in American culture.

Through collective intelligence, patient groups may produce greater wisdom than individual patients and even health workers, and this can meet patients' demand for health knowledge (Surowiecki, 2005). The internet is more important than personal resources in providing information related to sensitive issues such as sex education, HIV and AIDS and drug use because of its anonymity and timeliness, which enable people to quickly search for sensitive information without compromising their privacy (Chan & Fang, 2007). In addition, since there is no law in Hong Kong protecting homosexuals and bisexuals from discrimination, it may be difficult for them to affirm their sexual orientation and seek support. Social media provides channels for them to do so, which improves both their sense of belonging and mental health (Chong, Zhang, Mak & Pang, 2015). Furthermore, social media help lesbian, gay and bisexual groups exchange information and make emotional connections, while reducing the stigma from which they suffer.

## Social Media and Education in Hong Kong

Social media platforms based on Web 3.0 technology intelligently process and integrate massive amounts of information according to the needs, habits and preferences of users in order to aggregate personalised demands (James, 2010). Although social media use in educational settings is fairly new, its ability to offer individuals both personal and interpersonal interactivity makes it highly attractive as a learning tool. A high degree of information aggregation is believed to provide learners with an efficient learning environment by facilitating students' social participation, relationship development, interaction and communication (Watson, 2009). Since 2012, the Online Communication Research Centre has conducted an annual survey of secondary school graduates (Ma & Chan, 2012; Ma, 2014; Ma, Lau & Hui, 2014; Ma, Ng, Chow & Hui, 2015; Ma, Chow, Yip, Ng & Leung, 2016) (The survey report for 2013 was released in 2014). The survey focuses on the use of social media among Hong Kong youth and their tendency to consume news and establish interpersonal relationships via social media. Their findings indicate that with regards to sex education, the internet provides a private channel for young people to search for sensitive information and advice. In many situations, they find searching the internet preferable to communicating with personal sources such as parents or teachers (Chan & Fang, 2007).

In addition to enabling communicate between students and teachers, social media also improves students' collaborative engagement. For example, Facebook groups provide a convenient means of communication between peers, enabling students to experience online collaboration. Collaborative learning through social media helps enhance students' satisfaction with their studies in terms of the formation of a collaborative team, information exchange and resource sharing as well as the creation of learning contexts (Ma & Yuen, 2011; Li & Ma, 2014).

Collaborative team formation is based on the gathering of individuals with similar interests and experiences in the social media context. Social media users can learn without the limitations of time and space, and can instantly share resources with team members. Interactions based on video and audio sharing help to improve the effectiveness of group interactions. Shared content (e.g., GPS locations, pictures, videos and real-time audio) reflect users' lifestyles and are conducive to collaborative learners understanding of others' behavioural patterns and for imagining real-time user scenarios. Team members can thus deliver learning resources germane to these behavioural patterns and scenarios, and construct joint learning opportunities suitable for collaborative learning. Students' attitudes towards social media-based learning play an important role in online forum learning and in collaborative engagement (Chan & Chan, 2011).

Social media not only provide learners with creativity and a flexible space to perform initiatives but also facilitate teachers' guidance, monitoring and evaluating of a student's learning process. Internet discussion forums record the information searched and shared during the learning process and helps teachers maintain an accurate grasp on student progress. It also provides them with guidance and evaluation in real time. Additionally, it gives teachers a multi-dimensional means of evaluation, which makes the assessment of students more objective and effective (Murugesan, 2009). Mok (2013) has explored student-teacher behaviour in terms of teacher language awareness (part of a programme in Hong Kong aimed at improving the language awareness of teachers and students) and has shown the potential of using internet discussion forums to support learning and teaching.

## Conclusion

Based on secondary analysis and a literature review of social media usage in Hong Kong, this chapter examines four major issues: those pertaining to business, politics, health and education. Popular social media platforms in Hong Kong, such as Facebook and YouTube, originated in the West. However, Hongkongers' usage habits, including searching for social support from friends or family members and building close interpersonal relationships between members of small groups, reflect a sophisticated West-East fusion still bound by a common Eastern Asian cultural tradition and racial homogeneity. Traditional Chinese cultural values influence the way Hongkongers manage their virtual identity on social media, especially in terms of the distinctions between in-group and out-group members. There is also a growing trend of using popular social networking tools from Mainland China, such as WeChat and Weibo, particularly for personal communication between Hongkongers and Mainlanders as well as in business connections between Hong Kong enterprises and the Mainland market.

Much of the research on social media use in Hong Kong is concerned with the role of social media in democratic engagement and political mobilisation, though some scholarly efforts have explored social media use in interpersonal communication, education and health. There remains a dearth of studies related to various other disciplines affected by social media, such as culture, the arts, business and entertainment. Academic research has also consistently found that social media plays a positive role in citizens' political participation in Hong Kong. However, these studies often measure participation as protest-related activities, while neglecting other measures of participation. Civic participation encompasses a broader range of activities and takes on different forms, such as working with fellow citizens to find solutions to public issues in one's community.

The decline of local news in Hong Kong has been an area of growing concern for people who care about civic health, from policymakers and researchers to community groups and citizens. In an era when the public's time and attention is increasingly directed toward platforms such as Facebook and Twitter, the importance of social media as participatory spaces and sources of local information is growing. Future research should further explore the potential of social media to promote local involvement and to support community building.

## Note

This work was supported by a Faculty Research Grant of Hong Kong Baptist University (FRG2/15-16/066).

## References

Adorjan, M., &Yau, H.L. (2015). "Resinicization and Digital Citizenship in Hong Kong: Youth, Cyberspace, and Claims-making". *Qualitative Sociology Review*, 11(2),161–178.

APIS. (2017). "Gangqi shejiao meiti zhanlue shizaibixing, Danwei shendu yingyong" [Hong Kong enterprises social media strategy is imperative, But without deep application]. Retrieved from http://www.apifs.org/social-media.

"August 2017 Social Marketing Report Hong Kong". (2017). Retrieved from https://www.socialbakers.com/resources/reports/hong-kong/2017/august/.

Chan, C.K.K., & Chan, Y.Y. (2011) Students' Views of Collaboration and Online Participation in Knowledge Forum. *Computers and Education*, 57(1), 1445–57.

Chan, K., & Fang,W. (2007). "Use of the Internet and Traditional Media among Young People". Young Consumers, 8(4), 244–256.

Chan, M. (2015). Examining the Influences of News Use Patterns, Motivations, and Age Cohort on Mobile News Use: The case of Hong Kong. Mobile Media and Communication, 3, 179–195.

Chen, Y. R., Yang, C., Jin, Y., Hung-Baesecke, C. J. F., & Li, A. (June 2016). "Corporate WeChat communication in China: Examining Institutional Factors, Media Richness, Content Type, and Public Engagement". Paper presented at the Annual Conference of International Communication Association, Fukuoka, Japan. China Channel. (14 July 2017). Zuotian weixin zai xianggang fabule zuixin baogao: Rihuo yonghu dadao 8.77 yi [Yesterday WeChat released the latest report in Hong Kong: Daily living users reached 877 million]. Sohu. Retrieved from http://www.sohu.com/a/157224665_644778.

Chong, E.S.K., Zhang, Y., Mak, W.W.S., & Pang, I.H.Y. (2015). "Social Media as Social Capital of LGB Individuals in Hong Kong: Its Relations with Group Membership, Stigma, and Mental Well-being". *American Journal of Community Psychology*, 55(1–2), 228–38.

Chu, D. (2009). "Collective Behavior in YouTube: A Case Study of 'Bus Uncle' Online Videos". *Asian Journal of Communication*, 19(3), 337–53.

Chua, T. (20 July 2011). "Hong Kong Smartphone Users Keen on News Apps". *Hong Kong Business*. Retrieved from http://hongkongbusiness.hk/telecom-internet/news/hong-kong-smartphone-users-keen-news-apps.

"Connected for Life" — Press Release. (30 June 2016). CSRP. Retrieved from http://csrp.hku.hk/category/news/page/2/.

Ding, Y. (2 September 2016). Meimei: Shejiao meiti zhutui xianggang baoxian yinbi rexiao neidi [US media: Social media promotes Hong Kong Insurance Policy to be sold in the Mainland]. *Global Times*. Retrieved from http://news.ifeng.com/a/20160902/49882972_0.shtml.

Fichman, R., Kohli, R., & Krishnan, R. (2011). The Role of Information Systems in Healthcare: Current Research and Future Trends. *Information Systems Research*, 22(3), 419–28.

GlobalWebIndex. (2017). "Penetration of Leading Social Networks in Hong Kong as of 4th Quarter 2016". Retrieved from https://www.statista.com/statistics/412500/hk-social-network-penetration.

Hoebarth, J. (2013). "Art Organisations in the Age of Social Media: How Hong Kong's non-Profit Art Organisations are Dealing with the Use of Social Media to Address their Audiences". Restricted Access Theses and Dissertations. 1492.

"How LINE Captured Hong Kong Hearts". (2017). Retrieved from http://www.hysan.com.hk/how-line-captured-hong-kong-hearts/.

Huang, J. (4 February 2015). "Shejiao meiti maoqi, FB fahui geti zhan" [Social media emerges, FB plays individual warfare]. *Hong Kong Commercial Daily*. Retrieved from http://www.hkcd.com.hk/content/2015-02/04/content_3423733.htm.

"Internet Users in Asia". (June 2016). Retrieved from http://www.internetworldstats.com/stats3.htm.

Ithomenews. (5 September 2017). "Shouji zhuangge weixin juneng tongxing xianggang、Ao'men, Zhe yi bushi meng" [It is not a dream to pass Hong Kong and Macao by installing a WeChat in your mobile phone] [Web log comment]. Retrieved from https://mp.weixin.qq.com/s?__biz=MjM5Mzg4NzExMQ==&mid=2651195300&idx=2&sn=b7a99dafad09e137c690f0f24854ad2a&chksm=bd62814c8a15085a7a0f4eb6a6789e2242d63c68656f92cd86c6fcce93bb51ba79f15285753d&scene=27&open_source=weibo_search&pass_ticket=aWrBUMzWqrK1ql0%2BM42pGY5BkBXx5FOdV4PYLIxd%2F5Ll9eTJjDIel3aVGvPfKPsK.

James, K.L. (2010). *The Internet: A User's Guide*. New Delhi: PHI Learning Private Limited.

Jie Media. (28 September 2017). "Zhifubao, Weixin zhifu na'me huo, weishenme xianggang pian bu'ai? Yuanyin hen zhaguo" [Alipay, WeChat are so popular, But why are they not welcomed by Hong Kong people? The reason is incredible]. Sohu. Retrieved from http://www.sohu.com/a/195018614_710015.

Lee, F.L.F. (2014). "The Impact of Online User-Generated Satire on Young People's Political Attitudes: Testing the Moderating Role of Knowledge and Discussion". *Telematics & Informatics*, 31(3), 397-409.

Lee, F.L.F. (2015a). "Internet Alternative Media Use and Oppositional Knowledge". *International Journal of Public Opinion Research*, 27(3), 318–40.

Lee, F.L.F. (2015b). "Internet, Citizen Self-mobilization, and Social Movement Organizations in Environmental Collective Action Campaigns: Two Hong Kong Cases". *Environmental Politics*, 24(2), 308–25.

Lee, F.L.F. (2016). "Impact of Social Media on Opinion Polarization in Varying Times". *Communication & The Public*, 1(1), 56–71.

Lee, F.L.F., & Chan, J.M. (2015). "Digital Media Use and Participation Leadership in Social Protests: The Case of Tiananmen Commemoration in Hong Kong". *Telematics and Informatics*, 32, 879-89.

Lee, F.L.F., & Chan, J.M. (2016). "Digital Media Activities and Mode of Participation in a Protest Campaign: A Study of the Umbrella Movement". *Information, Communication and Society*, 19(1), 4–22.

Lee. Z.J., & Huang, D.L. (2016). "Xianggang shejiao meiti zhanlue" [Social media strategy of corporations in Hong Kong]. *Economy and Management*, 10, 24–6.

Lee, P.S.N., So, C.Y.K., & Leung, L. (2015). "Social Media and Umbrella Movement: Insurgent Public Sphere in Formation". *Chinese Journal of Communication*, 8(4), 356–75.

Leung, D.K.K. & Lee, F.L.F. (2014). "Cultivating an Active Online Counter-Public: Examining Usage and Political Impact of Internet Alternative Media". *International Journal of Press/ Politics*, 19(3), 340–59.

Leung, Z.C.S., Lam, C.W., Yau, T.Y., & Chu, W.C.K. (2010). "Re-empowering Social Workers through the Online Community: The Experience of SWForum in Hong Kong". *Critical Social Policy*, February 30(1), 48–73.

Li, B., & Wan, H. (11 August 2017). "Xianggang 7-Eleven quanxian jieru weixin zhifu" [Hong Kong 7-Eleven has fully access to WeChat payment]. Xinhuanet. Retrieved from http://news.xinhuanet.com/2017-08/14/c_1121482147.htm.

Li, S.M., & Ma, W.W.K. (2014). "Exploring Interpersonal Relationship and Growth Need Strength on Knowledge Sharing in Social Media". In *LNCS 8595, Hybrid Learning. Theory and Practice* (p. 288-299) edited by S.K.S. Cheung et al. Berlin Heidelberg: Springer-Verlag.

Lin, W.Y., Cheong, P.H., Kim, Y.C., & Jung, L.Y. (2010). "Becoming Citizens: Youths' Civic Uses of New Media in Five Digital Cities in East Asia". *Journal of Adolescent Research*, 25(6), 839–57.

Ma, W.W.K. (18 April 2014). "Shejiao meiti shiyong xingwei diaocha" [Social media use behaviour survey]. *Media Digest*. Retrieved from http://app3.rthk.hk/mediadigest/content.php?aid=1486.

Ma, W.W.K., & Chan, W.L. (12 October 2012). "2012 niandu xinwen meiti yu wangluo xingwei diaocha" [News media and online behaviour survey 2012]. *Media Digest*. Retrieved from http://app3.rthk.hk/mediadigest/content.php?aid=1305.

Ma, W.W.K., Chow, C.L., Yip, S.W., Ng, S.P. & Leung, C.Y. (21 September 2016). "2016 niandu xinwen yu shejiao meiti shiyong xingwei diaocha" [News and social media use behaviour survey 2016]. *Media Digest*. Retrieved from http://app3.rthk.hk/mediadigest/content.php?aid=2084.

Ma, W.W.K., Lau, H.Y., & Hui, Y.H. (12 September 2014). "2014 niandu xinwen yu shejiao meiti shiyong xingwei diaocha" [News and social media use behaviour survey 2014]. *Media Digest*. Retrieved from http://app3.rthk.hk/mediadigest/content.php?aid=1960.

Ma, W.W.K., Ng, S.P., Chow, C.L., & Hui, M.L. (1 September 2015). "Xinwen yu shejiao meiti shiyong xingwei diaocha 2015" [News and social media use behaviour survey 2015]. *Media Digest*. Retrieved from http://app3.rthk.hk/mediadigest/content.php?aid=2029.

Ma, W.W.K., Wong, T.K. & Hou, K.H. (19 August 2016). "Xianggang xinwen chuanbo meiti yu shejiao meiti zhong zhi yingyong diaocha: Facebook zhuanye" [The use of social media among Hong Kong news media: Facebook page]. *Media Digest*. Retrieved from http://app3.rthk.hk/mediadigest/content.php?aid=2079.

Ma, W.W.L., & Yuen, A.H.K. (2011). Understanding Online Knowledge Sharing: An Interpersonal Relationship Perceptive. *Computers & Education*, 56, 210–19.

Mei, J.S.N., Bansal, N., & Pang, A. (2010). New Media: A New Medium in Escalating Crises?, *Corporate Communications: An International Journal*, 15(2),143–55.

Mok, J. (2013). A Case Study of Developing Student-Teachers' Language Awareness through Online Discussion Forums. *Language Awareness*, 22(2), 161–75.

Murugesan, S. (Ed). (2009). *Handbook of research on Web 2.0, 3.0, and X.0, 2-volume set: Technologies, Business, and Social Applications*. Hershey: Information Science Publishing.

Ong, R. (2014). "The Writing is on the Forum: Liability of Internet Intermediaries in Hong Kong". *Asia Pacific Law Review*, 22(1), 119–30.

PRView. (2 September 2017). "Shejiao meiti shi ruhe yingxiang xianggang lifahui xuanju de?" [How do social media affect the election of the Hong Kong Legislative Council?]. Retrieved from http://www.vkandian.cn/article/2311012/.

Rudolph, S. (11 June 2015). "The State of Social Media Usage in Hong Kong". Retrieved from http://www.business2community.com/world-news/state-social-media-usage-hong-kong-01248891#IKBr88QFXJ2FPaCM.97.

Sbaih, L. C. (1995). "What Seems to be the Matter: Communication between Hospital and Patients". *Accident & Emergency Nurs*ing, 3(1), 51.

Song, H., Omori, K., Kim, J., Tenzek, K.E., Morey Hawkins, J., Lin, W.Y., Kim, Y.C., & Jung, J.Y. (2016). "Trusting Social Media as a Source of Health Information: Online Surveys Comparing the United States, Korea, and Hong Kong". *Journal of Medical Internet Research*, 18(3), 25.

Surowiecki, J. (2005). *The Wisdom of Crowds*. New York: Anchor Books.

Tang, G.K.Y., & Lee, F.L.F. (2013). "Facebook Use and Political Participation: The Impact of Exposure to Shared Political Information, Connections with Public Political Actors, and Network Structural Heterogeneity". *Social Science Computer Review*, 31(6), 763–73.

Watson, M. (2009). *Scripting Intelligence: Web 3.0 Information, Gathering and Processing*. New York: Apress.

"Why Internet Startups in Hong Kong are so Quiet?" (25 May 2015). TMTPost. Retrieved from http://www.tmtpost.com/233182.html

Wong, M.H., & Huang, J. (2012). "It's More than a Chatting Application: Will WeChat Take over WhatsApp?" *Hong Kong Institute of Marketing Quarterly*, Winter, 4-7.

Yan, L., & Tan, Y. (2014) "Feeling Blue? Go Online: An Empirical Study of Social Support among Patients". *Information Systems Research*, 25(4), 690–709.

Zhang, G. (13 July 2016). "Xingzhan xianggang tuichu zonghe zixun shejiao shuma pingtai" [DBS Hong Kong launched a comprehensive information social digital platform]. Retrieved from https://finance.sina.cn/2016-07-13/detail-ifxtwitr2141011.d.html?wm=3049_0015.

Zhiniuer Media. (16 March 2016). "Xianggang kuaiyun hangkong zai zhongguo shouge shejiao meiti xuanchuan huodong shangxian" [The first social media campaign in China of Hong Kong Express Airlines was launched] [Web log comment]. Retrieved from https://mp.weixin.qq.com/s?__biz=MzAxMTU0MDYzMA==&mid=402207426&idx=1&sn=db54fa363482a6102d92fe6552174461&mpshare=1&scene=1&srcid=100256PsOALjID9DQDa2uUMN&pass_ticket=aWrBUMzWqrK1ql0%2BM42pGY5BkBXx5FOdV4PYLlxd%2F5Ll9eTJjDIel3aVGvPfKPsK#rd.

Zhuo, M. (20 September 2017). "Maixiang 5G, 3 xianggang huo huawei jiancheng NB-IoT fugai quangang" [Towards 5G, 3 Hong Kong and Huawei built NB-IoT covering the whole Hong Kong]. *Apple Daily*. Retrieved from http://hk.apple.nextmedia.com/realtime/finance/20170920/57233349.

# Part III

## Media Credibility

# Chapter 8

# A Report on Public Evaluations of Media Credibility in Hong Kong

*Steve GUO*

## Introduction

Public discussions of media performance cannot avoid mentions of credibility. In Hong Kong, perhaps more than other similar regions, the issue is particularly pronounced because the local press is sharply divided along the political spectrum. Ideological contestations aside, credibility is also frequently evoked in controversies over boundaries of privacy, the prevalence of fake news and the value of user generated content.

A tightly-knit and information-rich society, Hong Kong has retained a sizable mass of its newspaper readers in the wake of the intrusion of digital media technology. Local residents holding up a newspaper, paid or free, continues to be a regular sight on-board public transportation, at breakfast tables, and in offices and parks.

This report is based on analyses of three waves of surveys conducted to discover, among other things: the most used forms of media among Hong Kong residents; the most read newspapers; those aspects of the newspaper they are loyal to that attract them the most; the top three newspapers rated to be the most credible; and differential salience of six indicators of credibility in the public mind. In addressing these issues, we are able to bridge people's newspaper consumption patterns and their credibility perceptions.

## Credibility as a Minor Gratification

To corroborate findings obtained from a focus group analysis that we conducted separately, we looked at data from these audience surveys gathered eight years apart. The focal point of triangulation remains centred on the public's definition of media credibility, news consumption patterns and evaluation of media performance. Our specific interest is not so much the absence of credibility in public assessment of media as the relative weight of credibility as a motive for exposure to public affairs content.

People who follow news do so to fulfil multiple needs (Wenner, 1985). More than half a century ago, communication scholars were already noticing that news use is a joint function of reality and pleasure motives (Schramm, 1949). Two issues emerge. First, if the myriad of motives, drives and gratifications sought are hierarchically stored in people's minds, then researchers can observe the importance of credibility relative to other needs. Second, the reasons why people use information from sources they do not trust are open to diverse interpretations. Neither a simple conclusion about people being irrational nor an inference about the inferior status of credibility in public assessment would do justice to the complexity of the phenomenon.

## Measuring Credibility

The most recent survey was conducted from May to June 2016 and commissioned by a local tertiary educational institution. We asked a sample of randomly selected respondents a series of questions concerning their media use habits, credibility judgments and evaluations of local media performance. All data were collected by trained interviewers using a computer assisted telephone interview (CATI) system, which automated the processes of interviewing, sampling and data collection for quality control purposes. Telephone numbers were randomly generated from the most recent extended fixed-line telephone book in Hong Kong. We chose our respondents by the next-birthday method. The selection rules also required that the respondents be native Cantonese speaking, permanent local residents, and aged 18 or above. The response rate was satisfactory at 66.4%. The final sample included 1,005 valid cases.

Two earlier waves of surveys conducted in August (n=1001) and December (n=1008) 2008 adopted exactly the same procedures. The three waves of surveys contained identical questions geared at measuring changes in the top three most credible newspapers in the eyes of the local reading public.

Our analysis involves four blocks of variables. First, respondents were asked to nominate their own ranking of the top three most credible newspapers in Hong Kong. Second, they were asked to indicate their agreement with six separate ingredients of media credibility, all measured on a Likert scale ranging from "extremely unimportant" to "extremely important". The six items were: accuracy, balance, comprehensiveness, supervision of power, public interest and local impact. Third, we asked respondents to rate, again on a Likert scale, the relative importance of five individual factors that most attracted them to the newspaper they read the most often. The factors were: entertainment, opinion, habit, popularity (i.e., many other people read it) and consistent views. Fourth, the number of years reading the newspaper, which is considered to be an indicator of loyalty, was included in the analytical model as a control.

For our analysis, we asked respondents to first tell us the newspaper or other forms and platforms of media they used the most frequently. In terms of the overall share of the readership market, the proportions of newspapers have remained remarkably stable over the years. The only exception was *Ming Pao* which suffered a fall from grace when its editorial policy began to favour Beijing (Chang & Liu, 2016). That being the case, a brief description of the placement of local newspapers on the political spectrum is in order before we move on to audience perceptions.

## The Political Spectrum of Hong Kong Newspapers

One can divide Hong Kong's newspapers by language, history of publication, size of circulation, target readers, elitism, mass appeal or political allegiance depending on their research focus. Although the issue of credibility is relevant no matter what the criteria are, we deem that it is intimately tied to a newspaper's perceived ideological position. The fate of the aforementioned *Ming Pao* is a case in point.

In January 2014, the then chief editor, Kevin Lau Chun-to of *Ming Pao* was suddenly and, to the surprise of the newspaper's staff and local residents, replaced by Malaysian pro-Beijing businessman Chong Tien Siong. Chong subsequently fired Executive Chief Editor Keung Kwok-yuen who had different opinions on editorial issues. The reason offered for the sacking was "to save resources". Together, the two episodes sent shockwaves into the community's media industry and many people were led to believe that *Ming*

*Pao*, which had long been a target for co-optation by Mainland China, had finally succumbed.

A recent study presented an ideology-oriented classification of seventeen local newspapers based on existing literature (Chang & Liu, 2016). The typology charts the newspapers along a continuum with "conservative pro-Communism" at one end and "democratic anti-Communism" at the other. Although, according to the authors, the entire body of the community's press has slowly but surely shifted their editorial stance toward the conservative end of the continuum, individual newspapers can still be separated into distinct groups by their identifiable political personality as reflected in news coverage and editorials (Table 8.1).

As shown in Table 8.1, at the extreme right end of the scale is *Apple Daily*, with *AM730* (free newspaper) and *Ming Pao* tagging along at some distance. While *Ming Pao* is believed to have slipped in editorial independence and *AM730* is regarded mainly as cultivating a niche market among young people, *Apple Daily* is said to have single-handedly upheld the discourse of radical democrats, which has earned the paper some points in credibility, at least among its committed readers (Huang, 2014).

## Table 8.1

### Political Orientation of Hong Kong's Main Commercial Newspapers from Conservative Pro-Communism (on left) to Democratic Anti-Communism (on right)

|  |  |  |  |  |  |  |
|---|---|---|---|---|---|---|
|  | *HK Daily News* | *HK Economic Times* |  |  |  |  |
| *HK Commercial Daily* | *Sing Pao Daily News* | *The Standard (f)* |  |  |  |  |
| *Ta Kung Pao* | *The Sun* | *Headline Daily (f)* |  | *Metropolis Daily (f)* |  |  |
| *Wen Wei Po* | *Oriental Daily* | *Sing Tao Daily* | *Economic Journal* | *Ming Pao* | *AM730* | *Apple Daily* |

Note: Newspapers marked with (f) are free.

Source: Chang & Liu (2016). From keying to interpretative boundaries: Occupy Central, commercial newspapers and independent media. Journal of Communication Research and Practice. Vol. 6(1): 45-77.

On the opposite extreme of the scale are the three Mainland backed newspapers: *Hong Kong Commercial Daily*, *Ta Kung Pao* and *Wen Wei Po*, jointly known as "the three big lefties." Subsidised by the Mainland government and serving as its political advocates, the three papers are known for being openly partisan and lacking in journalistic professionalism. Their joint circulation is less than 1% of the total readership market. The eleven newspapers in between the two political extremes lean predominantly towards the establishment side, with *Oriental Daily* and *Sing Tao* being most frequently pointed to as the speediest to turn their "steering wheels" towards Beijing, to use a popular slang phrase.

## Patterns of Media Use in Hong Kong

Hong Kong residents have long been known to have a more deeply rooted habit of reading newspapers than people in neighbouring societies. A study found that, in 2008, more than 50% of respondents in a survey sample read a newspaper for more than half an hour every day (Guo et al., 2010). Eight years later, the figure actually increased by about 2%, as shown in our 2016 survey. Despite the worldwide decline in people's fascination with news carried on paper (thanks to the impingement of the internet and social media), many print newspapers in the community have managed to maintain a decent readership. In our 2016 survey, a little over 25% of respondents nominated "newspaper" as their most frequently used media platform (top row of Table 8.2). Television also held its own with 35% of viewership, against the onslaught of new media and the internet, with 35% of viewership, although this pattern is likely to change in the future.

Given our primary interest in print newspapers and the public's perception of media credibility, we asked respondents to name their most frequently read local newspaper(s) in both 2008 and 2016. Distributions of their answers across the two years are presented in Table 8.3. In terms of within-media and between-year comparison, readership figures show dramatic changes for all newspapers, with the notable exception of those in the establishment group (i.e., *Commercial Daily*, *Ta Kung Pao* and *Wen Wei Pao*).

*Apple Daily* is the only newspaper that saw an increase in readership, with its circulation rising from 30% to 35%. Although a 5% rise over a period of eight years—mindful of the margin of error—is not impressive by any standard, the fact that a print newspaper could register a gain in circulation

**Table 8.2**

**Most Frequently used Media Platforms**

| Form of Media | Number of People | Valid Percent (%) |
|---|---|---|
| Print newspaper | 252 | 25.1 |
| TV | 355 | 35.3 |
| Radio | 40 | 4.0 |
| Internet/Social media/App | 354 | 35.2 |
| Other | 5 | 0.4 |
| Total | 1005 | 100 |

**Table 8.3**

**Most Read Print Newspapers**

| Name of Newspaper | Number of People | Valid Percent (%) |
|---|---|---|
| *Apple Daily* | 351[a] | 35.0 |
| | 272[b] | 30.4 |
| *Oriental Daily* | 189 | 18.9 |
| | 259 | 29.0 |
| *Headline Daily* (free) | 107 | 10.9 |
| *Metro Daily* (free) | 34 | 3.8 |
| *Ming Pao* | 32 | 3.1 |
| | 69 | 7.8 |
| *Commerce Daily/ Ta Kung Pao/ Wen Wei Po* | 2 | 0.1 |
| | 1 | 0.1 |
| All other print papers and internet (inclusive of non-readers) | 324 | 32.0 |
| | 258 | 28.9 |
| Total (N) | 1005 | 100 |
| | 893 | 100 |

Note: [a] Numbers in the top row were obtained in September 2016.

[b] Numbers in the second row were obtained in August 2008. A total of 108 system missing cases were recorded, bringing the valid cases down from 1001 to 893.

Since newspaper reading patterns are unlikely to change over a period of a few months, the 2008 December survey figures are not shown in the table.

at all in the digital and social media age is nothing short of a miracle. In retrospect, the observed win by *Apple Daily* in audience popularity is not without its logic. As mentioned earlier, this mass-appeal tabloid thrives not only on its daily staple of sensationalism, though this surely plays a role as an attractant. More importantly, it is the only local newspaper that flaunts an overt anti-Communist agenda, thus bearing the brunt of Mainland political pressures in the community and scoring on credibility along the way, particularly in the last several years when tensions between the Mainland and Hong Kong have loomed large in the everyday life of both institutions and individuals.

*Oriental Daily*, whose name used to be uttered in the same breath as *Apple Daily*, has over the years gradually detached itself from the camp of radical democracy in exchange for permission to land advertising revenue from the Mainland. Perhaps because of that, the paper took a heavy drop in circulation, going down from nearly 30% in 2008 to 19% in 2016. For reasons expounded on earlier, *Ming Pao* suffered an even greater drop, losing more than half its readers. Readership for the free newspaper, *Metro Daily* has stayed stable at a share of the readership market below 5%. All the other print papers and various new media platforms take up the remaining 30% or so of the news readership market.

## Public Rankings of the Most Credible Newspapers in Hong Kong

When it comes to public credibility ratings, the "three biggies" (i.e., *Oriental Daily*, *Ming Pao* and *Apple Daily*) have lived up to expectations and remain the top three most credible newspapers in Hong Kong, as reported by respondents in all three waves of surveys we conducted from 2008 to 2016. Consistent with findings from other sources and our own, longitudinal changes in public credibility perceptions of the three local newspapers have moved in a predictable direction and are congruent with the hardening or softening of Mainland-Hong Kong tensions in the broader political environment and the corresponding shifts in the editorial policy of different newspapers.

The short interval between the first two waves of the survey, from August 2008 to December of the same year, requires some explanation. The December survey was not in the original research plan. It was conducted because members of the research team were somewhat taken by surprise when they saw the August 2008 survey data showing that *Oriental Daily* ranked second in credibility, trailing *Ming Pao*. Since members had expected a lower ranking for *Oriental Daily*, a decision was made to follow up on the first wave and conduct a second and much shorter survey as a confirmatory study. Hence the third column in Table 8.4.

Looking down the last column, which shows the valid percentage of ratings, one can see that *Oriental Daily* has maintained a remarkably stable ranking across the three time points, holding onto second place for the first two rounds of surveys and climbing to number one in the latest survey. Despite its shrinking readership, *Oriental Daily* continues to be one of the bestselling papers in the community, due perhaps in part to its long publishing history, which is important in creating a loyal cluster of habitual readers. It may also be true that the paper's movement away from its traditionally hostile position toward the Mainland has won itself new readers who might appreciate the turn towards the consensus and harmony rather than conflict.

The story of *Ming Pao* is one of a reversal of fortune in a rather unflattering way. *Ming Pao* was ranked the highest in credibility in both surveys in 2008, although a downward slide was already apparent in the 6% drop in readership within the short period. At its peak, *Ming Pao*'s credibility ratings were more than thirteen percentage points higher than the second (*Oriental Daily*) and a good twenty percentage points higher than the third (*Apple Daily*) in the December 2008 survey. Looking back at Table 8.3, *Ming Pao*'s drop in credibility ratings seems to have occurred in parallel with the paper's sharp loss of regular readers (from 7.8% to 3.1%). However, the observed close associations between the loss of readers and perceived credibility are plausible and at this stage remain correlational because speculations about the impact of the paper's shift towards a pro-establishment editorial policy require more compelling evidence to sustain causal claims.

The figures for *Apple Daily*, in contrast to those of *Oriental Daily* and *Ming Pao*, are likely to be most heartening for the newspaper's staff because they are on the increase, defeating its peers in trend and new media in momentum. Although they are small and remain the lowest among the three newspapers in the three surveys, the 2016 numbers show a strong upward gain and may ultimately surpass *Ming Pao*. This is no trivial change considering that, in 2008, the proportion of people who perceived *Apple Daily* to be the most credible newspaper was barely a quarter of those who nominated *Ming Pao*.

On the whole, the general evolutionary trajectory of the top three most credible newspapers in the public mind in Hong Kong tells a tale of three

Table 8.4

**Most Credible Newspapers in Hong Kong**

| Name of Newspaper | Month & Year | Ranking | Number of Nominations | Valid Percentage (%) |
|---|---|---|---|---|
| Oriental Daily | 9.2016 | 1 | 164[a] | **16.3** |
|  | 8.2008 | 2 | 160[b] | 16.0 |
|  | 12.2008 | 2 | 145[c] | 14.2 |
| Ming Pao | 9.2016 | 2 | 126 | 12.7 |
|  | 8.2008 | 1 | 213 | **27.4** |
|  | 12.2008 | 1 | 281 | 21.3 |
| Apple Daily | 9.2016 | 3 | 112 | **11.2** |
|  | 8.2008 | 3 | 81 | 8.1 |
|  | 12.2008 | 3 | 73 | 7.1 |
| All others | 9.2016 | 4 | 602 | 59.8 |
|  | 8.2008 |  | 547 | 54.6 |
|  | 12.2008 |  | 519 | 51.3 |
| Total | 9.2016 |  | n= 005 | 100 |
|  | 8.2008 |  | n=1001 | 100 |
|  | 12.2008 |  | n=1018 | 100 |

Numbers in bold face were the highest within-newspaper ranking across the three time points.

distinct and yet interdependent patterns: rise for *Apple Daily*, fall for *Ming Pao*, and unchanged for *Oriental Daily*. Ideological alliance, rather than market competition and encroachment of new media, is likely the primary explanation. The only anomaly, if it can be called that, is that although both *Oriental Daily* and *Ming Pao* lost a large number of their readers, only the latter suffered a concomitant loss of public credibility. Again, shuffling the top management, the changing editorial policy and the recent stabbing of former outspoken Chief Editor Lau in the streets of Hong Kong in broad daylight in 2014 all contribute to the paper's misfortune.

To gain further insight into the connections between credibility standings of local newspapers and reading patterns, we cross-tabulated the nominations

**Table 8.5**

**Cross-tabulation: Most Credible Newspapers by Number of Reading Years**

| Name of Newspaper | Years of Reading | | Total |
| --- | --- | --- | --- |
| | ≤ 3 Years | > 3 Years | |
| *Oriental Daily* | 33 (35.1%) | 122 (40.8%) | 155 (39.4%) |
| *Ming Pao* | 42 (44.7%) | 85 (28.4%) | 127 (32.3%) |
| *Apple Daily* | 19 (20.2%) | 92 (30.8%) | 111 (28.2%) |
| Total | 94 (100%) | 299 (100%) | 393 (100%) |

Note: The sample size only includes Pearson Chi-Square Value: 9.256; $p < .05$.
September 2016; n=786.

of the most credible newspaper by the number of years a person has been committed to reading that paper with the line drawn at three years (Table 8.5).

Our decision to build into the questionnaire "years of reading one's favourite newspaper" was guided by previous studies on community integration whose multiple indicators included length of residence, habitual reading of local press, psychological attachment to community press news reporting and persona. Together, they form the basis of a sense of belonging to the community and loyalty to and, by extension, para-social relationship with the press and media persona (McLeod et al., 1996).

As Table 8.5 shows, residents who have read *Oriental Daily* longer than three years are more likely to rate it as the most credible newspaper than those who have spent less time reading the paper, with an increment of a little over 5%. The same pattern is found for *Apple Daily*, except that the margin of increase is twice as large, over 10%. By now, it should no longer surprise anyone that *Ming Pao* took a drop, although 16% is unexpectedly steep. Looking at the figures, one can easily imagine the disappointment loyal readers of *Ming Pao* must have felt with the paper's turn towards a pro-establishment stance and away from its long-cherished position of independence over the years. In Hong Kong, the claim that *Ming Pao* is number one in perceived credibility has long been assumed by its readers and is often the expectation of people who do not read the paper, as indicated in our focus group study.

Table 8.6

**Public Judgment of Media Credibility across Six Important Measures (%)**

| Response item | Extremely Unimportant | Unimportant | Neutral | Important | Extremely Important |
|---|---|---|---|---|---|
| Accuracy | 1.8 | 4.6 | 22.8 | 28.8 | **42.0** |
| Balance | 3.1 | 5.2 | 30.0 | 25.3 | **36.4** |
| Comprehensiveness | 2.2 | 6.1 | 30.8 | **31.4** | 29.6 |
| Supervision | 2.5 | 6.7 | **33.1** | 27.8 | 30.0 |
| Public interest | 1.2 | 5.8 | 23.0 | 32.2 | **37.8** |
| Local impact | 1.1 | 6.1 | 23.9 | **37.4** | 31.5 |

Note: Numbers in bold face indicate the highest value across the row.
September 2016; n=1004.

## Public Perceptions of Normative Aspects of Media Credibility

Drawing from existing literature and on inferences from our focus groups, we listed the six most common normative aspects of media credibility in the survey and sought respondents' views on each (Table 8.6). Without pointing to any specific media organisations, the questions were used to detect variance across the six items in terms of respondents' general inclinations toward and normative preferences for the attributes, which are: accuracy, balance, comprehensiveness, power supervision, public interest and local impact.

The overall pattern unveiled in Table 8.6 is that all the items were considered important or extremely important by two thirds of the respondents. If "neutral" is included, the figure jumps to over 90%, making the minuscule number of responses in the unimportant and extremely unimportant categories likely candidates for outliers.

If we separate the pattern into individual items, then the overall unidirectional impression becomes somewhat differentiated. Accuracy comes highest in the extremely important category at 42%, followed closely by public interest, which was at 37.8% in the same category. The fact that the latter covers a broader area of social phenomena than the former indicates that news readers either place great importance on a wide range of concerns subsumed under the six items or show, rather indiscriminately, due respect to all normative statements about media credibility. Evidence for the second possibility may come from the inclusion of more items stated in a normative tone and the observation of the heavy slant at the importance end of the scale.

Like accuracy, balance and comprehensiveness are content attributes closely related to the technical side of media professionalism. They represent the outer ring of the prevailing ideas about news objectivity. Balance was rated extremely important by most people and comprehensiveness important by most, with a slight difference from being rated most important (2%).

Compared with the four news attributes above, supervision of power has more to do with the expected function and image of media. This particular ingredient of media credibility implies a profound mistrust of state power and politicians and holds an assumption about news being the fourth estate, or an independent power base whose job is to offer an additional layer of checks and balances outside the existing system setup. As relevant and important as this could be to social health, public ratings of supervision were the lowest across all six attributes of media credibility (33.1%) and highest in the "unimportant" category. This was puzzling given that the source of growing tension between Mainland China and Hong Kong and the cause for much of the street politics in the community lies in the contestations between state power and so-called people power. In wave after wave of social movements in Hong Kong in the last several years, each local media outlet has pledged allegiance to its own ideological position and sided with either the establishment or the pro-democratic camp.

Local impact is more or less a stand-alone item in that it is indicative of parochial interest instead of most journalists' aspiration for metropolitan orientations as a valued pursuit of professionalism. Previous studies have documented, without exception, that Hong Kong readers are much more interested in local affairs than events farther away. News happening elsewhere typically goes through a process of "domestication" in which the reporter is trained to tease out the local angle from news events occurring elsewhere (Clausen, 2004). On the whole, local impact was rated important by most of the respondents (37.4%).

Having examined the public's perceptions of the credibility items in their own merit, we moved on to connect the six attributes with the top three most credible newspapers in the audience list: *Oriental Daily*, *Ming Pao* and *Apple*

**Table 8.7**

**Mean Differences of Public Judgment of Media Credibility across the Three Top-Ranking Newspapers**

| Questionnaire item | Oriental Daily | | Ming Pao | | Apple Daily | |
|---|---|---|---|---|---|---|
| | Mean | p-value | Mean | p-value | Mean | p-value |
| Balance | 3.71 | .04 | 3.88 | – | 3.88 | – |
| Comprehensiveness | 3.82 | – | 3.98 | .03 | 3.83 | .00 |
| Power supervision | 3.71 | – | 3.91 | .04 | 4.02 | .02 |

Note: Only significant t-test p-values are listed.
1=strongly disagree and 5=strongly agree.
September 2016; n=1004.

*Daily* (Table 8.7). The t-test analysis resulted in three of the six attributes being statistically significant: balance, comprehensiveness and power supervision. The three significant t-values, therefore, are the only ones shown in Table 8.7.

*Oriental Daily* was given credit for being balanced in reporting, a tribute due perhaps to the shift of its editorial policy from right wing to a more neutral middle ground. *Ming Pao* was lauded for comprehensiveness in coverage and its role in power supervision. As testimony to both, the paper ran a series of front page investigative stories on the illegal expansion of the chief executive's Peak house, which won the top place for best news reporting in Hong Kong's prestigious Best News Awards. *Apple Daily* performed well in exactly the same two realms, with a slightly higher mean score in power supervision than *Ming Pao*.

Next, we looked at factors that attract readers of the top three most credible newspapers to their favourite by self-reporting on six scales that were created on the basis of findings from the focus group discussions, our pilot study prior to the full survey and literature pointing to the diverse needs a person harbours when using news well beyond its referential values. Table 8.8 cross-tabulates the six factors with the three newspapers.

Consistent with expectations, *Ming Pao* (middle rows) was seen as both opinionated and objective, a somewhat unlikely pair of press qualities that could be interpreted as the newspaper's own act of sending mixed signals to readers. That is, on the one hand, the newspaper has no qualms about showing its position on major political issues, and on the other, it continues to

**Table 8.8**

**Mean Areas of Appeal ("which part of the newspaper attracts you the most?")
across the Three Top-Ranking Newspapers**

| Questionnaire item | Oriental Daily | | Ming Pao | | Apple Daily | |
|---|---|---|---|---|---|---|
| | Mean | p-value | Mean | p-value | Mean | p-value |
| Entertaining | 3.40 | .00 | 3.11 | – | 3.50 | .01 |
| Opinionated | 3.52 | .02 | 3.19 | .05 | 3.85 | .00 |
| Habitual | 4.15 | .03 | 3.82 | – | 4.41 | .00 |
| Popular | 3.84 | .00 | 3.32 | – | 3.92 | .00 |
| Similar view | 3.63 | .00 | 3.28 | – | 3.86 | .00 |
| Objective | 3.72 | .00 | 3.09 | .01 | 3.54 | .01 |

Note: Only significant t-test p-values are listed.
1=strongly disagree and 5=strongly agree.
September 2016; n=1004.

cling on to practices of media professionalism by providing factual accounts of news events and presenting various sides of social controversies. The lack of statistical significance for the other four factors suggests that *Ming Pao*, as many believe, is a serious and credible newspaper but is not much fun to read regularly, which might be the more important attractant.

In contrast, *Oriental Daily* and *Apple Daily* demonstrate strong appeal to readers across all six factors. Not only do people find the two papers fun to read (entertaining), worthy of long-term commitment (habitual) and boasting massive followings (popular), they also identify with the papers' prior existing stances on social issues (similar views) and think the papers have more distinct personalities (opinionated). Both papers were also thought to more closely abide by the journalistic code of conduct (objectivity) than *Ming Pao*, as indicated by the higher means on the last two items.

Looking at these findings, it is clear that media credibility and all the adjectives associated with it are only peripheral to certain central and pivotal motives that drive people to various media outlets. The results in Table 8.8 echo and provide further evidence for our earlier argument about media credibility being a minor source of gratification. The lack of significant differences between the figures for *Oriental Daily* and *Apple*

*Daily*, as opposite as they are in their editorial pursuits, seem to suggest that entertainment and utilitarian functions take precedence over political ideology in people's choice of media.

## Conclusion

Different views about people being tacit theorists converge on people's innate need to seek patterns and make sense of the world around them. This conception of the human mind assumes that individuals not only know what they need, but that they always actively look for ways to gratify these needs. Wenner (1985), for example, identified more than a dozen distinct motivations that prompt individuals to adopt a given pattern of media use, including ego-defense, self-expression, tension reduction, escapism, killing time, mood management and so on. Findings from our three rounds of surveys have confirmed our suspicion that news consumption has a built-in regularity whose continuity hinges on gratification of all the utilitarian and escapist urges a person has when faced with choice of media, which in an important way explains why the most favoured media channel was not the most credible one.

Although *Ming Pao*, *Oriental Daily* and *Apple Daily* remain the top three most credible newspapers in Hong Kong, only *Apple Daily* has seen any increase in circulation in recent years. The other two have lost half their readers, proving the superior ability of ideological consistency to cement the message-mind relationship. Of course, it is possible that some of the readers for all three newspapers have moved to their online platforms. We have not seriously distinguished the platform transition patterns among readers because in the current study we do not have any reasons for expecting variance for the three top newspapers.

Of the two main forces governing media production and consumption, political and commercial, the former appears to be holding the reins, at least in Hong Kong. In this study, we found that message-mind congruency in ideological stance determines the circulation and advertising revenue of the press. Fluctuations in audience reception across the years are invariably linked to the perceived changes in the papers' warmness to political authorities. This discovery is made possible because of the unique media ecology in Hong Kong where the press continues to enjoy sufficient editorial autonomy to express anti-establishment views.

Interestingly, ideological bondage is sealed more by each press' commitment to a professional code of conduct than its partisan bias. Judging by the respondents' preferences, it is clear that the essential ingredients of media professionalism, accuracy and balance, received higher scores than supervision of power and service to public interest. This is partial testimony to the rationality of audience members who are not blind followers of ideological zeal.

Researchers of media credibility need to be aware that this notion of media credibility carries with it certain normative weight such that when primed, people may feel some degrees of moral pressure to pronounce its relevance and importance. To the extent that this may be true, it is safe to assume that the nature of media credibility in the public mind is a more complex affair than existing studies have suggested.

## Note

This research was part of a larger project supported by the Hong Kong General Research Funding (Project Funding Number: 244242).

## References

Chang, T., & Liu, N. (2016). "From Keying to Interpretative Boundaries: Occupy Central, Commercial Newspapers and Independent Media". *Journal of Communication Research and Practice*. Vol. 6(1): 45–77.

Charnley, M. (1936). Preliminary Notes on a Study of Newspaper Accuracy. *Journalism Quarterly*. Vol. 13(4): 394–401 (in Chinese).

Clausen, L. (2004). Localizing the Global: 'Domestication' Processes in International News. *Media, Culture & Society*. Vol. 26(1): 25–44.

Guo, Z., Huang, Y., To, Y., & Chan, F. (2010). "Credibility, News Sources and Readership: The Case of Hong Kong Audience". Working Paper Series. David, C. Lam Institutes for East-West Studies.

Huang, W. (2014). "Hong Kong Review: Ming Pao's Replacement of its Executive Chief Editor Shook Hong Kong Media". (In Chinese) http://www.bbc.com/zhongwen/trad/hong_kong_review/2014/01/140114_hkreview_mingbao_editor.

McLeod, J., Guo, Z., Daily, K., Eveland, W., Bayer, J., Yang, S., & Wang, H. (1996). Community Integration, Local Media Use and Democratic Processes. *Communication Research*. Vol. 23(2): 179–209.

Schramm, W. (1949). "The Nature of News". *Journalism Quarterly*. Vol. 26(1): 159–269.

Wenner, L. A. (1985). "The Nature of News Gratification". In *Media Gratification Research*, edited by K. E. Rosengren, L. A. Wenner, & P. Palmgreen (p. 171–93). Beverly Hills, CA: Sage.

# Chapter 9

## Feel Real, Feel Credible:
# Animated News and Credibility

*Wai Han LO and Benjamin K. L. CHENG*

## Introduction

The study of media credibility has long been a focus among communication scholars (Brill, 2001; Ketterer, 1998; Lasica, 1998; Online News Association, 2002). Researchers have found that media organisation credibility has declined in the eyes of the public (Project for Excellence in Journalism, 2008), and 60% of Americans think that media reports are politically biased (Pew Research Center, 2005), up from 42% in 1986 (Pew Research Center, 2002). In 1985, more than half of respondents believed that the news was generally accurate—however, that dropped to 35% in 2002 (Pew Research Center, 2002). A similar situation exists in Asia, with Hong Kong as a prime example. The credibility of news in the eyes of the public has declined in the past twenty years, with notable drops in 2010, 2013 and 2016 (*Ming Pao*, 2017).

Media scholars always want to know what factors influence the audience's perception of news credibility (Flanagin & Metzger, 2000). Past studies have found that two main elements influence perceived news credibility: source credibility and medium credibility (Kiousis, 2001). Source credibility means that the public perceives a piece of information as credible or not according to the credibility of its source (Newhagen & Nass, 1989). Individual presenters, such as anchors, elites and world leaders are generally regarded as news sources (Kiousis, 2001). The perceived credibility of a news organisation is another important source of credibility (Cheng & Lo, 2012).

Medium credibility refers to the believability of a piece of information based on the medium in which it is delivered. Past research found that audiences are inclined to consider the medium credible when they judge the news credible, with newspapers regarded as a more credible medium than online news (Park, 2005). However, other studies have found that traditional news publications are perceived as less credible than their online versions (Johnson & Kaye, 1998).

Medium credibility is influenced by a number of presentation variables. For example, video editing affects an audience's perception of political candidates, and political candidates are perceived more positively if the advertisement contains more cuts (Reeves & Nass, 1996). News on a bigger screen size is also perceived as more credible than news on a smaller screen (Reeves & Nass, 1996). Presentation quality (Lee, 1978), aesthetic style (Slater & Rouner, 1996) and design of the website (Flanagin & Metzger, 2007) all matter in determining perceived credibility.

In this chapter, we investigate how animation, as a presentation feature, influences perceived credibility, its relationship with the concept of "presence" and with media dependency and use. It is a summary of our past studies about the use of animation in news, which is especially important because this is a developing area of research (Cheng & Lo, 2012). The findings of this study will aid in developing an understanding of the role this presentation variable plays in audience perceptions. This is particularly important because practitioners admit that not all details of animation are accurate, and this can blur the line between fact and fiction (Boykoff, 2010). So we want to find out whether the audience perceives animated news to be credible, and what factors contribute to the level of audience-perceived news credibility.

In the following pages, we first illustrate the recent development of melodramatic animated news and how media use and media dependency may interact with animation to influence perceived news credibility. We then discuss why the concept of presence can be a mediator of the relationship between animation and perceived news credibility.

## The Use of Animation in News

The development of new technology in the news industry has changed journalistic practices dramatically (Fahmy, 2008). Media organisations use different features across platforms to attract a diverse audience in the face of fierce competition (Aitamurto & Lewis, 2013). The use of digital skills and augmented reality technologies has become more frequent in the news-making process (Pavlik & Bridges, 2013), with animation being increasingly common (Cohen, 2009). We thus consider melodramatic animation to be an emerging news reporting format. In the past, animation was mainly used in a supplementary role in narrating the news with, for example, 3D models demonstrating natural phenomena. Recently, a more complex form of animation has been used in reporting news: "melodramatic animation" (Cheng & Lo, 2012; Lo & Cheng, 2013). Unlike the previous forms of news animation, melodramatic animation has at least three formal features. First, it re-enacts entire news stories with 3D animated characters in a digital environment, featuring dramatic facial expressions and action. Second, it provides a detailed story line. Third, it includes audio, with the videos usually having background music and sound effects as well as dialogue between the characters.

These features of melodramatic animation have been studied in terms of three testing variables in news reporting: the visual presentation (Kiousis, 2006; Seiler, 1971; Sundar, 2000), the vividness of the news stories (David, 1998) and the audio elements (Addington, 1971; Burgoon, 1978). Animation is used to fill gaps in news stories and describes details as if the reporters were witnessing the incidents in person.

Next Media Limited was the first news organisation to use this type of animation in a news story. Jimmy Lai, the owner of Next Media Limited, invested US$30 million and spent two and a half years launching the new business. A team of 180 employees create animations to fill the gaps in news stories every day (Boykoff, 2010). Next Media also has a partnership with Reuters, an international agency, to distribute the animated news videos to media organisations worldwide, including Time, The New York Times, CNN, and The Financial Times (Next Animation Studio, 2017). Next Media Limited was established in Hong Kong but now also has media outlets in Taiwan, Japan and New York (Cheng & Lo, 2015; Kigannon, 2011).

Next Media Limited often uses melodramatic animation to create news stories that feature international celebrities and significant international news events. These news videos have been featured on the websites for *Time* and the *New York Times* and have attracted audiences in the millions. Some of the videos have even gone viral (Next Animation Studio, 2017). Several critics have worried that the use of melodramatic animation provides unverified versions of news incidents (Coren, 2010). Indeed, the creators of such news items have admitted that they use fictional details in the news-making process (Wong, 2012) to fill in gaps in the news stories. Media scholars have thus questioned whether it is suitable to use animation to re-enact news stories and are concerned that it is contrary to the journalistic principle of objectivity (Cheng & Lo, 2012).

## Perceived News Credibility and Animation

Previous research has found that the medium in which news stories are narrated (Johnson & Kaye, 1998; Park, 2005), the source of the news (Kiousis, 2001), and audience variables (Bucy, 2003), such as age, educational background and gender, all of which contribute to perceived news credibility. The factors that influence online news credibility include the perceived credibility of the news presenter and the news organisation, the credibility of online media and audience attributes. As such, the factors influencing the perceived news credibility of animated news include the effect of the animation as a presentation format, the perceived credibility of the news source and the audience variables of media dependency and media use.

When introducing media dependency theory, Ball-Rokeach and Defleur (1967) claimed that audiences depend on media to achieve their goals and regard them as reliable sources of information. Individuals perceive information to be credible if they rely on media for gaining information (Austin & Dong, 1994; Wanta & Hu, 1994). For example, a study found that online news is perceived to be credible if internet users depend more on it to seek information (Yang & Patwardhan, 2004).

Media use is another theory that illustrates the relationship between perceived news credibility and news media. It differs from media dependency theory in that its focus is on how long and frequently a particular medium is used (Mackay & Lowrey, 2007) rather than the motives of the users. Past research has generated a range of results on the relationship between the use of media and perceived credibility. For example, the frequency of blog use has a positive relationship with the perceived credibility of blogs (Trammell, Porter, Chung & Kim, 2006). However, no relationship has been found between the use of online, television and newspaper news media and perceived news credibility (Kiousis, 2001), and no studies have examined the relationship between animated news reports and perceived news credibility.

Thus, we conducted an experiment to test the relationship between melodramatic news animation and news credibility. We recruited 153 college students in Hong Kong aged eighteen to twenty-four and randomly assigned them to one of two groups: one group watched a news video featuring melodramatic animation, while the other watched a manipulated and edited version of the video with the melodramatic animation removed. The first video was chosen from news produced by Next Media. It showed two men fighting inside a Hong Kong train. The forty-three-second video had two parts including actual footage and a seventeen-second animation. The second video had the animated content removed and replaced with shots of the subway.

We found that our participants' perceptions of news credibility were positively related to their perceptions of the news organisation's credibility and their dependence on the medium, but not with using the medium. In other words, our findings suggest that medium dependency contributes to perceived news credibility, whereas medium use is not a significant factor. This is consistent with previous findings that medium dependency is a stronger predictor of perceived news credibility than medium use (Yang & Patwarhan, 2004; Johnson & Kaye, 1998). Audiences could use media for many reasons: they may watch news videos for entertainment only, and thus, animation may not influence their perceptions of news credibility.

At the same time, we found that the use of melodramatic animation in news did not influence perceptions of news credibility. It is possible that animation use in the news may be outweighed by the effect of the news source—the perceived credibility of the news organisation. However, the use of animation as a news format may also be determined by how that animation is used. Different features of the melodramatic animation such as background music, sound effects and facial expressions of the animated characters contribute to a sense of "presence" that may play a role in the level of perceived news credibility.

## The Role of Presence in the Evaluation of News Credibility

The role of presence in influencing aspects of news perception such as credibility has been the focus of attention among scholars researching the effects of media, particularly those interested in researching new media. Previous studies have established the link between source credibility and audience involvement (Gunter, 1992), suggesting that audience immersion into a constructed media world influences the perceived source credibility of the news (Bracken, 2006). These results suggest that television images and footage seen in higher definition, which is more vivid, elicited a more intense media experience and enhanced news credibility (Bracken, 2006). From a similar perspective, Bracken, Neuendorf and Jeffres (2003), investigated the influence of screen size on the source credibility of candidates in a presidential campaign. Viewers who watched a larger screen reported a heightened experience of immersion and gave a more positive evaluation of a presidential candidate in terms of the candidate's trustworthiness. The results of these studies supported Couture's (2004) notion that if a simulation is perceived as looking like the real world—realism as a conceptualisation of presence—it is likely to be evaluated as more convincing and credible. Therefore, we can posit that perceived news credibility is linked to media use.

## Presence

Previous studies have shown that animation enhances perceived credibility because it creates an illusion that seems authentic (Cholodenko, 1991; Stoiber, Seguier & Breton, 2010). However, few studies have been conducted on the link between animation use and perceived credibility. Research does suggest that presence, a construct used to investigate how an audience experiences mediated or virtual environments (Baons et al., 2000), may serve as a mediator (Lombard, 2000). The sense of presence is enhanced, despite the fact that individuals are aware they are in a mediated environment different from the real environment (Lombard & Ditton, 1997; Bracken, 2006).

Presence has three dimensions. The first is transportation, a key feature of which is vividness, which enhances presence (Steuer, 1992). Vividness is the representational richness of the virtual medium and is driven by the stimulatory presentation features of the mediated environment. The sensory dimensions and clarity of the perceptual channels, such as music and graphics, are the primary aspects of vividness (Fortin & Dholakia, 2003; Steuer, 1992). They enhance a sense of presence if the videos have vivid images, high resolution and sound effects (Reeves, 1991; Steuer, 1992). Melodramatic animated news videos have action, animated characters with rich facial expressions and background music and sound effects. This presentational richness may increase the number of sensory dimensions, which in turn create a sense of presence for the audience.

The second dimension is immersion, with presence as a perceptual and psychological experience. The individual feels that he or she is surrounded and immersed in a mediated environment (Murray, 1997). Individuals experience a sense of perceptual immersion when physically submerged in the virtual environment, as with the use of a head-mounted display. Presence as immersion is a psychological experience, a sense of psychological involvement and mental absorption (Quarrick, 1989). It is the result of mental engagement in a virtual world (Lombard et al., 2000), such as when individuals read books or watch movies or television. McMachan (2003) found that moving objects can attract an audience's attention, and thus animation may be able to make people feel involved. Similarly, the use of melodramatic animation in news may provoke a sense of psychological involvement. Indeed, past studies have found that animation can arouse a physiological and emotional reaction (Detenber & Reeves, 1996; Detenber, Simons & Bennett, 1998; Lang, Dhillon & Dong, 1995).

The third dimension is realism, which is invoked when an individual believes that the virtual world is accurate and real (Lombard, Ditton & Weinstein, 2009). Realism can be categorised into social realism and perceptual realism. Social realism is measured by the degree of plausibility that the virtual description creates in the real world. Perceptual realism refers to the degree to which the media representation looks or sounds like a real person. An animated news report may be like science fiction, which has low social realism yet high perceptual realism (McMahan, 2003; Lombard, Ditton & Weinstein, 2009). The animated character has detailed facial expressions and engages in realistic dialogue.

## Transportation Imagery Model

The transportation imagery model (TIM) explains how animation, presence, and perceived credibility interact (Green & Brock, 2000). The TIM assumes that a vivid media representation allows an audience to leave the real world and be transported to a virtual world (Green & Brock, 2002). The attitude of the public toward a murder case changes after watching a scene. An individual's existing belief is suspended and he or she is more willing to believe the new content. Both the TIM and the theory of presence explain individuals suspending belief and being transported into the virtual environment (Bracken, 2002). These theories provide a framework within which to investigate the relationship between animation, presence and credibility. It is possible that animated news with its vivid description and rich sensory dimensions enables the audience to be transported into the mediated environment. Animation provides the audience with a sense of presence and may make the news story and medium more credible.

## Presence, Animation and Perceived Credibility: A Second Test

We conducted an additional study to test the relationship between the use of melodramatic animation, presence and perceived news credibility. A total of 187 college students were recruited at a university in Hong Kong. The participants were randomly assigned to one of two groups. In the first group, participants were asked to watch two videos including melodramatic animation. In the other group, the participants were asked to watch two videos without melodramatic animation. The videos shown in the first group were the same as those in the second except for the use of animation. The animated content was replaced by shot footage for the second group. The videos were selected from Apple Action News. The first was about a sexual assault on a university campus. The second video was about a maid physically assaulting her employer. These two news stories were chosen because many animated news videos are about sex and violence (Kaplan, 2010).

Our primary goal was to determine if there is a link between melodramatic animation in the news and presence and if presence is linked to the perceived credibility of a news story. We predicted that viewers watching a news report containing melodramatic animation would experience a greater sense of presence and, thus, perceive the news to be more credible. We conducted a separate path analysis using the maximum-likelihood method for both news stories. The software was used to create a bootstrap distribution of 5,000 samples. For the news story covering the maid assaulting her employer, the data was found to fit the model and all paths were significant. These results confirm that viewers have a more intensive experience of presence when melodramatic animation is used, through which they evaluate the news as being more credible (Lo & Cheng, 2015).

For the news covering a sexual assault at a university, the data also fit the model. However, the path between the use of melodramatic animation in news and presence was not found to be significant, suggesting that there was no difference between the effects on presence of news clips with or without melodramatic animation. Still, the path between presence and perceived credibility was significant, indicating that participants who had a more intense experience of presence found the news more credible.

In sum, our research shows a link between the use of melodramatic animation, presence and perceived news credibility, although the influence of animation on presence may depend on the content of the news story. These findings may explain why animation in news caused no difference in the audience perception of news credibility in our first study (Cheng & Lo, 2012). Presence plays a mediating role in the relationship between melodramatic animation and perceived news credibility. The use of melodramatic animation was found to enhance audience perceptions of news credibility if audience members experienced a higher level of presence. This proves that the TIM can be used to explain how an audience is transported into a virtual world where it tends to believe the messages broadcast (Green & Brock, 2002).

## Conclusion

The use of melodramatic animation in news reporting has allowed the development of a new, still under-explored research agenda among scholars in digital journalism. Our studies suggest that the use of animation per se may not influence a viewer's experience of presence, but how the technique is used may still be more important. Indeed, previous studies have suggested that the multidimensionality of a message influences a viewer's media experience (Steuer, 1992; Anderson, 1993; Kramer, 1995). It would, therefore, be worth investigating how each dimension of a message, such as visual presentation, sound elements, use of camera angles and so forth, affect presence. These results could then be used to provide guidelines for creating the optimum intensity of presence for animated news.

Another line of research into the use of animation in news stories considers the impact of culture and media education on viewer perceptions of animated news. As mentioned previously, the use of melodramatic animation has gained prominence among international news media, which source animated news from Next Media, now with its own outlets beyond Hong Kong (Next Media Animation, 2015). Thus, it will be important to conduct cross-cultural studies to examine cultural variation in viewers' attitudes toward melodramatic animation in news reports, especially when journalistic norms may differ between media systems (Schudson, 2001; Hallin & Mancini, 2004).

Demographic variables such as age should also be studied to ascertain how they affect viewers' perceptions of animated news. It is an observable trend, especially among younger generations, that social media have become popular channels for accessing news (Pew Research, 2016). Animated news videos that contain entertaining elements are likely to be relayed from one person to another on social networking sites (Lo & Cheng, 2012). Such online behaviour may further extend the media reach to these young viewers, and they could perceive news videos differently from older generations, who are used to traditional media. This line of research could use media dependency theory to investigate whether frequent viewers of animated news and users of social media find particular types of news content more trustworthy.

Most studies on melodramatic animation in news have been devoted to determining effects. However, it would also be interesting to investigate how animated news is produced and how credibility is manifested during the production of these news videos. The organisations that produce the videos hire performing arts graduates to re-enact news stories, and the production teams include not only journalists but also directors who orchestrate how the actors perform the story so animators can capture the actors' motions to create animated effects. It would be worthwhile taking a constructivist approach and investigating how these personnel work together to negotiate and construct animated news videos that potentially reach millions of people. More importantly, it is necessary to discern whether news credibility is on the agenda among producers when they negotiate how the story is presented during the production process. "Does credibility (still) matter?" is perhaps a question worth discussing from the perspective of news gathering, production and consumption in this era of innovation in news practices.

# References

Addington, D. W. (1971). "The Effect of Vocal Variations on Ratings of Source Credibility." *Speech Monographs*, 38, 242–7.

Aitamurto, T., & Lewis, S. C. (2013). "Open Innovation in Digital Journalism: Examining the Impact of Open Apis at Four News Organizations." *New Media & Society*, 15, 314–331.

Anderson, J. D. (1993). "From Jump Cut to Match Action: An Ecological Approach for Film Editing." Paper presented at the annual conference of the University Film and Video Association, Philadelphia, August.

Austin, E. W., & Dong, Q. (1994). "Source v. Content Effects on Judgments of News Believability." *Journalism Quarterly*, 91, 973–983.

Ball-Rokeach, S. J., & DeFleur, M. L. (1976). "A Dependency Model of Mass-Media Effects." *Communication Research*, 3, 3–21.

Banos, R. M., Botella, C., Garcia-Palacios, A., Villa, H., Perpina, C. & Alcaniz, M. (2000). "Presence and Reality Judgment in Virtual Environments: A Unitary Construct?" *Cyber Psychology and Behavior* 3 (3), 327–335.

Boykoff, P. (2 February 2010). "The Blurry Lines of Animated News." CNN. Retrieved from http://edition.cnn.com/2010/WORLD/asiapcf/01/30/taiwan.animated.news.

Bracken, C. C. (2006). "Perceived Source Credibility of Local Television News: The Impact of Television Form and Presence." *Journal of Broadcasting and Electronic Media*, 50(4), 723–741.

Bucy, E. P. (2003). "Media Credibility Reconsidered: Synergy Effects between On-air and Online News". *Journalism and Mass Communication Quarterly*, 80 (2), 247–264.

Burgoon, J. K. (1978). "Attributes of the Newscaster's Voice as Predictors of His Credibility." *Journalism Quarterly*, 55, 276–281.

Bracken, C. C. (2006). "Perceived Source Credibility of Local Television News: The Impact of Television Form and Presence." *Journal of Broadcasting and Electronic Media*, 50(4), 723–741.

Bracken, C. C., Neuendorf, K. A., & Jeffres, L. W. (2003). "Screen Size, Source Credibility, and Presence: Audience Reactions to the Televised 2000 Presidential Debates." Paper presented at the Communication Theory and Methodology Division at the annual conference of the Association for Education in Journalism and Mass Communication, Kansas City, July 30–August 2.

Brill, A. M. (2001). "Online Journalists Embrace New Marketing Function." *Newspaper Research Journal*, 22(2), 28–40.

Cheng, B. K. L., & Lo, W. H. (2012). "Can News be Imaginative? An Experiment Testing the Perceived Credibility of Melodramatic Animated News, News Organizations, Media Use, and Media Dependency." *Electronic News*, 6(3), 131–150.

Cheng, B. K. L., & Lo, W. H. (2015). "The Effects of Melodramatic Animation in Crime Related News." *Journalism and Mass Communication Quarterly*. doi: 10.1177/1077699015581799.

Cholodenko, A. (1991). *The Illusion of Life: Essays on Animation*. Sydney: Power Publications.

Cohen, N. (6 December 2009). "In Animated Videos, News and Guesswork Mix." *The New York Times*. Retrieved from http://www.nytimes.com/2009/12/06/business/media/06animate.html?_r=0.

Coren, A. (2 February 2010). "CNN Interviews Jimmy Lai on Animation News." CNN Asia Pacific, Retrieved from: http://www.cnnasiapacific.com/press/en/content/523/.

Couture, M. (2004). "Realism in the Design Process and Credibility of a Simulation-based Virtual Laboratory." *Journal of Computer Assisted Learning*, 20, 40–49.

David, P. (1998). "News Concreteness and Visual-verbal Association: Do News Picture Narrow the real Gap between Concrete and Abstract News?" *Human Communication Research*, 25, 180–201.

Dentenber, B., & Reeves, B. (1996). "A Bio-Informational Theory of Emotion: Motion and Image Size Effects on Viewers." *Journal of Communication*, 46(3), 66–84.

Dentenber, B. H., Simons, R. F., & Bennet, G. G. (1998). "Roll' em: The Effects of Picture Motion on Emotional Responses." *Journal of Broadcasting and Electronic Media*, 42, 113–127.

Fahmy, S. (2008). "How Online Journalists Rank Importance of News Skills." *Newspaper Research Journal*, 29(2), 23–39.

Flanagin, A. J., and Metzger, M. J. (2007). "The Role of Site Features, User Attributes, and Information Verification Behaviors on the Perceived Credibility of Web-based Information." *New Media and Society*, 9 (2), 319–342.

Fortin, D. R., & Dholakia, R. R. (2003). "Interactivity and Vividness Effects on Social Presence and Involvement with a Web-based Advertisement." *Journal of Business Research*, 58, 387–96.

Green, Melanie C., and Timothy C. Brock. (2000). "The Role of Transportation in the Persuasiveness of Public Narratives." *Journal of Personality and Social Psychology*, 79, 701–21.

Gunther, A. C. (1992). "Biased Press or Biased Public? Attitudes toward Media Coverage of Social Groups." *Public Opinion Quarterly*, 56, 147–167.

Johnson, J. T., and Kaye, B. K. (1998). "Cruising is Believing? Comparing Internet and Traditional Sources on Media Credibility Measures." *Journalism and Mass Communication Quarterly*, 75, 365–386.

Kaplan, M. (30 August 2010). "Taiwan Tabloid Sensation Next Media Re-creates the News." Wired. Retrieved from http://www.wired.com/magazine/2010/08/mf_appledaily/all/1?pid=2886.

Ketterer, S. (1998). "Teaching Students How to Evaluate and Use Online Resources." *Journalism & Mass Communication Educator*, 52(4), 4–14.

Kilgannon, C. (20 November 2011). "Bringing Animation Where the News is." *New York Times*. Retrieved from http://cityroom.blogs.nytimes.com/2011/11/20/bringing-animation-where-the-news-is/.

Kiousis, S. (2001). "Public Trust or Mistrust? Perceptions of Media Credibility in the Information Age." *Mass Communication and Society*, 4, 381–403.

Kiousis, S. (2006). "Exploring the Impact of Modality on Perceptions of Credibility for Online News Stories." *Journalism Studies*, 7, 348-359.

Kline, R. B. (2005). *Principles and Practice of Structural Equation Modelling*. New York: Guildford.

Kramer, G. (1995). "Sound and Communication in Virtual Reality." in *Communication in the Age of Virtual Reality*, edited by Biocca, F. and Levy, M. R. 259–276. Hillsdale: Lawrence Erlbaum.

Lang, A., Dhillon, K., & Dong, Q. (1995). "The Effects of Emotional Arousal and Valence on Television Viewers' Cognitive Capacity and Memory." *Journal of Broadcasting and Electronic Media*, 39(3), 313–327.

Lasica, J. D. (16 December 1998). "Online News: A Credibility Gap Ahead?" *Online Journalism Review*. Retrieved from http://www.ojr.org/ojr/ethics/ 1017969396.php.

Lee, R. S. H. (1978). "Credibility of Newspaper and TV News." *Journalism Quarterly*, 55 (1), 282–87.

Lo, W. H., & Cheng, B. K. L. (2013). "Fuelling the Debate: Predictive Relationships among Personality Characteristics, Motives and Effects of Animated News Viewing." *Journal of Applied Journalism & Media Studies*, 2, 135–160.

Lombard, M., & Ditton, T. B. (1997). "At the Heart of It All: The Concept of Presence." *Journal of Computer-Mediated Communication*, 3(2).

Lombard, M., Ditton, T. B., & Weinstein, L. (2009). "Measuring (Tele)presence: The Temple Presence Inventory." Paper presented at the twelfth international workshop on presence, Los Angeles, November 11–13.

Lombard, M. (2000). "The Concept of Presence: Explication Statement." International Society for Presence Research. Retrieved from http://ispr.info/about-presence-2/about-presence/.

Lombard, M. and Ditton, T. B. (1997). "At the Heart of It All: The Concept of Presence." *Journal of Computer-Mediated Communication*, 3 (2). Retrieved from http://jcmc.indiana.edu/vol3/issue2/ lombard.html.

Mackay, J., & Lowrey, W. (2007). "The Credibility Divide: Reader Trust of Online Newspapers and Blogs." Paper presented at International Communication Association, San Francisco, CA. Retrieved from http://citation.allacademic.com/meta/p_mla_apa_research_citation/1/ 7/3/2/6/pages173266/p173266-1.php.

McMahan, A. (2003). "Immersion, Engagement, and Presence: A Method for Analyzing 3-D Video Games." in *The Video Game Theory Reader*, edited by Wolf, M. J. P. &. Perron. B., p. 67-86. New York: Routledge.

Murray, J. (1997). *Hamlet on the Holodeck: The Future of Narrative in Cyberspace*. Cambridge: MIT Press.

Next Animation Studio. (2017). "News Animation." Retrieved from http://nextanimationstudio.com/en/.

Next Media Animation. (2015). "Next Media Animation." Accessed http://www.multiplejournalism.org/case/next-media-animation.

Newhagen, J., & Clifford N. (1989). "Differential Criteria for Evaluating Credibility of Newspapers and TV News." *Journalism & Mass Communication Quarterly*, 66, 277–84.

Online News Association. (2002). "Digital Journalism Credibility Study." Retrieved from http://banners.noticiasdot.com/termometro/boletines/docs/marcom/prensa/ona/2002/ona_credibilitystudy/2001report.pdf.

Park, C.Y. (2005). "Decomposing Korean News Media Credibility in the Internet Age." *International Journal of Public Opinion Research*, 18(2), 238–245.

Pavlik, J. V., & Bridges, F. (2013). "The Emergence of Augmented Reality (AR) as a Storytelling Medium." *Journalism & Communication Monographs*, 15, 4–59.

Pew Research Center. (2002). "News Media's Improved Image Proves Short-lived." Retrieved from http://people-press.org/reports/print.php3?ReportID=159.

Pew Research Center. (2005). "Public More Critical of Press, but Goodwill Persists." Retrieved from http://people-press.org/reports/display.php3?ReportID=248.

Quarrick, G. (1989). *Our Sweetest Hours: Recreation and the Mental State of Absorption*. Jefferson, NC: McFarland.

Reeves, B., & Clifford N. (1996). "The Media Equation: How People Treat Computers, Television, and Sources Relate to Beliefs about Media Bias." *Newspaper Research Journal*, 20(4), 41–51.

Reeves, B. R. (1991). "Being There: Television as Symbolic Versus Natural Experience". Unpublished Manuscript. Stanford University. Institute for Communication Research, Stanford, CA.

Seiler, W. J. (1971). "The Effects of Visual Materials on Attitudes, Credibility, and Retention." *Speech Monographs*, 38, 331–334.

Slater, M. D., & Rouner, D. (1996). "How Message Evaluation and Source Attributes May Influence Credibility Assessment and Belief Change." *Journalism and Mass Communication Quarterly*, 73 (4), 974–91.

Steuer, J. (1992). "Defining Virtual Reality: Dimensions Determining Telepresence." *Journal of Communication*, 42 (4) (1992), 73–93.

Stoiber, N., Seguier, R., & Breton, G. (2010). "Facial Animation Retargeting and Control Based on Human Appearance Space." *Computer Animation and Virtual Worlds*, 21(1), 30–54.

Sundar, S. S. (2000). "Multimedia Effects on Processing and Perception of Online News: A Study of Picture, Audio, and Video Downloads." *Journalism and Mass Communication Quarterly*, 77, 480–99.

Trammell, K., Porter, L., Chung, D., & Kim, E. (2006). "Credibility and the Uses of Blogs among Professionals in the Communication Industry." Paper presented at Association for Education in Journalism and Mass Communication, San Francisco, CA. Retrieved from http:// www.aejmc.org/home/2012/01/ctec-2006-abstracts/.

Wanta, W., & Hu, Y. W. (1994). "The Effects of Credibility, Reliance and Exposure on Media Agenda-setting: A Path Analysis Model." *Journalism Quarterly*, 71, 90–98.

Wong, A. (2012). "Animated News is Animating the News." *The Journalist*, 3, Hong Kong: HKJA's Publication. Retrieved from http://hkthejournalist.blogspot.hk/2010/01/animated-news-isanimating-news.html.

Yang, J., & Patwardhan, P. (2004). "Determinants of Internet News Use: A Structural Equation Model Approach." *Web Journal of Mass Communication Research*, 8. Retrieved from http://www.scripps.ohiou.edu/wjmcr/vol08/8-1a.html.

蘇鑰機: 香港傳媒公信力又見新低. (2016). Retrieved from http://news.mingpao.com/pns/dailynews/web_tc/article/20160908/s00012/1473270958100.

# Part IV

Public Relations and Advertising

# Chapter 10

## Public Relations Developments in Hong Kong:
### Twenty Years after the Handover

*Angela K. Y. MAK, Regina Y. R. CHEN, Lennon L. L. TSANG and Hyun Jee OH*

## Introduction

The role of public relations (PR) relies heavily upon the business environment. There have been many significant changes in Hong Kong in terms of politics, economic development and sociocultural values in relation to Mainland China and the region in the past twenty years. However, academic discussions about the PR landscape in the post-handover period are scarce. In one of the few examples of these discussions, Martin (2009) highlighted some key changes, including increased attention to social responsibility related to three things: the rise of advocacy and citizen activism, more balanced business-partner bonding in the agency-client relationship, and the building of long-term relationships with stakeholders. Lee (2007) discussed changes in the government's PR practices, which might have resulted from concern over relations with China and the fear of losing Hong Kong's economic edge. Martin (2009) pointed out that Shanghai and Hong Kong are competing against each other in the international financial arena, not to mention facing a challenge from other first- and second-tier cities in China that are emerging as commercial centres. The trend in the PR industry in Hong Kong is to try to stay competitive with the Mainland while at the same time finding ways to complement PR practices in greater China.

To understand the changing landscape of the PR industry in the post-handover period, we interviewed six PR gurus who have been in the industry for more than thirty years or currently hold a leadership role in professional PR associations. They are:

1. Dr Linda Tsui (崔綺雲), Honourable President of the Hong Kong Public Relations Professionals' Association;

2. Mr Richard Tsang (曾立基), Chairman of the Strategic Public Relations Group and Global Chairman of Public Relations Organisation International (PROI) Worldwide;

3. Mr C. F. Kwan (關則輝), Assistant Director of Corporate Communications, Hang Lung Properties;

4. Mr Chris Liu (廖國偉), Director of Corporate Communications, Sun Hung Kai Properties Limited;

5. Ms Pamela Leung (梁綺蓮), President of the Hong Kong Public Relations Professionals' Association; and

6. Ms Virginia Chi (池文皓), President of the International Association of Business Communicators (IABC) Hong Kong.

We also analysed government data on the industry, trend reports from agencies operating in Hong Kong and PR awards to produce a profile of PR practitioners over the years and to discover some key elements for PR excellence in Hong Kong and the Asia-Pacific region.

## PR Guru Interviews

From our in-depth interviews with the PR gurus, we identified four salient areas in the changing landscape of the PR industry in Hong Kong—namely, the political economy, localisation and leadership qualities, the effects of new media, and the rise of community stakeholders.

### The Political PR Economy

Political and socio-economic developments are essential components that shape the environment of PR practices, and recent changes in Hong Kong have brought about a greater complexity in decision-making. The main role of PR was once product promotion, but current PR practitioners spend more time handling relationships with different public groups and dealing with issues of corporate social responsibility. Taking public groups or stakeholders into consideration is now key to effectiveness. This requires the PR industry to engage more with its audience and to be ready for unexpected questions from the general public. It must be well prepared for the unexpected.

Since the return of sovereignty of Hong Kong back to Mainland China in 1997, a number of changes to the political scene have taken place. First, society has become more politicised than ever, with the public paying a lot of attention to political issues. Second, the room for negotiation on many issues has decreased, because, whereas members of the Legislative Council used to care deeply about public interest and were highly knowledgeable about issues, today some members just want to win media exposure and votes and apparently do not leave much room for discussion. For these reasons, it has been increasingly important for organisations to work hard to build a sustained and friendly relationship with policymakers.

As a result of the changing business and political environment, corporate communication, integrated marketing communication and financial relations have emerged as the top three specialities for local PR practitioners. In the past two decades, many non-governmental organisations (NGOs) have been successful in their advocacy through effective communication. This has convinced commercial organisations of the importance of proper corporate communication in order to achieve good business results. Thus, a lot of commercial organisations have increasingly applied corporate communication strategies in recent years to disseminate corporate information. The main function of an integrated marketing communication department is business development. With the success of early attempts to implement integrated marketing communication, more organisations are engaging in this form of communication when they conduct market promotions. Financial PR has also come into its own. With Hong Kong being a major financial centre, a large number of companies need financial PR consultants to help them with their initial public offerings. Companies have also learnt that their stock prices are affected by the information put out about them, and therefore employ financial PR consultants to handle dissemination of their financial news.

## PR Localisation and Leadership Qualities

Hong Kong was once a stepping stone for multinational corporations (MNCs) to enter the Chinese market, but according to the PR gurus, it lost this unique position about ten years ago. Now the PR agencies in Hong Kong work primarily for the local market. Their ability to work with Mainland Chinese clients is limited because these clients are looking for PR firms with a good understanding of Mainland culture and conditions, and Hong Kong PR agencies do not have such familiarity. They are put off by the fact that practising PR on the Mainland may be too political as it may require involvement with the central or municipal government of China.

However, Hong Kong PR firms are doing well. In the two decades since the handover, they have overtaken international PR firms in the territory and occupy the majority of the market share. This is not unusual: markets all over the world are witnessing the same trend. Local professionals understand the local market and work well with the local media, government and other stakeholders. International PR firms are still active here, but their main function is to manage business in the regional market, and a regional director plays the role of communicator and manager rather than just executing PR ideas. For this reason an expatriate manager is usually sent here to facilitate communication with the head office.

Another area of change is the rising awareness of the need for PR by public organisations and its increasing importance in public affairs. While many commercial organisations devote much effort to PR to communicate with their consumers, public organisations—government offices, NGOs and advocacy groups—now need to promote their ideas and values to the local community, and this is where public affairs have created a niche for PR. The gurus also mentioned the high public expectations of organisations with regard to corporate social responsibility. When a commercial organisation makes a decision today, it takes into consideration its social responsibility as well as the interests of its shareholders. For example, the real estate investment fund Link REIT cannot just raise rents to increase its profits and stock price, but they have to consider the government, social groups, NGOs, political groups and other stakeholders in their decision.

As a result of these developments, more PR practitioners are performing a managerial function in organisations, often acting as counsellors for top management. This takes some special skills. In order for PR practitioners to have a direct reporting line to top management, they must achieve three essential leadership goals. First, they need to prove themselves. Second, they need to be able to work with all departments, so that each performs its function. Third, they need to make the top management understand the importance of having PR counsellors. Another important developing role for PR managers is to build a "trust bank" for their organisations. Given these changes, PR professionals need to develop management capabilities and in particular pay attention to ESG (environmental, social and governance) reporting, where many listed companies and other organisations have to fulfil some requirements to build public trust and goodwill. Indicators are available in the market for measuring the performance of a business in each of these areas—for example, the Global Reporting Initiatives and the Hang Seng Sustainability Index.

Despite rapid changes in the industry, the requirements for becoming a PR practitioner remain largely unchanged. After all, PR is still at its core a matter of communication, and language is the key to communication. Language skills, including oral and written skills in Chinese and English, and the ability to grasp the key points of a message are the most important requirements, though today practitioners also need to be able to understand and apply various types of new media.

## The Effects of New Media on PR

All the PR gurus interviewed in this chapter mentioned the importance of and challenges posed by new media. Some of them, however, observed that most people are looking at these issues too superficially, often ignoring innovative strategies for using new media. At present new media are mainly used for short-term promotion of products and are seldom used for image-building or long-term public affairs. The PR gurus also noted that the emergence of new media had changed the time span and degree of control in messaging. The viral nature of message delivery in new media may produce unexpected consequences in a very short period of time. PR practitioners have to be sensitive, with a sense of crisis preparedness, because many who see their messages are ready to express their opinions using readily available means of expression in new media. When brands and organisations recruit staff today, they are beginning to look for applicants with online and social media skills to more effectively monitor new media.

If such changes mean that monitoring new media is a round-the-clock job, then in general, the work of PR is actually much easier than before. For example, the availability of digital media has simplified PR production because much of the tedious preparation work is no longer necessary. Besides, social media enable faster dissemination of news to the general public, and the use of big data makes it easier to target a particular segment of the audience. In terms of content, simple, direct language is the key to new media messages, since social media users seldom devote a lot of time to a single message. But there are also added duties. Written press releases are no longer the only staple, with graphics, animations, audios and videos being required today to arouse substantial interest.

Some of the PR gurus expressed concern that new media and current journalism practices may be negatively affecting relationship management by PR practitioners. With new media, in-depth reporting and discussion are rare, and the general public receive a more simplified picture than it did in the past, possibly leading audiences to unsupported conclusions. Today, local communities pay attention to local news at the expense of an international perspective. In the past, international news often made the headlines, but now the headlines and front pages are dominated by local news. The media also covers more news about political events than other news topics. Moreover, instead of providing information and leaving it to the public to form opinions, online media sources are often the first to pass judgement.

Public organisations are often hindered by issues such as privacy, and may not be fully transparent in information disclosure. With the rise of new media, the general public often judge issues on the basis of the type of information they absorb from new media. As a result, the government is drawing overwhelming criticism from the public. Deterioration of the relationship between the government and citizens has caused some public organisations close to the government to be attacked by citizens.

## The Rise of Community Stakeholders

Most of the PR gurus described new media as a double-edged sword and said that it is up to PR practitioners to use it strategically and properly. New media offer opportunities because information can be shared with the target audience quickly and widely. However, controlling public opinion is much more difficult than before. Today, the wealth of information available makes it hard to determine whether each piece of news is true or not. After brewing on the internet, a small problem may become a major PR disaster. PR practitioners have to monitor public opinion trends carefully and exercise control before a crisis strikes. Shaping public opinion today requires the co-creation of messages and meanings by netizens and organisations.

Another problem is that the message an organisation wants to spread may easily be submerged in the mass of information out there. To stand out among the crowd, PR practitioners need a head start—for instance, finding influential people to speak for them—and they should act before a PR disaster strikes. This requires PR practitioners to look for and to know key opinion leaders (KOLs) and influential media sources. All the PR gurus said that engaging the audience is what new media promotion is about, especially using Facebook and other social networking sites. PR practitioners need to learn how to engage netizens using language familiar to them while maintaining a positive image and credibility.

## The PR Industry in Hong Kong

This section is drawn from a secondary analysis of two surveys conducted in Hong Kong: the Hong Kong PR Industry Benchmarking Survey (HKPRBS) conducted by the Council of Public Relations Firms of Hong Kong (CPRFHK) in 2012, 2013 and 2014; and the Asia-Pacific Communication Monitor (APCM) conducted in 2015 (Macnamara, Lwin, Adi & Zerfass, 2015).

HKPRBS surveyed PR firms in Hong Kong via an online and print questionnaire consisting of seven sections that sought to ascertain the status and views of participating firms. Our analysis is based on the data of four of the sections: clients, staff profile and remuneration, firm profile, and macro industry issues. In total, thirty-four firms completed the survey in 2012, thirty-two in 2013 and sixteen in 2014. It should be noted that the 2012 and 2013 surveys covered January to December of those years while the 2014 survey covered June 2014 to June 2015. Due to confidentiality issues, detailed information about the participating firms is not available for this analysis, though it was confirmed by CPRFHK that the participants were eligible firms in Hong Kong that included both CPRFHK members and non-members.

The APCM surveyed PR professionals in the private and public sectors in twenty-three countries in the Asia-Pacific region using an online questionnaire. In Hong Kong, 128 PR professionals in the private or public sectors completed the survey (Baesecke, Chen, Macnamara, Zerfass, Boyd & Zhang, 2016). As with HKPRBS, APCM's aim was to understand the state of the PR and communication management industries and the directions of its future development from the perspective of individual practitioners. The survey covered seven sections: future relevance of mass media, communication channels and instruments, social media skills and knowledge, strategic issues and value contribution, measurement and evaluation in communication departments, job satisfaction, and characteristics of excellent communication functions. The following section discusses the trends in the PR industry in Hong Kong as suggested by our secondary data analyses of the two surveys.

## Client Spending Fuels Steady Industry Growth

The HKPRBS participants reported three consecutive years of growth. In 2012, 79% of the surveyed firms indicated an increase in client spending and, although the figure fell to 53% in 2013, it bounced back somewhat to 67% in 2014/15. To look more closely, a majority (60%) of the firms in the 2014 HKPRBS indicated a 20% increase in total client spending in the twelve-month period, while in 2012 and 2013 most firms (53% and 45%, respectively) surveyed reported a client spending increase below 10%. It is also worth noting that 2014 saw the largest proportion of new retainer clients (that is, those who have not used the firm as a retainer before) for the surveyed firms among the three years (2012: 42%, 2013: 38%, 2014: 46%). Retainers are clients who pay a PR agency in advance for its overall service. Because retainer clients tend to have a larger budget than project-based clients and it is harder to secure new clients as retainers than project-based clients, an increase of such clients suggests growth in the Hong Kong PR industry.

## A Possible Change of Business Portfolio

The top three business sectors providing income for the HKPRBS respondent firms in 2012 were (in decreasing order of importance): consumer goods, financial/professional services and technology. In 2013, consumer goods remained as the top sector followed by technology and others. Financial/professional services dropped out of the top three in 2013 but came back to the top again in 2014, followed by travel/lifestyle and technology. The results indicate a growth in the travel/lifestyle industry in Hong Kong in 2014. However, it should be noted that travel/lifestyle was not an answer option in the 2012 and 2013 surveys. Whether this industry will continue to grow and change the business portfolio of PR firms in Hong Kong, or whether it is only a short-term phenomenon, remains to be seen.

## Rapid Growth of Digital Communications in Client Campaigns

More firms used social media and digital communications as their main communication tool for client campaigns and fewer used direct marketing and mixed channels in 2014/15 than in the preceding two years (Figure 10.1). The use of digital communications grew rapidly over the three years, moving from the eighth most frequently used communication channel in 2012 to the fourth in 2013 and the second in 2014/15 among the eleven channels recorded. On the other hand, direct marketing rapidly lost popularity, dropping from the fourth most frequently used communication channel in 2012 to the sixth in 2013 and the tenth in 2014. Meanwhile, experiential events (i.e., a strategy to engage target audiences in real-life events which enables them to experience and memorise a campaign's key messge) and media publicity remained important throughout the period, being in the top three most frequently used communication channels over all three years.

**Figure 10.1**
**Communication Channels in Client Campaigns**

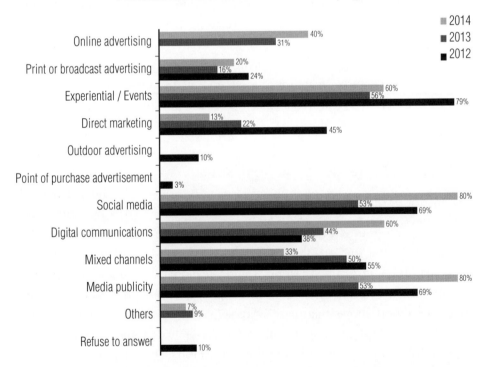

Adapted from Hong Kong Public Relations Benchmark Study 2014-2015: Redacted Findings for HKBU (p. 7), by The Council of Public Relations Firms of Hong Kong and Centre for Communication and Public Opinion Survey, the Chinese University of Hong Kong. Unpublished manuscript. Copyright 2015 by The Council of Public Relations Firms of Hong Kong. Adapted with permission.

## Media Relations Remain Important

The APCM results show that 81.3% of the Hong Kong participants still considered print newspapers and magazines very important for reaching stakeholders, gatekeepers and audiences today, while just under 67% of them also considered mobile communication (phone/tablet apps, mobile websites) and events very important (Macnamara et al., 2015). These results support the HKPRBS's finding that media publicity is still being used more than digital communication in client campaigns (Figure 10.1). It is worth noting that more participants in Taiwan (78.2%) and Mainland China (69.7%) believed that using mobile communication to target the public was a key communication practice rather than media relations with print newspapers or magazines (69.1% in Taiwan and 68.9% in Mainland China; Macnamara et al., 2015).

When asked about the main reasons for interacting with traditional mass media (online or offline), 81.3% of the APCM Hong Kong participants said they did so to monitor news and public opinion, 54.7% indicated they did so to source content for internal services and 36.7% to jointly produce quality content with the media (e.g., native advertising or advertorials) or to create topical platforms. More importantly, 56.3% of the Hong Kong participants, as opposed to 66.8% of the Asia-Pacific participants overall, were confident that over the next three years the mass media would grow in relevance as a strategic partner of PR professionals in content production or other related practices (Macnamara et al., 2015).

## Profile of PR Professionals in Hong Kong

### A Snapshot of Manpower Composition in PR

The report on the 2014 Manpower Survey of the Mass Communication Industry (hereafter the 2014 Manpower Report) published by the Hong Kong Vocational Training Council (Hong Kong Vocational Training Council, 2014) contains the most recent statistics on manpower in the PR industry in Hong Kong. The report shows that there were 4,735 PR practitioners in Hong Kong as of January 2014. Among them, 968 (20.4%) had a managerial position while 1,373 (29.0%) had a supervisory position. The majority (49.3%) of the practitioners were at the executional level and the rest (1.2%) played a supporting and technical role. Using labour market analysis and an adaptive filtering method, the report projected an increase of manpower demand for the advertising and PR sector in the years 2014 to 2018 ranging from 1.6% to 8.7% (Hong Kong Vocational Training Council, 2014).

## Educational Level

The survey found a positive relationship between the job level and educational level of PR professionals. All those at the managerial level who reported their educational level had a bachelor's degree or above. At the supervisory level, 82.7% had a bachelor's degree or above, but only 44% of those at the executional level had a bachelor's degree or above, while the education level of most (78%) practitioners at the supporting or technical level was below secondary 5.

## Professional Experience

According to the 2014 Manpower Report, nearly half of the professionals at the managerial level (49%) had ten or more years of experience. Most (61%) at the supervisory level had five to ten years of experience. Most at the executional level (39%) had experience of two to five years, while 34% had been in the industry for less than two years. The majority of the professionals at the supporting or technical level (90%) had worked in the industry for less than two years.

## Remuneration

According to the 2016 Hong Kong Salary Guide published by Morgan McKinley (Morgan McKinley Hong Kong, 2016), the monthly salary of PR professionals as assistant managers is between HK$20,000 and HK$30,000 while for managers (equivalent to the supervisory level in the 2014 Manpower Report), the monthly salary is between HK$35,000 and HK$55,000. The minimum monthly salary of PR directors (equivalent to the managerial level) is HK$80,000.

## Job Satisfaction

APCM investigated the level of job satisfaction among PR professionals in Hong Kong and other countries using a five-point Likert-type scale, the average score being 3.66. By comparison, in Mainland China it was 3.64, in Taiwan 3.56 and in Singapore 3.69. A further look at the seven attributes of job satisfaction using the scale revealed that career opportunities (mean = 3.21), work-life balance (mean = 3.24) and adequate salary (mean = 3.34) were perceived as more problematic attributes among the Hong Kong participants than others (i.e., interesting and manifold tasks, job security and stability, social status of the job, and appreciation from the supervisor and clients) (Macnamara et al., 2015). Since the top three effective strategies for advertising and PR employee retention identified in the 2014 Manpower Report were increasing job autonomy, shortening working hours and salary increment, we see that the working environment in the PR industry in Hong Kong has not changed much in the past two years.

## Staff Turnover

Staff turnover has been a challenging issue for the PR industry in Hong Kong. The reasons for staff turnover in the past three years (Figure 10.2) are connected with the following:

1.  PR professionals look for opportunities to move to the in-house side (i.e., working in organisations rather than for agencies) and to larger companies. Moving to an in-house role usually allows PR professionals in Hong Kong to have a better work-life balance, and moving to a larger company is seen to provide better career opportunities.

2.  Salary increase remains a crucial determinant for employee retention. This result is also consistent with the APCM's, as mentioned above.

3.  On the other hand, family or personal reasons seemed to be of fluctuating importance for employee retention because it was one of the top three reasons for staff turnover in 2013 but not in the other two years.

4.  It seems that firms in the industry have improved their promotion system and client profile as indicated by the data showing decreasingly important roles of promotion and exposure to different clients in staff turnover over the three years.

5.  The data show a decreasing trend for opportunities to receive training as a reason for staff turnover. There are two possible explanations: One is that firms have made a great effort to increase their provision of training, and the other is that training has a lower priority given the

**Figure 10.2**
**Top Three Reasons for Staff to Leave**

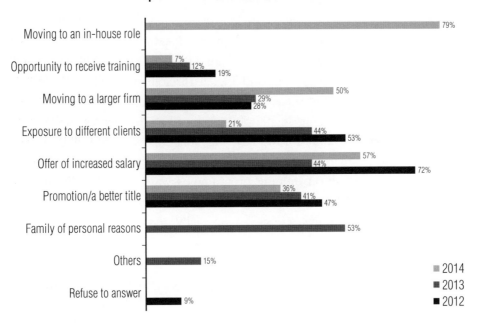

Adapted from Hong Kong Public Relations Benchmark Study 2014-2015: Redacted Findings for HKBU (p. 4) ), by The Council of Public Relations Firms of Hong Kong and Centre for Communication and Public Opinion Survey, the Chinese University of Hong Kong. Unpublished manuscript. Copyright 2015 by The Council of Public Relations Firms of Hong Kong. Adapted with permission.

everyday demand on driving the business and long working hours. In fact two participating firms in the 2014 HKPRBS commented that training had little impact on employee retention.

## The Biggest Issues Facing the PR Industry

### Findings of the HKPRBS

The main issues at the industry and the firm levels as pointed out by the respondent firms in the HKPRBS surveys were largely identical and had changed little over the past three years. The good news is that the industry does not face new challenges. The bad news is that the industry has not come up with solutions to the old challenges. The issues can be divided into three categories: talent; industrial sustainability and professionalism.

## Issues Concerning Talent

The PR industry is highly dependent on its people. It has always been a challenge to recruit people with sufficient PR knowledge and skills, but today the industry needs people with more than this. Recruits must be able to work with the changing media and social landscapes; be able to keep up with the integration of PR, marketing and digital disciplines; and have mid-level managerial knowledge and skills.

Once recruited, investing in people is important because of the need to equip people with the right knowledge and skills for today's rapidly changing media and social environments. However, firms reported that staff retention was costly, and putting on training programmes was unattractive because of the low return on the investment due to high staff turnover and the limited number of quality training courses (especially in Chinese or Cantonese) available in Hong Kong.

A few areas in which staff training is needed were identified, including analytics, storytelling, content marketing, strategic insights, time and stress management, and social media skills. One firm surveyed suggested that PR accreditation is needed in Hong Kong.

## Issues about Industrial Sustainability

Industrial sustainability refers specifically to the issues of a tightening budget, write-offs, loss of retainer clients and the difficulty of business scaling up. The tightening of clients' budgets has resulted from a sluggish economy, allocating resources to the Mainland China market over the Hong Kong market, misunderstanding of digital communication (e.g., assuming that social media communication is cheap) and clients' moving their social media practice from PR people to advertising, marketing, digital firms or to in-house teams.

## Issues about Professionalism

The emerging issues about professionalism in Hong Kong have mainly resulted from the fast-changing media landscape in the digital era. The issues pinpointed by the respondent firms included insufficient consulting and digital skills, lack of strategic consultations for social and digital media communication, lack of innovation, an inability to integrate all media channels into a cohesive whole and to integrate an overseas client's Hong Kong and China programmes. Issues in this category also included the unclear strategic position of PR in today's marketing/communication mix. In addition, once the industry has a position that is well justified, firms will need to educate their clients about it. The results are consistent with those of interviews with the PR gurus as reported in the previous section. The professionalism of PR, therefore, should be advanced by the knowledge and skills of multimedia applications and content creation that result in strategic value to communication between an organisation and its public in the context of Hong Kong.

## Findings of the APCM

Unlike the HKPRBS, the APCM asked participants to identity the top three issues for strategic communication management in 2018. There were eleven answer options, as follows:

1. Strengthening the role of the communication function in supporting top-management decision-making.
2. Dealing with the speed and volume of information flow.
3. Coping with digital evolution and the social web.
4. Linking business strategy and communication.
5. Dealing with sustainable development and social responsibility.
6. Matching the need to address larger audiences and more channels with limited resources.
7. Building and maintaining trust.
8. Dealing with the demand for more transparency and active audiences.
9. Explaining the value of communication to top executives.
10. Supporting organisational change.
11. Implementing advanced measurement and evaluation routines.

Four of these options were identified as key issues in Hong Kong. They were (in descending order): option 3 (57.0%), option 4 (39.1%), option 2 (35.9%) and option 7 (42%). These issues are consistent with the the Asia-Pacific data, albeit with the latter two being swapped in order. Comparing country-to-country rankings of the most important issues, it is interesting to find that linking business strategy and communication was a much less important issue in Korea and New Zealand. Information flow (option 2) was not a serious challenge for Mainland China, Japan and Korea but trust (option 7) was. In contrast, trust was not an issue for communication professionals in the Oceania countries, Taiwan and Singapore (Macnamara et al., 2015).

## Social Media Capabilities of PR Professionals

While the industry is using more digital, mobile and social media as communication tools, the proficiency of communication professionals in social media is worth exploring. Using the APCM data, Hung-Baesecke et al. (2016) found that knowing about social media trends is on the top of the skills participants considered they were capable of (mean=3.22, SD=1.03), while they said their lowest capabilities were knowing the legal framework of social media (mean=2.61, SD=1.16) and initiating web-based dialogues with stakeholders (mean=2.66, SD=0.07). These results imply that, despite the emergence of digital technology enabling organisations to engage with members of the public more interactively via mobile and social media communication, the practice of social media by the industry in Hong Kong remains largely for one-way communication rather than for triggering dialogues with the public. Corporate communicators have argued that engaging in dialogue with stakeholders is important for building quality relationships, but they are actually rather limited in their ability to do so. Interestingly, the Hong Kong participants rated their overall social media skills and most (six out of nine) rated their specialised social media skills lower than the Mainland Chinese participants did (Hung-Baesecke et al., 2016). This suggests that PR professionals in Mainland China have a higher level of confidence in their social media skills than their Hong Kong counterparts.

Hung Baesecke et al. (2016) further compared the social media skills and knowledge among corporate communicators working in organisations with those working in agencies. They found that agency professionals in Hong Kong reported a significantly higher level of overall social media capability than their corporate counterparts. As for their capabilities in specific areas, agency participants reported a significantly higher level of the following skills than their corporate counterparts: delivering messages, initiating web-based dialogues with stakeholders, setting up social media platforms, managing online communities and developing social media strategies. Agency participants also claimed to have more advanced knowledge about risk avoidance and crisis management on social media, interpretation of social media monitoring data and evaluation of social media activities than those working in organisations. These findings are consistent with the pattern across the twenty-three countries surveyed in the 2015 APCM which showed that professionals working in corporations were lagging behind those in agencies, non-profit organisations and government in their social media skills (Macnamara et al., 2015).

## PR Awards in Hong Kong and the Asia-Pacific Region

Although sceptics think that award competitions just involve making money through sponsors, entry fees and expensive tickets to a glamorous gala dinner, it is clear that through such competitions the PR field can recognise well-planned, creative work, share good practices and evolve better.

Exchanges with PR practitioners in Hong Kong revealed the following motivations for submitting their PR efforts to a competition: promoting their organisation to the public, including current and potential clients; strengthening relationships with current clients; honouring employees' good work and building the organisation's brand; boosting employees' morale; promoting the organisation through third-party endorsements; and promoting personal branding. This section discusses some PR awards that are highly regarded by Hong Kong PR practitioners.

### The Public Affairs Asia Gold Standard Awards

These awards are operated by Public Affairs Asia Ltd. and recognise innovation and achievement in communications, corporate citizenship and public affairs. Individuals, corporations, communications consultancies, government agencies, NGOs and diplomatic missions are all eligible.

### The Asia-Pacific Stevie Awards

This business awards competition is organised by the U.S.-based organisation Stevie Awards. They are open to all organisations in the twenty-two nations of the Asia-Pacific region and judges are recruited worldwide. The relevant categories for the PR community are the Corporate Communications, Investor Relations and Public Relations Awards.

### PRWeek Awards Asia

The awards are hosted by PRWeek, a trade magazine for the PR industry. The awards are open to PR consultancies, solo practitioners and in-house departments from all countries in the Asia-Pacific region. The work must be carried out and conceptualised within the Asia-Pacific for the Asia-Pacific market, including Australia and New Zealand.

## Asia-Pacific SABRE Awards

The SABRE awards are organised by the Holmes Group and it is the world's largest PR awards competition, with separate awards for the various regions across the world. PR programmes eligible for the Asia-Pacific SABRE Awards should be conducted in whole or in part in the Asia-Pacific or should originate from the region.

## Marketing PR Awards

The awards are organised by Marketing magazine, which is published in Hong Kong, Singapore and Malaysia. PR work eligible for the awards must have been carried out in Hong Kong for the Hong Kong or the China market or for a regional or global market that includes Hong Kong or China.

## Asia-Pacific Excellence Awards

These awards are hosted by Communication Director, a magazine for corporate communications and PR which has a special edition for the Asia-Pacific. They are open to public relations and communications operatives and other professionals. They are part of the worldwide Excellence Awards, which are organised in Africa, Europe, Latin America and North America.

## Asia-Pacific Communications Awards

These are organised by the Asia-Pacific Association of Communication Directors and Communication Director Magazine. Campaigns or projects in all areas of communications can enter the competition, but they must be initiated and implemented by in-house communication departments rather than agencies or consultancies.

## The Mumbrella Asia Awards

These awards are organised by Focal Attractions Pty Ltd. and recognise creative work in the media, marketing and advertising industries. The Mumbrella Asia Awards span the regions of Southeast Asia, South Asia and greater China and include categories such as PR idea of the year and PR agency of the year.

## Scope of the Data and Analysis

To show overall trends in reputable PR awards available in the Hong Kong market, we examined awards for the period between January 2014 and May 2016. The total number of 129 awards is included in our analysis. The analysis included gold, silver, and bronze awards.

We divide the awards into five categories: digital and social media; corporate social responsibility; crisis and issues management; public affairs and government relations; and financial and investor relations.

Table 10.1 shows whether each of the above awards contains these categories. Hong Kong was ranked in the top three in digital and social media, CSR, crisis and issues management, and financial and investor relations, but not in public affairs or government relations, compared with China, Australia, Singapore and South Korea.

### Table 10.1

### Award Categories

|  | Digital and Social Media | Corporate Social Responsibility | Crisis and Issues Management | Public Affairs and Government Relations | Financial and Investor Relations |
|---|---|---|---|---|---|
| The Public Affairs Asia Gold Standard Awards | Y | Y | Y | Y | Y |
| The Asia-Pacific Stevie Awards | Y | Y | N | Y | Y |
| PRWeek Awards Asia | Y | Y | Y | Y | Y |
| Asia-Pacific SABRE Awards | Y | Y | Y | Y | Y |
| Marketing PR Awards | Y | Y | Y | Y | Y |
| Asia-Pacific Excellence Awards | Y | Y | Y | Y | N |
| Asia-Pacific Communications Awards | Y | N | Y | Y | N |
| The Mumbrella Asia Awards | Y | N | N | N | N |

"Y" means the awards in the first column of the table contain awards in this category and "N" means otherwise.

## Two Case Studies

We closely examined two cases to highlight what makes an award-winning case. For each case, we invited a PR practitioner who was closely involved in it to comment.

### Case 1: Ketchum — Kiss Him or Not? (P&G)

This project (http://publicaffairsasia.com/goldstandard/the-gold-standard-award-for-stakeholder-engagement/) won a Public Affairs Asia Gold Standard Award in 2015. The campaign was done by Ketchum to promote P&G Gillette's products in Hong Kong and Taiwan. The agency launched surveys through an app and Facebook and asked people their opinions about two things: shaving and kissing. It used user-generated comments for the campaign. On-the-street events, contests, and invitations to key opinion leaders to blog on the issue followed in later stages. The campaign results endorsed the attractiveness of a clean shave to women. Total social media views in both markets exceeded seven million and the "Kiss Him or Not" video was ranked second on Hong Kong YouTube. A total of 118 print and online media reports were generated.

### Insider Insights

Simeon Mellalieu, Partner, Client Development APAC, Ketchum, provided the following insights about the campaign.

> Integrating Research Into The Campaign —
> Rather than doing a single field survey, we actually used the social media over an extended period of time to come up with both the social media content and also the attitude questions we were looking for. In normal cases, the survey is done behind the scene and below the campaign to test consumer attitudes. In this particular case, the survey was almost at the forefront. The production of the campaign was not the end point in the campaign; rather it was a starting point of the campaign. We put a lot of effort in the campaign development, starting appropriate research to develop meaningful insights that have an impactful resonance with our target audience. And with this particular campaign, the research into the insights was essentially done by the consumers. That was something unique and different about the campaign.

Sharable Content Generation For Social Media —

The client wanted a viral video. Therefore, we did a lot of research so that we could develop something that could be successfully sharable. We wanted something people genuinely wanted to share. We also used the results of the survey to generate further content and put the sharable content in a variety of different formats. Some of it used cartoons, and some of it used graphics or fast facts. These actually helped us to generate more content and to sustain the whole campaign as well, rather than just relying on the series of questions.

Differentiating Research And Insights —

I believe research and insights are uniquely different. The content that we were creating was directly relevant to those people we were actually putting those questions to. We packaged it and turned it to something which is fun and sharable. The approach was successful. We did not necessarily rely on likeability, and we did not rely on just a couple of Facebook posts on the video. The whole campaign was sustainable.

## Case 2: Edelman and Samsung Electronics — Samsung Solve for Tomorrow

The project (http://www.samsung.com/hk_en/solvefortomorrow/2014/) won a Silver Marketing PR Award for Best Corporate Social Responsibility in 2014.

The Samsung Solve for Tomorrow 2014 campaign was a competition that invited students in Hong Kong to share their ideas about how technology could be used to solve environmental issues. The competition was open to all students in primary and secondary schools and tertiary institutions. Prizes included cash and Samsung products. Winning entries had the chance to be put into practice through funding from the Samsung Realisation Plan. The competition received 1,133 submissions from 250 schools.

### Insider Insights

Stephanie Chan, manager of Edelman, provided the following insights about the project.

Large Campaign for a Social Issue—

Samsung Solve for Tomorrow targeted primary, secondary and tertiary students. More than 90,000 members of the public voted on the entries. A campaign with as many stakeholders as this one is rare.

Encouraging People to Make a Difference—

A recent study showed that although Hong Kong people believe it is important to do their part to protect the environment, about half of them do not see how one person can make a difference. Samsung Solve for Tomorrow challenges students to think how technology can be used to drive environmental change. Results of the campaign show Hong Kong that one person's idea can make a difference. We leveraged the client's brand to great advantage. The campaign had very interactive mentor-mentee training sessions where participants exchanged feasible and creative ideas to make the world a greener place.

Joint Effort of Multiple Stakeholders—

The campaign was a joint effort of the company, the government, NGOs and academics. On top of that, parents and teachers were involved. The whole idea was to create a movement in Hong Kong. We wanted to say every effort counts and there is no action too small for the environment. For awareness building, the strategy was to reach as many people as we could. The campaign partnered with some of Hong Kong's leading environmental NGOs, including Hong Kong's Business Environment Council and Ecovision Asia. These organisations shared Samsung's vision for a greener, smarter Hong Kong and pledged their support to help students to realise the potential technology has to improve the environment.

## Conclusion

Finally, we asked the interviewed PR gurus about their views on the future development of PR in Hong Kong and in the greater China region. Blending new media with relationship management remains the top priority. New media have subverted the whole process of communication and a business may quickly lose its competitive edge if it does not take timely action. To excel in PR, a business needs to find out promptly and accurately what the public cares about and keep its finger on the public pulse. Organisations in the public sector may now face opposition from various groups, and PR practitioners need to distinguish true stakeholders from people who are actually irrelevant but who just want to attract media exposure. When PR practitioners meet true stakeholders they should work hard to bridge gaps. The hot topic of the day is how to make use of big data to improve PR strategies. Besides getting their client's message across they should understand the stakeholders' demands and relate them appropriately to the management of their client, to steer them towards better decisions.

Many PR gurus mentioned the Belt and Road (B&R) Initiative, the new project of the Chinese government to engage the countries around its periphery. They commented that if Hong Kong grasps this golden opportunity, it will be able to reposition itself as a stepping stone for B&R countries to enter the China market and, conversely, for China to enter markets in B&R countries. At present, the initiative is more important militarily and politically than economically, so its economic effects have yet to be seen.

Ten years ago Hong Kong had an advantage in its geographical position and was a regional centre of communication, but its importance has declined since. This has greatly affected the profits of PR companies in Hong Kong. At present Hong Kong is more like a testing ground for brands, since it has a mature consumer market with Chinese elements. For Chinese state enterprises or private enterprises that wish to enter the international market or foreign companies that wish to enter the Chinese market, Hong Kong is a good place for running trials, enabling brands to avoid big losses for recklessly entering an unfamiliar market. This fact may provide an opportunity for Hong Kong to turn itself around in the next ten years, but a precondition is that young people in Hong Kong have to do away with their local focus and to develop a truly international outlook. The Hong Kong market, though relatively small, still has the advantage of being a financial centre, but if Hong Kong people do not change their mode of thinking, then it will fall into recession, and the PR industry will be hit, since it is closely tied to the city's economic development.

There are three keys to a PR company's success: a localised marketing strategy, good local talent and good clients who respect the role of a PR company. PR companies in various countries have formed alliances. Public Relations Organisation International, for example, has members who help each other to their mutual benefit and serve big clients that have global business. The B&R initiative will provide opportunities to local PR companies, because they are familiar with local issues and the way local media work.

## References

Council of Public Relations Firms of Hong Kong. (2012). *Industry Benchmark Study 2012*. Hong Kong: CPRFHK.

Council of Public Relations Firms of Hong Kong. (2013). *Industry Benchmark Study 2013*. Hong Kong: CPRFHK.

Council of Public Relations Firms of Hong Kong. (2015). *Industry Benchmark Study June 2014 to June 2015*. Hong Kong: CPRFHK.

Hong Kong Vocational Training Council. (2014). "2014 Manpower Survey Report". Hong Kong: Hong Kong Vocational Training Council.

Hung-Baesecke, C. J. F., Chen, Y. R., Macnamara, J., Zerfass, A., Boyd, B, & Zhang, N. (2016). "Social Media Competence And Public Trust In Chinese Speaking Region And The Oceania: A Comparison Study". Paper presented at the 8th International Public Relations Research and Advertising Forum, Wellington, New Zealand, 2016, January.

Lee, B. K. (2007). "The HKSAR Government's PR Sense and Sensibility: Analysis of its SARS Crisis Management." *Asian Journal of Communication*, 17(2), 201–214.

Macnamara, J., Lwin, M. O., Adi, A., & Zerfass, A. (2015). "The State of Strategic Communication and Public Relations in a Region of Rapid Growth. Survey Results From 23 Countries". *Asia-Pacific Communication Monitor 2015/16*. Hong Kong: APACD.

Martin, E. F. (2009). "Hong Kong Public Relations: Resilient in the Face of Challenges." *Media Asia*, 36(2), 72–79.

Morgan McKinley Hong Kong. (2016). *2016 Hong Kong Salary Guide*. Hong Kong: Morgan McKinley Hong Kong.

# Chapter 11

## Media Change and the State of the Advertising Industry in Hong Kong

*Kineta H. K. HUNG*

## Introduction

While advertising remains a robust industry, with an annual global growth rate of 5% (Trefis Team, 2015), change is the name of the game today as the drivers that fuel its progress shift from traditional to social media. Advances in internet and mobile technology have changed user behaviour and proliferated user-generated content. Advertisers' traditional reliance on one-way communication, which gives them strong control over the message and how it is communicated, is giving way to efforts to entice and engage consumers, who may reiterate, enrich and disseminate advertising content in a network of social communication. This new emphasis on user involvement is leading the advertising industry into the internet plus era, where the availability of big data, cross-platform (desktop, mobile and tablet) marketing and improved advertisement measuring techniques allow for better audience targeting and drive advertising effects. However, at the same time these developments are posing serious challenges to traditional content generation sources such as television and print media that are less interactive and lack CRM-based data to facilitate individual targeting.

An interesting question is: to what extent are these global trends affecting the advertising industry in Hong Kong? What are the growth areas in the local advertising market, and what are the implications for talent development?

This chapter attempts to answer these questions by examining several sets of data: advertising expenditure in Hong Kong over the past decade, Nielsen Hong Kong's Media Index Report for 2015, the mass communication industry manpower survey report from the past six years and current advertising job listings. The data will be analysed to identify the qualities and skills advertising professionals need to equip themselves with in the changing industry. In sum, this chapter identifies salient issues in talent development that need to be addressed to ensure future growth of the advertising industry in Hong Kong.

That the data came from diverse sources and were collected using different methods contributes to its comprehensiveness and objectivity. The advertising expenditure data was provided by admanGo, a leading advertising monitoring service firm in Hong Kong, and was broken down by media categories as well as within media categories for the years 2005, 2010 and 2015 to review a ten-year trend. Analysis of the data can show changes over time both across and within media use. These results are supplemented by Nielsen's rating report for magazines in 2015. The manpower report is a survey report of industry professionals on human resources needs in mass communication industries and is published biennially by the Vocational Training Council. We obtained copies of the report published in 2012, 2014 and 2016 to ascertain human resources challenges in the industry. Finally, the job postings were listed on the job recruitment website of the *South China Morning Post* (*SCMP*)and downloaded in early July 2016.

## Advertising Expenditure and Media Change

The advertising industry in Hong Kong is no exception to world trends and is enjoying robust growth. Ad expenditure, which stood at HK$43,292 million in 2005, grew by 67% to $72,327 million in 2010 and from there by 57% to $113,478 million in 2015. This growth rate was higher than those in global advertising expenditure and in Hong Kong's GDP. Hidden in this growth pattern, however, is the shift towards new media. In line with global trends, ad expenditure on TV, which enjoyed 41% of the total in 2005, dropped to 35% in 2010 and 31% in 2015. Print media also declined. Ad expenditure on newspapers dropped from 34% of the total in 2005 to 32% in 2010 and then 29% in 2015. The situation for magazines was even more drastic, going down from 15% of total ad expenditure in 2005 to 13% in 2010 and 9% in 2015—a 31% drop over the five-year-period. At the same time, expenditure

**Table 11.1**

**Adspend by Media in Millions of Dollars (% of overall adspend)**

|        | TV        | Newspapers | Magazines | Radio    | Interactive | Mobile   |
|--------|-----------|------------|-----------|----------|-------------|----------|
| 2015   | 35,295.34 | 33,410.15  | 10,566.51 | 4,155.1  | 11,532.58   | 3,505.06 |
|        | (31.10%)  | (29.44%)   | (9.31%)   | (3.66%)  | (10.16%)    | (3.09%)  |
| 2010   | 25,223.79 | 23,240.45  | 9,741.42  | 3,332.82 | 3,130.11    | 0        |
|        | (34.87%)  | (32.13%)   | (13.47%)  | (4.61%)  | (4.33%)     |          |
| 2005   | 17,546.5  | 14,929.49  | 6,377.83  | 1,442.22 | 0           | 0        |
|        | (40.53%)  | (34.49%)   | (14.73%)  | (3.33%)  |             |          |

on interactive advertising grew from HK$3,130 million in 2010 to $11,533 million in 2015, representing a jump from 4% to 10% of total ad expenditure. Expenditure on mobile advertising also picked up, with interactive and mobile together accounting for 13% of total ad expenditure in 2015 (Table 11.1).

The ad expenditure by media category in Hong Kong shows a pattern similar to the global trend, with social media gaining importance at the expense of television and print media. Print ads have dropped 17.5% worldwide over the past five years (Trefis Team, 2015). In Hong Kong, the decline in print is similar, though the drop is much steeper for magazines than for newspapers. One possible explanation for the difference is the wide availability of free newspapers, which commuters can pick up at transit stations and read during their morning ride. There is concern that print may drop to the bottom tier and make up only a minor portion of advertising in the future as consumers become used to obtaining news free of charge.

The shift from print to social media is also indicated in the jobs available. Among the 134 jobs listed under "advertising" on the *SCMP* website, 42% were related to account management, sales and the business side of advertising; 32% were related to design, graphics, copywriting and the creative aspects of advertising; and 26% were related to digital and online media. Thus, about one quarter of the jobs currently available concern social media. The shift from print to social media is also shown in consumers' differential media habits across age groups, as indicated in Nielsen Hong Kong's Media Index Report for 2015. Whereas all magazine readers preferred hard copies, younger readers were more likely than older readers to read the same magazines using

**Table 11.2**

**Weekly Magazine Readership across Age Groups (in 000s)**

|  | 25–34 | 35–44 | 45–54 | 55–64 |
|---|---|---|---|---|
| *East Week* |  |  |  |  |
| Hardcopy + web + app | 69 | 75 | 125 | 88 |
| Hardcopy only | 53 | 66 | 108 | 83 |
| *Ming Pao Weekly* |  |  |  |  |
| Hardcopy + web + app | 46 | 26 | 64 | 44 |
| Hardcopy only | 34 | 22 | 59 | 44 |
| *Cosmopolitan* |  |  |  |  |
| Hardcopy + web + app | 66 | 61 | 51 | 1 |
| Hardcopy only | 50 | 55 | 47 | 1 |
| *Capital* |  |  |  |  |
| Hardcopy + web + app | 55 | 57 | 43 | 4 |
| Hardcopy only | 46 | 53 | 40 | 3 |

an online platform, such as a website or app. Thus, the salience of online media is likely to grow as young readers take up a larger proportion of the population due to demographic shifts (Table 11.2).

## Out-Of-Home Adspend

Aside from the trend toward increased online media use, there is also a growing trend toward out-of-home advertising. In 2005, compared to television (41%) and print (49%), the major advertising media at the time, out-of-home played a secondary role and took up just below 7% of the overall ad expenditure. By 2010 it had grown to over 10% and by 2015 to more than 13%, and its dollar value had grown five times over the same period, from HK$2,996 million to $15,013 million. This growth in out-of-home ad expenditure may partly be a result of changing technology, such as the availability of outdoor LED displays and digital light boxes, which make advertisements more eye-catching. Even areas that were little used in the past, like bus body advertising, have grown (Table 11.3).

**Table 11.3**

**Adspend on Out-of-Home Media in Millions of Dollars (% of overall adspend)**

|      | MTR | Bus Body | Other Out-of-Home | Total Out-of-Home |
|------|-----|----------|-------------------|-------------------|
| 2015 | 6563.61 (5.78%) | 838.89 (0.74%) | 7610.7 (6.71%) | 15013.2 (13.23%) |
| 2010 | 1968.2 (2.72%) | 192.9 (0.27%) | 4397.64 (7.60%) | 7658.74 (10.59%) |
| 2005 | 922.93 (2.13%) | 0 | 2072.75 (4.79%) | 2995.68 (6.92%) |

Note: MTR, mass transit railway.

It is not only Hong Kong residents who are exposed to advertising, but the large numbers of visitors to the city are also targeted. Tourist numbers have soared over the past decade following improvements in local attractions and favourable policy changes. Hong Kong Disneyland opened in 2005 and four years later the Beijing government approved a scheme to allow Shenzhen households to apply for one-year multiple-entry permits to visit Hong Kong (Legislative Council Secretariat, 2015). Many tourists are heavy shoppers, and out-of-home channels offer exposure opportunities to catch their attention.

## Essential Skills and Knowledge among Advertising Practitioners

In its biennial survey of companies involved in advertising and public relations, the Mass Communication Training Board of the Vocational Training Council examined the essential skills and knowledge that practitioners in the industry need to develop to cope with the changing environment. While these specific skills and knowledge have varied over the past three rounds of the survey (2010, 2012 and 2014), they can be categorised into three areas: social media, language skills and cultural sensitivity, as indicated in Table 11.4. Interestingly, language skills were highly relevant in 2010. Among the eight top ranked skills/knowledge listed under that year, three of them were language-related: Putonghua, spoken English and written English. Putonghua remained an important skill, ranked second in 2014. Similarly, creativity and cultural insights, along with knowledge about practices in China, were found to be important in both 2010 and 2014. This is not unexpected since China is a leading global advertising powerhouse, as indicated by Euromonitor

International. Advertising revenue in China, the second highest in the world, is expected to expand by 15% in 2016 to close the gap with the United States, which has the largest global advertising industry (Krasodomskyte, 2016).

Skills and knowledge related to digital media are also important, being listed in all three years surveyed. Multimedia knowledge and applications and innovative media research and applications both ranked among the top eight in both 2010 and 2014. But most notable was the explosion in the requirement for social media skills and knowledge in 2012, when all top eight items listed involved some aspect of social media (Table 11.4).

## Conclusion

This chapter shows that the Hong Kong advertising industry's growth is in the social media and out-of-home channels. However, whereas the growth in the former is in line with global trends, especially among young consumers, the rise in out-of-home advertising is less expected. This may, at least in part, be a result of the growth in tourism in Hong Kong, as tourists can be reached more

**Table 11.4**

**Essential Skills/Knowledge Areas Ad/PR Employees Need to Enhance**

| Rank | 2010 | 2012 | 2014 |
|---|---|---|---|
| 1 | Putonghua | Web research | Multimedia knowledge & application |
| 2 | Multimedia knowledge & application | Sharing platforms (e.g., YouTube) | Putonghua |
| 3 | Spoken English | Social networking platforms (e.g., Facebook, Twitter) | Political systems, social & economic development in Mainland China |
| 4 | Website design & supporting skills | Microblogging | Sales/marketing strategic planning |
| 5 | Written English | Web analytics | Account & strategic planning |
| 6 | Creativity & cultural insights | Search engine optimization | Market research applications |
| 7 | Innovative media research & applications | Web monitoring & surveillance | Innovative media research & applications |
| 8 | Industry practices in Mainland China | App development | Creativity and culture insights |

easily using out-of-home advertising. Television and print advertising are both declining, but magazine advertising has experienced the biggest drop and there is serious concern about its future.

The skills and knowledge advertising practitioners need to equip themselves with in this changing environment are also in flux. We found that social media-related skills were essential, which is not surprising given the rapid development in these channels. We also noted the continuing importance of language skills and cultural sensitivity in the profession. Another point that emerged from this study was the differential media habits of younger and older consumers, which highlights the need for advertising practitioners to understand millennial consumers. Finally, as the tourist market is highly salient in Hong Kong, advertising practitioners need insights not only into Hong Kong residents but also visitors.

While this chapter examines media changes in advertising in Hong Kong, the remaining chapters in this section cover the following topics: the top advertisers in Hong Kong, perception of creativity, consumers' attitudes towards television advertising, and advertising complaints in Hong Kong. Together, these chapters provide an overview of the state of advertising in Hong Kong as well as people's perceptions and behaviour towards advertising.

## References

Krasodomskyte, V. (3 January 2016). "Key Trends for Advertising Industry in 2016." *Euromonitor*. Retrieved from http://blog.euromonitor.com/2016/01/key-trends-for-advertising-industry-in-2016-2.html.

Research Office Legislative Council Secretariat. (5 August 2015). "Hong Kong's Tourism Industry" Research Brief. Retrieved from http://www.legco.gov.hk/research-publications/english/1415rb06-hong-kongs-tourism-industry-20150805-e.pdf.

Trefis Team. (28 September 2015). "Trends in Global Advertising Industry: Winners and Losers – Part 1." *Forbes*. Retrieved from http://www.forbes.com/sites/greatspeculations/2015/09/28/trends-in-global-advertising-industry-winners-and-losers-part-1/#2b1085d523a1.

Vocational Training Council. (2010). "Mass Communication Industry Manpower Survey Report 2010." Retrieved from http://www.vtc.edu.hk/uploads/files/publications/mass_communications_training_board/Manpower%20Survey/MCTB%202010%20report.pdf.

Vocational Training Council. (2012). "Mass Communication Industry Manpower Survey Report 2012." Retrieved from http://www.vtc.edu.hk/uploads/files/publications/mass_communications_training_board/Manpower%20Survey/MCTB%202012%20report.pdf.

Vocational Training Council. (2014). "Mass Communication Industry Manpower Survey Report 2014." Retrieved from http://www.vtc.edu.hk/uploads/files/publications/mass_communications_training_board/Manpower%20Survey/MCTB%202014%20report.pdf.

# Chapter 12

## Contemporary Advertising Industry:
## Profiling Top Advertisers in Hong Kong

*Terri H. CHAN*

## Introduction

The ever-increasing popularity of digital and online advertising is reshaping the communication landscape in Hong Kong. This trend challenges advertisers to rethink how they can better connect to and engage with their audiences. Renowned for their creativity and ability to adapt, marketers and advertisers in Hong Kong are reacting to this rapid change by structurally revising their communication mix. This chapter profiles recent Hong Kong top advertisers in terms of ad expenditure and awards, thus allowing us to detail the trends in this industry with respect to the unprecedented changes in advertising context and content in the region.

## Top Ten Ad Spend By Industry Categories

Total advertising spending in Hong Kong rose steadily from HK$43.3 billion in 2005 to HK$113.5 billion in 2015, according to data published by the media monitoring company, admanGo. Total ad expenditure in the city in 2015 increased 3.7% compared to that in 2014. As shown in Table 12.1, banking and investment services topped all industry categories in advertising expenditure. Maintaining its leading position since 2005, banking and investment services accounted for almost 10% of the share of voice (SOV) in the whole market in 2015. The pharmaceuticals and healthcare industry improved its position

**Table 12.1**

**Top Ten Ad Spend by Industry Categories**

| Ranking | | | Industry Categories | Revenue in billion HK$ (SOV (%)) | | | Change in SOV (%) (2005–2015) |
|---|---|---|---|---|---|---|---|
| 2005 | 2010 | 2015 | | 2005 | 2010 | 2015 | |
| 1 | 1 | 1 | Banking & investment services | 3.35 (7.73) | 7.91 (10.93) | 11.32 (9.98) | +2.25 |
| 2 | 3 | 3 | Toiletries & household | 2.85 (6.58) | 5.07 (7.01) | 9.15 (8.06) | +1.48 |
| 3 | 6 | 9 | Property & real estate | 2.75 (6.36) | 3.07 (4.25) | 4.44 (3.91) | −2.45 |
| 4 | 4 | 4 | Cosmetics & skincare | 2.53 (5.85) | 4.93 (6.82) | 7.41 (6.53) | +0.68 |
| 5 | 2 | 2 | Pharmaceuticals & healthcare | 2.44 (5.64) | 5.28 (7.29) | 9.37 (8.25) | +2.61 |
| 6 | 8 | – | Entertainment | 2.37 (5.47) | 2.81 (3.88) | – | −5.47 |
| 7 | 5 | 5 | Travel & tourism services | 2.22 (5.12) | 3.15 (4.25) | 5.99 (5.28) | +0.16 |
| 8 | 9 | – | Food | 2.16 (4.98) | 2.73 (3.78) | – | −4.98 |
| 9 | – | 8 | Media | 1.78 (4.12) | – | 4.58 (4.04) | −0.08 |
| 10 | – | – | Restaurant | 1.66 (3.83) | – | – | −3.83 |
| – | 7 | 6 | Beverages | – | 2.83 (3.91) | 5.76 (5.08) | +5.08 |
| – | 10 | 7 | Jewellery, watches & luxury products | – | 2.65 (3.66) | 4.61 (4.06) | +4.06 |
| – | – | 10 | Retail | – | – | 4.41 (3.89) | +3.89 |

Note: SOV, share of voice.

Source: admanGo.

from fifth in 2005 to second in 2015 with a rise of 2.6% in its SOV. The toiletries and household industry recorded the third largest ad spend. Though witnessing a slight drop from second position in 2005 to third, this category constituted 8% of SOV. Maintaining their fourth and fifth positions from 2010 are the cosmetics and skincare industry and the travel and tourism industry, accounting for 6.5% and 5.3% of SOV, respectively. Beverages, jewellery and luxury products and property and real estate have also remained in the top ten since 2010. The entertainment, food and restaurant sectors, which were among the top ten in 2005 and 2010, were no longer there in 2015. Despite global economic uncertainty, marketers in Hong Kong anticipated a steady influx of visitors from Mainland China, and because of this, advertising for the retail sector reached a top ten position in 2015 for the first time, with almost 4% of SOV. That the digital revolution propelled the media category back into a top ten position in ad expenditure in 2015 is also notable.

## Top Ten Advertisers In 2015

Table 12.2 lists the top ten advertisers in the years 2005, 2010 and 2015 in terms of advertising expenditure. The top spender on the 2015 list was the Hong Kong government, which invested about HK$1.7 billion in public campaigns. Consistent with the list of top spenders, the banking and investment services sector was well represented on the list, with Hong Kong and Shanghai Banking Corporation (HSBC), the Hang Seng Bank Group and United Asia Finance at second, third and eighth positions, respectively. Dropping by one place, McDonald's finished fourth on the 2015 list with an ad spend of HK$867 million and almost 10% SOV. Leading the pharmaceuticals and health industry's ad expenditure was Friesland Campina and Fortune Pharmacal, which took the fifth and ninth positions, respectively. Wellcome, representing the toiletries and household sector, spent HK$767 million on advertisements in 2015 and ranked sixth. L'Oreal, top in the cosmetics and skincare industry, finished in seventh on the list in 2015, accounting for 8.3% of SOV. Samsung, which was not in the top ten in 2005 or 2010, was tenth in the top ten advertisers in 2015, spending HK$618 million on its campaigns.

**Table 12.2**

**Top Ten Advertisers by Ad Spend**

| Ranking | | | | Revenue in million HK$ (SOV (%)) | | |
|---|---|---|---|---|---|---|
| 2005 | 2010 | 2015 | Advertiser | 2005 | 2010 | 2015 |
| 1 | 3 | 4 | McDonald's | 393.6 (12.89) | 545.5 (10.77) | 866.7 (9.85) |
| 2 | – | – | Midland Realty | 370.8 (12.14) | – | – |
| 3 | 2 | 2 | HSBC Group | 368.1 (12.05) | 697.8 (13.78) | 1,032.0 (11.72) |
| 4 | – | – | Aji Ichiban | 324.3 (10.62) | – | – |
| 5 | 4 | – | Wrigley | 308.9 (10.11) | 524.8 (10.36) | – |
| 6 | – | – | Sun Hung Kai Properties | 280.6 (9.19) | – | – |
| 7 | 8 | – | PCCW | 265.2 (8.68) | 404.7 (7.99) | – |
| 8 | – | – | SmarTone | 255.7 (8.37) | – | – |
| 9 | – | – | Centaline Property Agency | 253.0 (8.29) | – | – |
| 10 | – | – | Sewame | 233.5 (7.65) | – | – |
| – | 1 | 1 | The government of the Hong Kong Special Administrative Region | – | 785.4 (15.51) | 1,708.3 (19.41) |
| – | 5 | 9 | Fortune Pharmacal | – | 480.1 (9.48) | 663.7 (7.54) |
| – | 6 | – | Canon | – | 445.8 (8.80) | – |
| – | 7 | – | Citibank | – | 445.1 (8.79) | – |
| – | 9 | – | SK-II | – | 367.7 (7.26) | – |
| – | 10 | – | MTR Corporation | – | 367.1 (7.25) | – |
| – | – | 3 | Hang Seng Bank | – | – | 886.8 (10.08) |
| – | – | 5 | Friso | – | – | 861.5 (9.79) |
| – | – | 6 | Wellcome | – | – | 766.5 (8.71) |
| – | – | 7 | L'Oreal Paris | – | – | 728.2 (8.27) |
| – | – | 8 | United Asia Finance | – | – | 670.5 (7.62) |
| – | – | 10 | Samsung | – | – | 617.0 (7.02) |

Note: SOV, share of voice.

Source: admanGo.

## Advertising Awards and Agency Performance in Hong Kong

Attaining high positions in advertising agency rankings has long been a high priority for many advertisers. Besides judging agencies on their incomes, these awards are now widely recognised as professional indicators of advertising effectiveness with specific emphasis on creative excellence (Kübler & Proppe, 2012). Agencies achieve not only professional recognition through these events but also use them as a promotional instrument. Other reasons they take part include acquisition of new customers, enhanced loyalty among existing clients and recruitment of potential talent (Tippins & Kunkel, 2006). In this regard, industry actors today put increasing resources into taking part in the award presentation (Wentz, 2005) and strive for leading positions in widely recognised creative rankings (e.g., the Ad Age rankings in the United States).

Advertising award events are a global phenomenon. Some events, such as the Cannes Lions, the One Show and the Clio Awards, are internationally prestigious, drawing contestants from all over the globe. Other events are organised on a national or local level. In addition, some are general in scope, covering a wide range of advertising channels, products and techniques, while some are specific in relation to media or other contexts. Regardless of the many differences among the awards and events, the emphasis on creativity emerges as a strong common denominator. This section outlines the achievements of top Hong Kong advertising agencies in local industry awards.

We focus on three Hong Kong-based awards in 2015, namely the Kam Fan Awards, the Television Broadcasters Limited (TVB) Most Popular TV Commercial Awards and the Marketing Excellence Awards. In total, 181 entries were gathered from the three websites where they were announced. There are a few points to note here. First, the benchmarking and profiling of top Hong Kong advertising agencies in this study are based only on awards obtained in the three local events, thus they do not take into account national and international awards. Second, the ranking of agencies for each award is based purely on the number of award-winning entries, not on the weight and hierarchy of awards. Third, the sampled awards highlight a spectrum of values that the advertising industry tries to pursue.

The Kam Fan Awards are organised annually by the Association of Accredited Advertising Agencies of Hong Kong (HK4As) to recognise the best creative work in the Hong Kong market. To be eligible, entries must be created and developed by an agency based in Hong Kong and launched for the local market. Hence, it is a representative accolade for the Hong Kong advertising industry. On the other hand, the TVB Most Popular TV Commercial Awards and the Marketing Excellence Awards are context-specific awards that focus more on effective execution than creativity. They are included because of their high visibility. Many important stakeholders such as clients, marketers and media buyers use them as reference tools to assess agencies' competence.

## 2015 Kam Fan Awards

Finalists in the Kam Fan Awards are awarded a gold, silver, bronze or merit medal in the following categories: print, outdoor, design, film, radio, cyber, media and integrated. The Grand Kam Fan award is chosen from among all Kam Fan winners (Association of Accredited Advertising Agencies of Hong Kong, 2015). First, we will look at how many awards it takes to be among the top advertising agencies based on statistics from the Kam Fan Awards: of the twenty-one award-winning agencies (with a total of 127 winning entries), four won one award each and two won two awards each, but five agencies had won ten or more each. The three with eleven or more awards were the top three agencies, and the top two had seventeen and twenty-three winning entries, which were high numbers indeed. Table 12.3 shows the award-winning agencies at the 2015 Kam Fan Awards. It is not surprising that the majority are world-renowned multinational advertising agencies, with McCann & Spencer as the leading awardee, the DDB Group Hong Kong coming second and Cheil finishing third in terms of numbers of award-winning entries.

## TVB Most Popular TV Commercial Awards

Television has long been an important and effective medium of advertising in Hong Kong. TVB, having a penetration rate as high as 82% of the Hong Kong population (TVB, 2015), is the organiser of the TVB Most Popular TV Commercial Awards (TVB Awards), which recognise and honour the teams behind successful commercials. The TVB Awards have made advertising stakeholders and the general public aware of outstanding commercials.

All entries must have been first aired on TVB in order to be eligible for the award. Awards in various categories are given, such as the Most Creative Award, Best Visual Effects Award, Audience's Choice Award and Best of the Best Award. A total of nineteen commercials won awards in 2015. In terms

**Table 12.3**

**Winners of the 2015 Kam Fan Awards**

| Agency | Grand Kam Fan | Promo & Activation Kam Fan | Integrated Kam Fan | Best | Gold | Silver | Bronze | Merit | Total |
|---|---|---|---|---|---|---|---|---|---|
| McCann & Spencer | 1 | 1 | 1 | 2 | | 2 | 2 | 14 | 23 |
| DDB Group Hong Kong | | | | | | 3 | 5 | 9 | 17 |
| Cheil | | | | | | 1 | 4 | 6 | 11 |
| Ogilvy & Mather Group, Hong Kong | | | | | 1 | 1 | 4 | 4 | 10 |
| Grey Group Hong Kong | | | | | | | 4 | 6 | 10 |
| Leo Burnett Hong Kong | | | | | | | 2 | 7 | 9 |
| PHD Hong Kong | | | | | | | | 7 | 7 |
| Carat Media Services Hong Kong Limited | | | | | | 1 | 1 | 5 | 7 |
| Dentsu Hong Kong Limited | | | | | | | | 4 | 4 |
| J. Walter Thompson Hong Kong | | | | | | 1 | | 3 | 4 |
| Maxus Hong Kong | | | | | | | | 4 | 4 |
| TBWA\Hong Kong | | | | | | | 3 | 1 | 4 |
| OMD Hong Kong | | | | | | | | 3 | 3 |
| BBDO | | | | 1 | | 2 | | | 3 |
| Mindshare Hong Kong Limited | | | | | | | 2 | 1 | 3 |
| The Gate Worldwide Ltd | | | | | | 1 | 1 | | 2 |
| PCCW Media Ltd - NOW TV | | | | | | | 1 | 1 | 2 |
| Starcom MediaVest Group | | | | | | | | 1 | 1 |
| Touches Ltd | | | | | | | | 1 | 1 |
| Saatchi & Saatchi Services (Hong Kong) Limited | | | | | | | | 1 | 1 |
| Geometry Global | | | | | | | | 1 | 1 |
| Total | 1 | 1 | 1 | 3 | 1 | 12 | 29 | 79 | 127 |

## Table 12.4
## Winners of the 2015 TVB Most Popular TV Commercial Awards

| Agency | Professional Selection | Most Popular TV Commercial | Most Popular Male Talent | Most Popular Female Talent | Audience's Choice | Best Visual Effects | Most Creative | Best of the Best | Powerhouse Agency | Total No. of Awards |
|---|---|---|---|---|---|---|---|---|---|---|
| Metta Communications Limited | 3 | 3 | 1 | | | 1 | 1 | 1 | 1 | 11 |
| Grey Group Hong Kong | 1 | 1 | | 1 | 1 | | | | | 4 |
| McCann & Spencer | 2 | 1 | | | | | | | | 3 |
| Dentsu Hong Kong Limited | 2 | | | | | | | | | 2 |
| DDB Group Hong Kong | | 1 | | | | | | | | 1 |
| Publicis Worldwide (Hong Kong) Limited | | 1 | | | | | | | | 1 |
| J. Walter Thompson Hong Kong | | 1 | | | | | | | | 1 |
| Twohundred Limited | 1 | | | | | | | | | 1 |
| BBDO | | 1 | | | | | | | | 1 |
| Uth Creative Group Limited | | 1 | | | | | | | | 1 |
| The Right Side Limited | 1 | | | | | | | | | 1 |
| Bliss Concepts Limited | 1 | | | | | | | | | 1 |
| Total | 11 | 10 | 1 | 1 | 1 | 1 | 1 | 1 | 1 | 28 |

of judging, an online public poll was used to select the "Audience's Choice Award" while a panel of professional judges selected the other awards.

Twelve agencies won one or more TVB Awards. The majority of agencies (67%) had only one winning entry, while the agency that did the best had eleven and the second best had four. These two agencies had more award-winning entries than all the other agencies combined, resulting in a skewed frequency distribution. Table 12.4 shows that of the twelve agencies that won TVB Awards, six agencies—Grey Group Hong Kong, McCann & Spencer, Dentsu Hong Kong Limited, DDB Group Hong Kong, J. Walter Thompson Hong Kong and BBDO—were Kam Fan Award winners. The other six—Metta Communications Limited, Publicis Worldwide (Hong Kong) Limited, Twohundred Limited, Uth Creative Group Limited, The Right Side Limited and Bliss Concepts Limited—were not.

## Marketing Excellence Awards

The Hong Kong Marketing Excellence Awards celebrate the best campaign work across the integrated marketing communication spectrum, ranging from excellence in advertising, branded content and digital marketing to corporate social responsibility. As with the other awards, entries to the Marketing Excellence Awards must have been conceptualised and launched in Hong Kong for the local market, emphasising indigenous features and challenges in a broader marketing discipline (Marketing Excellence Awards, 2015).

In 2015, there were a total of 102 awardees in a wide range of marketing categories. Sixty per cent of them had one winning entry, 24% of them had two, while the top winner had eight. Table 12.5 lists all fifty-eight awardees. Among the six agencies with four or more awards, Maxus Hong Kong, Uth Creative Group Limited and PHD Hong Kong were also winners of Kam Fan or TVB Awards. The other three, Razorfish (HK) Co., Havas Worldwide Hong Kong and CMRS Digital Solutions, did not win these awards.

## Conclusion

Being at the top in various agency rankings is of high importance for many advertising agencies. This priority can be explained from various perspectives. From a business strategy perspective, major brands as well as new marketers often refer to ranking systems to look for potential new agencies. As the media landscape is transforming quickly with increasing audience scepticism

**Table 12.5**

**Winners of the Marketing Excellence Awards 2015**

| Agency | Number of Winning Entries |
|---|---|
| Razorfish (HK) Co. | 8 |
| Maxus Hong Kong | 5 |
| Uth Creative Group Limited | 5 |
| Havas Worldwide Hong Kong | 4 |
| PHD Hong Kong | 4 |
| CMRS Digital Solutions | 4 |
| Grey Group Hong Kong | 3 |
| OMD Hong Kong | 3 |
| UM Rally | 3 |
| Agenda | 2 |
| Anonymous | 2 |
| Cherrypicks | 2 |
| DDB Group Hong Kong | 2 |
| ET Promotions | 2 |
| McCann & Spencer | 2 |
| MEC Hong Kong | 2 |
| MediaCom Hong Kong | 2 |
| Metta Communications Limited | 2 |
| NMC Interactive | 2 |
| Pixels | 2 |
| Speedy | 2 |
| Starcom MediaVest Group | 2 |
| The Great European Carnival | 2 |
| Alpha 245 | 1 |
| BBDO | 1 |
| The Bread Digital | 1 |
| Daylight Partnership | 1 |
| Edelman | 1 |
| FevaWorks Solution | 1 |
| Fimmick | 1 |

**Table 12.5 (continued)**

| Agency | Number of Winning Entries |
|---|:---:|
| Guru Online | 1 |
| iClick Interactive Asia | 1 |
| iProspect Hong Kong | 1 |
| Isobar | 1 |
| J. Walter Thompson Hong Kong | 1 |
| Leovation | 1 |
| Mazarine Asia Pacific | 1 |
| Mindshare Hong Kong | 1 |
| Object Valley | 1 |
| Ogilvy & Mather Group, Hong Kong | 1 |
| Phenomena | 1 |
| Pixo Punch | 1 |
| Publicis Worldwide (Hong Kong) Limited | 1 |
| Resolution Hong Kong | 1 |
| RSVP | 1 |
| Secret Tour Hong Kong | 1 |
| Sinclair Communications | 1 |
| Social Power | 1 |
| Soho Square | 1 |
| Strategic Public Relations Group | 1 |
| TBWA\Hong Kong | 1 |
| The Thing | 1 |
| Turn Plus Communication | 1 |
| Untitled | 1 |
| VIS Communications | 1 |
| WRG Creative Communication (Asia) | 1 |
| Xaxis Hong Kong | 1 |
| Y&R | 1 |
| Total | 102 |

towards advertisements, the challenge remains for communicators, in both the public and private sectors, to get across their desired messages in a synergised and effective way. From an advertising performance perspective, awards events are widely perceived as a benchmark for creativity (John, 2011). Advertising awards are thus fiercely sought after by members of the advertising industry as trophies of creativity. The findings from this chapter are encouraging as they suggest that while multinational advertising agencies are dominant in winning accolades in Hong Kong, local agencies also shine in context-specific awards that reflect local tastes, wisdom and culture.

## References

Association of Accredited Advertising Agencies of Hong Kong. (2015). "2015 Kam Fan Awards". Retrieved from http://aaaa.com.hk/main/awards/2015-kam-fan-awards/.

John, J. (2011) "Why You Should Care about Awards." *Strategy* February 1, 56. Retrieved from http://strategyonline.ca/2011/02/01/ forumjohn-20110201/.

Kübler, R. V., & Proppe, D. (2012). "Faking or Convincing: Why Do Some Advertising Campaigns Win Creativity Awards?" *Business Research*, 5(1), 60–81.

Marketing Excellence Awards. (2015). Retrieved from http://www.marketing-interactive.com/mea-awards/hk/.

Tippins, M. J., & Kunkel, R. A. (2006). "Winning a Clio Advertising Award and its Relationship to Firm Profitability." *Journal of Marketing Communications*, 12(1), 1–14.

TVB. (2015). "TVB 2014 Annual Report". Retrieved from http://img.tvb.com/corporate/_upload_/article/en/f6d973d95f4aa24cce36e351fe8eeb63.pdf.

Wentz, L. (2005). "At Cannes, the Lions say 'Grrr'". *Advertising Age*, 76 (26), 1–2.

# Chapter 13

## Creative Professionals' Perceptions of Creativity in Hong Kong

*Vivienne S. Y. LEUNG*

### Introduction

Creativity is commonly defined as developing a product that is novel, valuable, useful, appropriate and consistent for a given society (Sternberg et al., 2005). In the advertising sector, creativity consists of three dimensions: novelty, meaningfulness and connectedness (Ang, Lee & Leong, 2007). Jewler and Drewniany (1998) previously suggested that a creative advertisement should be new and take risks as well as include divergent thinking and humour. According to the social-psychological framework of creativity (Glăveanu, 2010), the perception of creativity by advertising creatives is an interaction between the creator, the creation and the audience in the specific cultural context.

In an advertising agency, different parties often believe that a good, effective advertisement should possess different qualities (Cagley & Robert, 1984; Fam & Waller, 1999; Hackley & Kover, 2007). Creative directors or copywriters tend to view originality as being the most important aspect in an advertisement (Koslow et al., 2006). Hackley and Kover (2007) interviewed senior advertising creatives in New York to explore their sense of personal and professional identity. The participants indicated that organisational bureaucracy damaged their sense of reassurance and security. They preferred peer approval, as represented by industry awards, to that of their clients, since they believed that their peers understand their work better in terms of aesthetic values. Another study conducted in New Zealand showed that interpersonal relations were considered the most important, followed by creative ability rated by a group of agency account managers (Fam & Waller, 1999; Hui et al., 2012). The third- and fourth-ranked factors were the quality of account personnel and integrity and shared purpose, while the fifth and sixth were agency resources and marketing and strategy development. While account management talents place more importance on strategy and interpersonal relationships than creative business development, production mangers focus more on artistry and emotional expression (Koslow et al., 2006). Often, there is tension between the concepts of novelty and appropriateness, which in turn creates discord and rivalry between the client and the agency, and sometimes even within parties working in the same agency.

Factors of creativity, such as originality, strategy and artistry, can be enhanced when clients are open to exploring new ideas and give advertising creatives sufficient time, and when unsophisticated clients, having less experience, expertise, and understanding of advertising, provide a clear strategy (the reverse is true when the client is sophisticated) (Koslow et al., 2006). In contrast, creativity can also be viewed as a key performance factor affecting the agency-client relationship, in addition to deadlines, campaign results, experience, price, relationships between the agency, media and other operators as well as agency size, reactivity and proactivity and personnel turnover (Triki et al., 2007). An open and supportive organisation nurtures creativity (Cummings et al., 1975), enabling different opinions and ideas to be formed and voiced during advertising strategy development and enhancing the execution of new and innovative ideas.

Previous studies show that differences and disagreements between the agency and the client have a negative impact on their relationship and lead to failures in collaboration. For instance, Thamhain and Wilemon (1975) suggest that mismatches around human resources management, prioritisation and scheduling for a project are harmful to the relationship because they lead to problems with, or even the termination of, existing projects. Therefore, coordination and effective communication are essential for maintaining the agency-client relationship.

The rest of this chapter is based on the previous study by Leung and Hui (2014). The purpose of this study is to present an up-to-date picture of how creativity is defined and communicated from agencies to clients in the advertising industry in Hong Kong. Our findings are intended to enhance our understanding of advertising creativity in Asia as well as to enlighten both advertising practitioners and clients to strive for better agency-client communication in the future. This study posed three research questions:

1.  What does "creativity" mean to advertising creative talents in Hong Kong?
2.  What do advertising professionals in Hong Kong consider to be top quality advertising?
3.  Does the agency-client relationship affect creative development in Hong Kong? And how?

## Qualitative Interviews of Advertising Professionals

The study employed qualitative interviews. Seven advertising creative professionals (four males and three females) working in Hong Kong were recruited. All of them were involved in creative advertising work on a daily basis. All had three or more years of experience working in the advertising industry. Most held senior positions. Five of them were interviewed at their workplaces face-to-face in April 2016. Two of them were interviewed via email. All face-to-face interviews were audio recorded and transcribed for analysis.

Regarding research question 1, all interviewees believed that creativity is crucial and is not limited to advertising. They said that advertising was an integral part of the creative industry. To a large extent, everyone is a creative talent in daily life.

Creativity is not about the division of art base or copy base. Everyone can be a creative and possess some sort of creative talents. Kids, adults... Our mothers are creative too. (Creative director, male)

All industries need creativity... You need to be creative even when you bargain before you buy something. (Creative director, male)

Echoing previous research (Rudowicz, 2004; Rudowicz & Hui, 1997), the interviewees said that creativity involves the "betterment" or "improvement" of existing ideas. In contrast to Western societies, in which creativity is perceived as novelty and invention, creativity in Chinese culture refers more to modification, adaptation, renovation or re-interpretation in the form of intellectual and societal revision (Rudowicz, 2004).

> Creativity is usually based on or built on something that already existed but adds a new twist or new angle. It also means you have a new or different perspective on something. Sometimes, you can be creative when you bring unrelated things together. (Co-executive creative director, female)

> Creativity is an uncovered angle or perspective which you can see but others cannot. If you can bring in a new perspective, that's creativity. Creativity does not need to be something totally new. It could be a combination of different existing elements together with a new interpretation. (Head of digital, male)

> Creativity is fun. If you can modify or change one thing into something else, that's creativity. Creativity is a thinking process. (Group creative director, female)

> Creativity is about turning something ordinary into something never seen or thought of before. (Creative group head, female)

Interestingly, almost all interviewees stated that creativity in advertising has its boundaries. For one thing, industry professionals have to strive for a balance between creativity and practicality. Good advertising has to help clients achieve their objectives, which to a large extent means to boost sales.

> Besides being creative, good advertising has to have a positive impact on the brand or product. As the creatives working on the project, we need ideas that are based on the advertising brief and results agreed on with the clients. It doesn't mean you can't be creative. Our ideas have to be effective in terms of raising awareness or changing consumer behaviour. (Co-executive creative director, female)

> Creativity is a means of communication that allows the clients to achieve a business goal. (Creative director, male)

Creativity is a planning process. It's about the consumer journey. We need to see how an idea can help raise awareness, generate viral impacts and ultimately lead to transactions. (Head of digital, male)

Advertising aims to achieve some commercial goals through creative means. It can't deviate from the original brief too much, or be "off-brief" in advertising terms. (Strategic planner, male)

The interviewees think that clients in Hong Kong are generally not very creative because they are too business-oriented. Because of budget constraints, clients are often not willing to spend too much on a campaign, and their goals are mainly short-sighted, such as to increase sales or "likes" on social media. They tend to put more weight on promotion (product or sales advertising) than branding (brand and corporate advertising), which limits the development of creativity.

Clients focus on promotion but not branding. They emphasize ad hoc results. That's due to the influence of digital media. Clients only count click rates or the number of "likes". (Co-executive creative director, female)

Creativity is difficult to measure. Clients always think that an idea that is entertaining is creative. And they tend to judge an idea based on a rational, business standard. (Creative director, male)

Clients think something they have not seen before is creative. It's different from how creative talents see creativity. (Creative director, male)

Some clients define creativity as an idea that has never been done before in their product category. Some see creativity as a marketing idea that has PR value, wins awards and increases sales. (Creative group head, female)

In particular, two interviewees think that local advertising agencies are more creative than 4As agencies because they provide more flexibility and freedom, and there are more restrictions in international advertising groups.

Since 4As agencies are less flexible, many people leave them and start working in local agencies or boutique agencies. I think it's a good move. (Head of digital, male)

Creative talents do not have bargaining power in 4As agencies. They are not flexible. And since some clients started to contact local agencies, some creative talents follow suit. In a small local agency, it's about relationships and trust. Trust enables creative talents to have room for idea generation. They do not have to give in too much as they have a close relationship with their clients. (Strategic planner, male)

Regarding research question 2, the interviewees tended to agree that a good advertisement should be able to create resonance with its audience and should be executable. A sound strategy with good insight can help to foster the development of a creative idea.

A good strategy is the foundation of a good idea. A strategy is built upon rational and scientific data. Normally, clients are knowledgeable in that regard. They understand the full picture. (Strategic planner, male)

Actually, there's no definition for a good or bad advertisement. Whether it is good or not depends on the target audience. In my opinion, an effective advertisement fits the target group. (Head of digital, male)

For research question 3, almost all interviewees believed that a friendly and close relationship with clients is preferred but not necessarily beneficial for idea generation. Disagreement is inevitable. Open, continuous communication between agency and client is needed.

In my company, creative talents will take the brief together with the account servicing team and the clients. Hence, as creative talents, we better understand what the clients expect. This lets the clients know that we are committed to the project as well. (Co-executive creative director, female)

There is no one-size-fits-all formula in the agency-client relationship. Both parties need to keep up open, continuous dialogue and be flexible. It takes time to convince clients to accept an idea. (Head of digital, male)

When a conflict arises, the majority of the interviewees tend to compromise and avoid direct confrontation with their clients. They understand that clients are more knowledgeable about their brand and products.

> If a client does not like my idea, I won't think that is the client's problem. I'll try my best to see how we can come up with a solution that is beneficial to both parties. The clients usually have a better understanding of their brands. We have to understand their expectations. If we can do that, it's easier to convince them since they'll see that we are trying to think from their perspective. It's a long trust-building exercise. If the client trusts you, your ideas will be accepted more easily. (Creative director, male)

> I avoid direct confrontations with my clients. Normally I will let the clients know that their concerns are well understood but there are other options, which can help them solve the problem. Advertising is a people business. Both parties can agree on the disagreements. Our job is to let them know that there are many ways to achieve the same goals. Communication is the key to success. (Co-executive creative director, female)

> [A conflict] is not necessarily a bad thing because this situation can be a good gauge of the client's creative appetite. From an agency's point of view, it's good to meet clients' expectations. But it's even better when we exceed them (in a good way). And that is what we aim for each and every time. (Creative group head, female)

Lastly, the interviewees think that Hong Kong advertising is creative in general. With the changes in the media landscape over the last decade, it is hard to judge whether advertising in Hong Kong is better or worse than it was ten years ago. Many creative talents who used to work for international 4As agencies are now working for local agencies and injecting their creative experience into the local scene. Being local, their ideas may strike a chord with target audiences.

> Some campaigns run by Metta Communication are good, for example the campaign 'Lion Rock Spirit' for Fortune Pharmacal Co. Ltd in 2015. It demonstrated the Hong Kong spirit, that is, perseverance and determination. (Co-executive creative director, female)

## Striving for a Balance between Creativity and Practicality

This study shows that creative professionals in Hong Kong need to be both logical and intuitive. Many interviewees acknowledged that research and consumer insights were important for creative development, which led to a comprehensive strategy for campaign planning. Creative professionals realise that their clients are working with limited budgets but are under severe pressure to boost sales of their products. Creative professionals therefore are responsible for generating a creative idea which contributes to a favourable business performance, in terms of sales, market share and the number of "likes" or click rates. A good advertisement does not need to be groundbreaking. It can be a re-interpretation of existing ideas.

> Creativity is subjective. It ought to be able to help to achieve some goals in the end. (Strategic planner, male)

> A good advertisement is usually derived from a good strategy. A strategy is supported by research, facts, figures and analysis. Hence, a creative advertisement is a combination of facts and emotions. (Co-executive creative director, female)

## A Good Agency-Client Relationship is Crucial for Creativity

All interviewees agreed that a friendly, healthy relationship with clients is beneficial to creative development. It is important to gain the trust of clients. Therefore, open communication is important. Creative professionals realise that having ideas rejected is common in the advertising industry. It is crucial to keep the clients informed to ensure that they are aware of the creative rationale and to convey respect. When the clients reject an idea, creative professionals should not take it personally. To solve the problem, they should try to provide different options to the clients. Ongoing communication and respect is the key to success.

> In the past, a creative department was rather independent. Now it is different. Creative departments have more contact with clients. Sometimes creative talents join the account servicing team to socialise with the clients. We can try to convince the clients of our ideas in an informal setting…

Once trust is built, it shortens the distance between the client and the creative team. (Co-executive creative director, female)

When a client rejects my idea, I won't insist. The client makes the final decision. I don't take it too personally. I ask them why they don't like my idea, what is bad about it, what are their ideas and so forth. Perhaps when we understand each other better, we can work out a solution. It is our job to find a solution for the client. (Creative director, male)

Building a strong relationship with the client, and having a good track record are important. Agencies must do their homework, e.g., know the client's business and the target audience... We always put our best foot forward because we believe in our work. Of course, there are situations where both agency and client will find middle ground in order to move forward with the project. We always have our client's best interest in mind. (Creative group head, female)

## Advertising in Hong Kong is Creative and the Advertising Business in Mainland China is Catching Up

When comparing creative developments between Hong Kong and Mainland China, almost all interviewees believed that Hong Kong advertising is more creative. However, it is hard to compare the markets in Hong Kong and Mainland China directly as their audience sizes and profiles are so different. One key difference lies in the role of strategic planning. While strategic planning is a key driver of promotional effectiveness in Hong Kong, it is not always perceived to be important to brand communications in China. Some clients in China, for instance, do not rely on research findings for strategy planning because of the diversity of the target market. In general, brands in China target a mass audience. Clients want ideas which everyone in the mass market can understand. When the general goal is only to let everyone know about the brand, there is no need to explore a specific strategy.

Clients in Hong Kong are more tolerant and open to creative ideas than clients in Mainland China. The Mainland Chinese population is huge. Most of the time a brand just wants everyone in China to know about it. That's why they don't need a complicated strategy. What they want is a one-size-fits-all idea. In the Mainland, brands have bigger budgets than in Hong Kong. They do not like to take risks. The Hong Kong market is relatively small. To make your brand outstanding in such a small market, you need a good strategy with a creative idea. (Creative director, male)

Some interviewees believed that Hong Kong advertising is in good shape in terms of innovation and ideas. Examples such as Expedia, HKTV, Fortune Pharmacal Co. Ltd. and Solvil et Titus were cited as producing successful and effective campaigns in the local Hong Kong market.

## Conclusion

In summary, we found that it is important for advertising agencies to have continuous communication with clients and to understand their business goals so as to develop a beneficial relationship. When there is a disagreement, a compromise is needed. This study found that mutual trust and understanding between the agency and the client is achieved through effective communication and respect. The creatives we interviewed stated that a creative advertisement does not need to be completely novel. It can be an "improvement" on an existing idea but with a different perspective.

Although only seven interviews were conducted, this study provides an understanding of how advertising professionals perceive creativity in Hong Kong nowadays. In addition, this study has shown that cultural factors are clearly important in the appreciation of creativity. Western concepts of creativity are not completely suitable in this case. In Chinese culture, where harmony and personal prestige are valued, it is important to strike a balance between creativity and practicality.

Future research is necessary to examine the impact of creative industries in emerging markets like Mainland China, Thailand and Korea and to better evaluate creative development in Hong Kong.

# References

Ang, S. H., Lee, Y. H., & Leong, S. M. (2007). "The Ad Creativity Cube: Conceptualization and Initial Validation." *Journal of the Academy of Marketing Science*, 35(2), 220–32.

Cagley, J. W., & Robert, C. R. (1984). "Criteria for Advertising Agency Selection: An Objective Appraisal." *Journal of Advertising Research*, 24(2), 27–31.

Cummings, L. L., Hinton, B. L., & Gobdel, B. C. (1975). "Creative Behavior as a Function of Task Environment: Impact of Objectives, Procedures, and Controls." *Academy of Management Journal*, 18(3), 489–99.

Escalas, J. E., & Stern, B. B. (2003). "Sympathy and Empathy: Emotional Responses to Advertising Dramas." *Journal of Consumer Research*, 29(4), 566–78.

Fam, K. S., & Waller, D. S. (1999). "Factors in Winning Accounts: The Views of Agency Account Directors in New Zealand." *Journal of Advertising Research*, 39(3), 21–32.

Glăveanu, V. P. (2010). "Creativity as Cultural Participation". *Journal for the Theory of Social Behaviour*, 41(1), 48–67.

Hackley, C., & Kover, A. J. (2007). "The Trouble with Creatives: Negotiating Creative Identity in Advertising Agencies." *International Journal of Advertising*, 26(1), 63–78.

Hui, A. N.-N., Yeung, D. Y. L., Sue-Chan, C., & Cheng, S.-T. (2012). "Team Processing and Creative Self-Efficacy in Professionals from Creative and Non-Creative Industries." Paper presented at the International Symposium on Creativity, Culture and Related Industries: Implication for Greater China Region, Hong Kong.

Jewler, A. J., & Drewniany, B. L. (1998). *Creative Strategy in Advertising* (6th ed.), Belmont, CA: Wadsworth.

Koslow, S., Sasser, S. L., & Riordan, E. A. (2006). "Do Marketers Get The Advertising They Need Or The Advertising They Deserve?: Agency Views Of How Clients Influence Creativity." *Journal of Advertising*, 35(3), 81–101.

Leung, V. S. Y., & Hui, A. N. N. (2014). "A Recent Look: Creative Professionals' Perceptions of Creativity in Hong Kong." *Services Marketing Quarterly*, 35(2), 138–154.

Miniard, P. W., Bhatla, S., Lord, K. R., Dickson, P. R., & Unnava, R. H. (1991). "Picture-Based Persuasion Processes and the Moderating Role of Involvement." Journal of Consumer Research, 18(1), 92–107.

Rudowicz, E. (2004). "Applicability of the Test of Creative Thinking: Drawing Production for Assessing Potential of Hong Kong Adolescents." Gifted Child Quarterly, 48(3), 202–218

Rudowicz, E., & Hui, A. (1997). "The Creative Personality: Hong Kong Perspective." *Journal of Social Behavior and Personality*. 12(1), 139–157.

Sternberg, R. J., Lubart, T. I., Kaufman, J. C., & Pretz, J. E. (2005). "Creativity." in *The Cambridge Handbook Of Thinking And Reasoning*, edited by Holyoak, K. J. and Morrison, R. G., 351–370. Cambridge: Cambridge University Press.

Thamhain, H. J., & Wilemon, D. L. (1975). "Conflict Management in Project Life Cycles." *Sloan Management Review*, 16(3), 31–50.

Triki, A. M., Redjeb, N., & Kamoun, I. (2007). "Exploring the Determinants of Success/Failure of the Advertising Agency-firm Relationship". *Qualitative Market Research*, 10(1), 10–27.

# Chapter 14

## Attitudes towards Advertising

*Kara CHAN*

### Introduction

Overall attitudes towards advertising are important because they affect attitudes towards specific advertisements, and hence consumers' responses to the advertisements. For example, a person who believes that advertising is misleading is unlikely to be convinced by any advertisement. This chapter describes a 2016 study on the attitudes toward advertising in Hong Kong. The study was based on the framework established by Alwitt and Prabhaker (1992) and analyses the perceived functions and consequences of particular advertisements that were used in the local market.

### Framework Introduction and Application to the 2016 Data

According to Alwitt and Prabhaker (1992), attitudes toward advertising have two components: the perceived functions of advertising and the perceived consequences of advertising. The perceived functions of advertising are to: provide information about products and services, enhance consumers' confidence in a purchase, inform consumers about the social image of using a product, and entertain consumers. These functions are called knowledge, buying confidence, social image and entertainment functions, respectively. Moreover, according to Alwitt and Prabhaker's framework the perceived consequences of advertising are: materialistic values, adverse effects on children, economic costs, economic benefits, and consumer manipulation. Using this framework, we conducted a random telephone survey in Hong

**Table 14.1**

**Demographic Profile of the Sample**

| | % of Sample Population |
|---|---|
| **Sex** | |
| Male | 45.1 |
| Female | 54.9 |
| **Age** | |
| 18–29 | 17.6 |
| 30–49 | 36.4 |
| Above 50 | 46.0 |
| **Education** | |
| Primary school or below | 23.7 |
| Secondary school | 48.1 |
| College or university | 28.3 |
| **Residence** | |
| Public housing | 45.1 |
| Home Ownership Scheme housing | 14.3 |
| Private housing | 40.5 |
| **Personal monthly income** | |
| No income/no steady income | 25.1 |
| Under $10,000 | 25.9 |
| $10,000–$19,000 | 25.0 |
| $20,000+ | 24.1 |
| **Occupation** | |
| Professionals/executives | 21.5 |
| Clerical/services | 24.4 |
| Manual workers | 5.8 |
| Students | 8.2 |
| Homemakers | 14.9 |
| Others | 25.3 |

Percentages may not add up to 100% due to rounding.

N=1005

Kong in May and June 2016 to study respondents' opinions about the two criteria as well as government regulation of advertising. The random sample included 1,005 valid cases. The demographic breakdown of the sample is shown in Table 14.1.

Earlier, we had studied public attitudes towards television advertising in Hong Kong using the same framework in 1994 and 2002 (Chan, 1995; Chan, 2006). The 2016 study differed from the two previous studies in three major aspects. First, the 2016 study covered advertising in general while the previous studies covered television advertising only. Second, the 2016 study was based on probability sampling while the previous studies adopted convenience sampling. Third, the convenience samples in the previous studies were obtained by undergraduate students through their social networks and contained a high proportion of young respondents. For example, in the 2002 survey only 4% of the respondents were aged fifty or above. In the 2016 study, the sample contained a much higher proportion (46%) of respondents aged fifty or above. Because of the three major differences, we have not compared the attitudinal questions at the three time points.

## Overall Attitudes toward Advertising

Our study shows that Hong Kong consumers generally hold positive attitudes towards advertising in general (Table 14.2). Forty per cent of respondents considered advertising very good or somewhat good, with only 8% considering it very bad or somewhat bad. Twenty-seven per cent of respondents strongly or somewhat liked advertising and 17% strongly or somewhat disliked it, but the majority (55%) neither liked nor disliked advertising. Overall, the respondents had doubts about advertising. Only 10% found advertising mostly trustworthy, while 36% found advertising absolutely not trustworthy or somewhat not trustworthy.

Compared with the results in Chan (2006) on television advertising, obtained from a sample of younger respondents, the current sample shows a lower level of advertising enjoyment.

## Perceived Functions of Advertising

The frequency distribution, mean and standard deviation of respondents' perceived functions of advertising are summarised in Table 14.3. The

**Table 14.2**

**Overall Attitudes Towards Advertising**

| Question | Year | Very Bad (%) | Somewhat Bad (%) | Neither Good nor Bad (%) | Somewhat Good (%) | Very Good (%) |
|---|---|---|---|---|---|---|
| Overall, do you consider advertising a good or bad thing? | 2016 | 3 | 5 | 51 | 34 | 6 |
| | 2002* | 2 | 15 | 33 | 39 | 11 |

| Question | Year | Strongly Dislike It (%) | Somewhat Dislike It (%) | Neither Like nor Dislike (%) | Somewhat Like It (%) | Strongly Like It (%) |
|---|---|---|---|---|---|---|
| Overall, do you like or dislike advertising? | 2016 | 3 | 14 | 55 | 25 | 2 |
| | 2002* | 2 | 12 | 31 | 45 | 10 |

| Question | Year | Absolutely not Trustworthy (%) | Somewhat not Trustworthy (%) | Half and Half (%) | Mostly Trustworthy (%) | Absolutely Trustworthy (%) |
|---|---|---|---|---|---|---|
| Overall, do you think advertising is trustworthy or not trustworthy? | 2016 | 6 | 30 | 52 | 10 | 0 |

* based on attitudes towards television advertising, from Chan (2006)

Percentages may not add up to 100% due to rounding

majority of respondents (88%) said that advertising provided them with up-to-date information about products and services. Just over two-thirds (68%) considered advertising a main source of information about products and services, and just under two-thirds (64%) thought that advertising could inform them about brand features that they were looking for.

The respondents were neutral about the buying confidence function of advertising. Forty-three per cent disagreed with the statement that people

**Table 14.3**

**Perceived Functions of Advertising**

| Function | Mean* | Standard Deviation (S.D.) | Disagree (%) | Neutral (%) | Agree (%) |
|---|---|---|---|---|---|
| **Knowledge** | | | | | |
| Advertising helps me keep up-to-date about products and services. | 4.1 | 0.7 | 4 | 8 | 88 |
| Advertising is a main source of information about products and services. | 3.6 | 1.0 | 18 | 15 | 68 |
| Advertising tells me which brands have the features I am looking for. | 3.5 | 0.9 | 16 | 20 | 64 |
| **Buying Confidence** | | | | | |
| Advertising helps consumers buy the best brand for the price. | 3.1 | 1.1 | 31 | 23 | 46 |
| If there were no ads, deciding what to buy would be difficult | 3.0 | 1.2 | 40 | 18 | 42 |
| One can put more trust in products seen in ads than in those not in ads | 2.8 | 1.0 | 43 | 30 | 27 |
| **Social Image** | | | | | |
| Ads tell me what people like me are buying and using. | 2.9 | 1.1 | 42 | 22 | 36 |
| Ads help me know which products reflect my personality and taste. | 2.7 | 1.2 | 48 | 21 | 31 |
| From ads, I learn what is in fashion and what I should buy for keeping a good social image. | 2.7 | 1.1 | 50 | 22 | 28 |
| **Entertainment** | | | | | |
| I enjoy some TV commercials. | 3.9 | 0.9 | 10 | 13 | 77 |
| Sometimes I take pleasure in thinking about what I saw in ads | 3.5 | 1.0 | 22 | 17 | 61 |
| Sometimes ads are even more enjoyable than other media content. | 3.2 | 1.0 | 28 | 25 | 47 |

Percentages may not add up to 100% due to rounding

*1=disagree strongly; 5=agree strongly

could put more trust in advertised products than unadvertised products. Forty-two per cent agreed that consumers would have difficulty making buying decisions if there were no advertising, while roughly the same number of respondents (40%) disagreed. However, 46% of the respondents agreed that advertising helped them to get the best buy.

The respondents agreed least with the social image function of advertising. Just over one-third (36%) agreed that advertising informed them about what people like them were buying. Nearly half of them (48%) disagreed with the statement that advertising could inform them about products that reflect their personality and taste. Exactly 50% disagreed with the statement that they could learn from advertising what to buy to give themselves a good social image.

The respondents had a good opinion of the entertainment function of advertising. Most respondents thought that some TV commercials were enjoyable, and 61% took pleasure in thinking about them. Near half of the respondents (47%) believed that sometimes commercials were even more enjoyable than other media content.

## Perceived Consequences of Advertising

The frequency distribution, mean and standard deviation of consumers' perceived consequences of advertising are summarised in Table 14.4. Sixty-one per cent of the respondents believed that advertising promotes materialistic values. Roughly equal numbers agreed and disagreed that advertising causes people to live in a fantasy world or to buy unaffordable products to show off.

One of the criticisms of advertising is its adverse effects on children. Two-thirds (67%) of the respondents thought that advertising led children to pester their parents for unreasonable purchases. Forty-one per cent agreed that advertising encourages children to consume snacks and candies. More than one-third (36%) agreed that advertising takes undue advantage of children.

The respondents felt strongly about the economic costs of advertising. Eighty-six per cent of them agreed that advertising increases the costs of products. Sixty-nine per cent agreed that some advertising budget could be diverted to product improvements. However, near half of the respondents (49%) disagreed with the statement that consumers would be better off if advertising were eliminated.

Regardless of the undesirable economic costs of advertising, this study shows that Hong Kong consumers are aware of its economic benefits. Seventy-

**Table 14.4**

**Perceived Consequences of Advertising**

| Consequence | Mean* | Standard Deviation (S.D.) | Disagree (%) | Neutral (%) | Agree (%) |
|---|---|---|---|---|---|
| **Materialistic Values** | | | | | |
| Advertising encourages materialistic values and fuels people's desires to buy and own things. | 3.5 | 1.2 | 26 | 13 | 61 |
| Advertising sometimes makes people live in a world of fantasy. | 3.0 | 1.2 | 43 | 17 | 40 |
| Advertising makes people buy unaffordable products just to show off. | 3.0 | 1.3 | 43 | 16 | 41 |
| **Adverse Effects on Children** | | | | | |
| Advertising leads children to make unreasonable purchase demands on their parents. | 3.7 | 1.2 | 18 | 15 | 67 |
| Advertising encourages children to eat snacks and candies. | 2.9 | 1.3 | 43 | 15 | 42 |
| Advertising takes undue advantage of children. | 2.9 | 1.2 | 43 | 21 | 36 |
| **Economic Costs** | | | | | |
| Advertising increases the costs of products. | 4.2 | 1.0 | 10 | 4 | 86 |
| It would be better to save money on advertising and invest it in product improvements instead. | 3.8 | 1.1 | 15 | 16 | 69 |
| If advertising were eliminated, consumers would be better off. | 2.8 | 1.1 | 49 | 27 | 24 |
| **Economic Benefits** | | | | | |
| We need advertising to support TV programming. | 3.9 | 0.9 | 8 | 14 | 78 |
| Advertising helps raise the living standard. | 3.1 | 1.1 | 37 | 19 | 44 |
| **Manipulation of Consumers** | | | | | |
| Advertising encourages people to buy what they do not need. | 3.0 | 1.2 | 37 | 21 | 42 |

*1=disagree strongly 5=agree strongly.

eight per cent of the respondents agreed that advertising supports free TV programming. Forty-four per cent of them agreed that advertising helps raise living standards.

Regarding advertising being manipulative, 42% of the respondents agreed that it encourages people to buy what they do not need.

## Opinions on Government-Regulated Advertising

The frequency distribution, mean and standard deviation of the respondents' opinions on the regulations of advertising are summarised in Table 14.5. In general, do Hong Kong people think that advertising content should be under government control? The answer is yes. Eighty-seven per cent of respondents disagreed with removing government control. Seventy-four per cent believed that advertising content should be more closely regulated, and 46% thought a limit should be put on the number of times a TV commercial may be repeated. Forty-seven per cent agreed that advertising should be banned on TV programmes for children.

## Public Attitudes toward Advertising Vary by Demographic

This section presents the results of overall attitudes towards advertising by sex, age, educational level, personal income and type of housing. T-tests were used to evaluate differences in attitudes by sex or by type of housing. ANOVA tests and Duncan pairwise tests were used to uncover differences in attitudes by age, educational level or personal income.

Generally speaking, there were no differences in the perceived trustworthiness of advertising among all demographic groups. Younger respondents neither liked nor disliked advertising in general, while older respondents showed some liking of advertising. Respondents with a personal monthly income above HK$10,000 were more likely to consider advertising a good thing than respondents with no income or respondents whose monthly income was less than $10,000. Respondents residing in private housing were also more likely to consider advertising a good thing than respondents residing in public housing.

**Table 14.5**

**Public Opinions on Government Regulation of Advertising**

| Opinion | Mean | Standard Deviation (S.D.) | Disagree (%) | Neutral (%) | Agree (%) |
|---|---|---|---|---|---|
| Advertising should be free from government control so that advertisers may say what they want to. | 1.7 | 0.9 | 87 | 6 | 7 |
| The government should regulate advertising content more closely. | 3.9 | 1.0 | 12 | 14 | 74 |
| There should be a limit on how many times a TV commercial may be repeated | 3.2 | 1.3 | 36 | 18 | 46 |
| Advertising should be banned on TV programmes for children. | 3.3 | 1.2 | 29 | 24 | 47 |

## Conclusion

To conclude, public attitudes toward advertising in Hong Kong appear to be consistent over time. Most of the respondents were indifferent to advertising. They considered advertising neutral and did not have strong feelings about it. The perceived function of advertising was to provide market information and some entertainment. They strongly believed that advertising leads to cost inflation. They were also concerned about the persuasive effect of advertising on children's purchase requests.

### References

Alwitt, L. F., & Prabhaker, P. R. (1992). "Functional and Belief Dimensions of Attitudes to Television Advertising: Implications for Copytesting." *Journal of Advertising Research*, 32(5), 30–42.

Chan, K. (1995). *Hong Kong Television Advertising: The Good, The Bad and The Ugly*. Hong Kong: Department of Communication Studies, Hong Kong Baptist University.

Chan, K. (2006). "Criticism and Public Opinion of Advertising." in *Advertising and Hong Kong Society*, edited by Chan, K., (77–94). Hong Kong: Chinese University Press.

# Chapter 15

## Public Complaints against Advertising on Licensed Broadcasting Services in Hong Kong

*Maggie S. K. FUNG*

### Introduction

Hong Kong's advertising management system combines aspects of governmental regulation with industry self-regulation (Shaver & An, 2015). Hong Kong has a laissez-faire approach to the advertising industry within the business environment (Chan, 2006). An individual (as a member of the public) who perceives a problem in an advertisement may lodge a complaint (Lawson, 1985). On the other hand, advertisers are under relatively high pressure to reach their potential customers while facing issues like media fragmentation (Douglas, 2002), the explosion of new media (Petty, 1992) and fierce competition in the market (Phillips, 2013). Some advertisers opt for advertising puffs (Lawson, 1985) and exaggerated claims (Greyser, 1972), or even resort to using substantial social issues to sell something trivial (Douglas, 2002). Such advertisements might be considered misleading by consumers and inappropriate by others (Anderson & Cunningham, 1972). This chapter reviews Hong Kong's advertising standards and regulations for licensed broadcasting services, its complaints channel and actual complaints about advertising made to the Communication Authority (CA).

Day (1980) suggests that consumer dissatisfaction acts as a trigger from which the consumer finds the voice to act on their feelings of dissonance. Prior research has established that consumers have three basic options when faced with a dissatisfying consumption experience: bad-mouthing, complaining to the service provider and lodging a complaint with a third party (Singh, 1988).

## Complaint Channel for Licensed Broadcasting Services

In Hong Kong, the main third party for complaints about television and radio advertising is the CA, an independent statutory body whose role is to regulate the broadcasting and telecommunications industries in accordance with a number of Hong Kong ordinances. The CA issues the code of practice with which the Hong Kong advertising industry must comply. It is well known to the public for its regulatory role and there are no other comprehensive channels to gather complaints from about individual advertising media, such as portal sites, social network sites and traditional print and out-of-home media. The CA analyses complaints regularly and produces reports. The comprehensive nature of the code of practice administered by the CA in categorising the complaints it receives provides useful insights and available data. For these reasons, the CA's complaints reports are used for analysis here.

For any complaint lodged against an advertisement with the CA, the complainant should provide sufficient concrete information about the advertisement as soon as possible after it appears because late complaints may not be processed due to the unavailability of the relevant recording (Office of the Communications Authority, 2012).

## Advertising Standards and their Challenges

According to the CA's advertising standards (CA, 2013), television advertising should be legal, clean, honest and truthful. Further, all television advertising material must comply with the laws of Hong Kong, be clearly identified as advertising, be presented in good taste, be without disparagement, be truthful in its presentation, should not imitate the name or advertising slogans of a competitor and should not unduly play on fear. All sponsor involvement must be declared so that the viewer knows who is funding the programme. Standards for advertising on radio are similar. In general, good advertising not only tells the literal truth but also avoids possible deception through subtle implication or omission (Freer, 1949). In most countries, false advertising is illegal. However, many deceptive claims are implicitly manipulative rather than absolutely false (Shanahan & Hopkins, 2007).

In today's fiercely competitive and media convergent market, advertisers go to great lengths to increase the visibility of their products and there is some concern about whether regulatory measures are able to keep up with the dynamic changes and radical transformations of the digital age, especially in terms of the diversity of advertising channels. Online advertising methods, in particular, and the expansion of new communication platforms such as blogs and social media networks have enabled a more accurate and efficient relationship between consumers and advertisers. With consumers keen to be participants in the media process (Hanna et al, 2011), many of their opinions and complaints appear in forums and blogs (Kerr at el, 2012) as well as alongside search engine advertisements (UCPD, 2016). However, these comments and complaints are often scattered.

## Issues Related to Advertising Standards

In Hong Kong, the issues related to advertising standards can be divided into the following categories (Communications Authority, 2013): deception, unacceptable products or services, appeal to fear or exploitation of credulity and advertising to children.

### Deception

Deception refers to consumers making a purchase under the influence of an advertisement which contains one or more of the following:

- claims which involve the use of all-encompassing adjectives or superlatives such as "all", "the best", "the most successful", "the safest" or "the quickest" or project an impression of professional advice and support (e.g., by doctors, dentists or related experts) without the necessary substantiation or approval;
- exaggerations of the special qualities of a product.

### Unacceptable Products or Services

The following are not acceptable in advertisements:

- products or services related to firearms, betting, fortune telling, unlicensed employment services or night clubs;
- tobacco or tobacco-related products;
- treatment of conditions requiring medical attention or encouragement of excessive use of any medical preparation or treatment.

## Appeals to Fear or Exploitation of Credulity

An advertisement should not:
- dramatise distress;
- show a dreadful situation involving sickness;
- suggest that negative consequences may result in not using the product being advertised;
- show a patient receiving treatment which might imply the cure of any condition;
- describe bodily functions or matters which are generally considered not acceptable;
- make derogatory references to a physical or mental affliction.

## Advertising to Children

No products or services that might harm children physically, mentally or morally may be advertised. The method used to advertise to children should not take advantage of their natural credulity. Particular care should be taken in the following areas:
- No advertisement may encourage children to take part in anything that may be dangerous to them.
- There are restrictions on the transmission time of advertisements which are not suitable for children.
- Children in advertisements should be seen as safe, under supervision and well behaved. They should not be associated with medicines, alcoholic drinks or tobacco products.

## An Analysis of Complaints Made to the CA

In 2014 and 2015, the director-general of Communications ("DG Com") who is under the delegated authority of the CA dealt with 11,812 and 6,586 complaints cases, respectively. Of these, 258 and 153 were considered classified complaints, 10,313 and 5,605 were considered unsubstantiated complaints, and 1,241 and 828 were the remaining complaints, respectively. In this study, a total of twenty CA monthly reports released between 2014 and 2015 were selected and used as the source of data for our analysis.

Altogether, seventy of complaint cases filed with the CA were related to advertising: sixteen substantiated and fifty-four unsubstantiated. Table 15.1 shows that thirteen cases were related to the embedding of advertising material within TV and radio programme content and extensive display of sponsorship material. There were two misleading claims in TV commercials, and one case involving children participating in an alcoholic drink advertisement.

In response to the complaints, the CA imposed one financial penalty of $100,000 and issued two serious warnings, two moderate warnings, one strong advice and five moderate advices. The breakdown of the verdicts of the CA on the complaints it dealt with in 2014–15 is summarised in Table 15.2.

Table 15.3 lists the fifty-four unsubstantiated complaints about advertising-related cases of dissatisfaction. Of these, forty-eight cases were classified as unsubstantiated, four cases were found to be outside the remit of the CA, one case was classified as a minor breach and one case was classified as unsubstantiated and outside the remit of the CA. Out of all fifty-four complaints, fifteen of the complaints concerned television advertisements and four concerned radio advertisements. The remaining thirty-five cases were related to television programmes and weather reports.

## Conclusion

In conclusion, the complaints reported about advertising on television and radio were about 0.38% of all complaints lodged to the CA in Hong Kong in 2014 and 2015. The majority of the complaints were related to categories defined as deception, unidentified product placement or sponsor involvement. One was made against advertising to children. However, the figures might not reflect the true situation of Hong Kong consumers' dissatisfaction toward advertising as the number of cases reported to the CA is in fact quite small. Additional complaints may have been expressed via other online platforms, such as social media or discussion forums.

The absence of legislation or regulations for online media and emerging advertising platforms may result in possible gaps in collecting consumer complaints towards advertising. Therefore, an extensive review of advertising regulations applicable to both traditional and online media channels should be developed to integrate the new technologies and make them accountable for providing acceptable advertising to society (Harker, 2008).

**Table 15.1**

**List of Substantiated Complaints Handled by the CA**

| Date | Programme nature | Programme Title | Channel | Substance of complaint | Verdict |
|---|---|---|---|---|---|
| 7 Jun 2013 | Television programme | *Come Home Love* (愛・回家) | Jade and HD Jade Channels of TVB | Indirect advertising | Serious warning issued |
| 8, 15 & 29 Sep 2013 and 6, 13, 20 & 27 Oct 2013 and 22 Sep 2013 | Television programme | *Cook away Lady May* (May姐有請) | Jade and HD Jade Channels of TVB | Indirect advertising | No further action |
| 2–6 & 9–13 Sep 2013 | Television programme | *The Taste of Taipan Snowy Mooncakes Mini 2013* (大班冰皮月餅特約：大班群星添戲Fun) | HD Jade Channel of TVB | Indirect advertising | Penalty of $100,000 |
| 28 Sep 2013 | Television programme | *Dolce Vita* (明珠生活) | HD Jade Channel of TVB | Indirect advertising | No further action |
| 4 Sep 2013 | Television advertisement | Abbott Eye-Q Plus (雅培Eye-Q Plus) | Jade Channel of TVB | Misleading claims | Warning issued |
| 25 Oct 2013 | Television programme | *Will Power* (法外風雲) | Jade and HD Jade Channels of TVB | Indirect advertising | Serious warning issued |
| 23 Jan 2014, and 1 & 4 Feb 2014 | Television advertisement | PARKnSHOP (百佳超級市場) | Jade and HD Jade Channels of TVB | Child participation in an advertisement of alcoholic drinks | Advice issued |
| 15 Mar 2014 | Television programme | *Zhuhai Chimelong Ocean Resort Presents: Mega Missions* (珠海長隆海洋度假區：超級任務) | Jade and HD Jade Channels of TVB | Indirect advertising | No further action |
| 23 Dec 2013 | Television programme | *Tech Biz* (潮玩科技) | Now TV | Indirect advertising | Advice issued |
| 31 Jul 2013 | Television programme | *Dolce Vita* (明珠生活) | HD Jade Channel of TVB | Indirect advertising | Advice issued |
| 17 May 2014 | Television programme | *Cartoon Park* (第一動畫樂園) | CCTV-1 Channel of ATV | Indirect advertising | Advice issued |
| 6 Aug 2014 | Television advertisement | Country Garden —Ten Miles Coast (碧桂園・十里銀灘) | Jade Channel of TVB | Misleading illustrations | Advice issued |
| 13–17 and 20–22 Oct 2014 | Radio programme | *Circles* (1圈圈) | CR1 Channel of Commercial Radio Hong Kong | Indirect advertising | Strong advice issued |
| 2, 7, 16 and 23 Oct 2014 | Television programme | *The Chef's Choice* (天天飲食) | CCTV-1 Channel of ATV | Extensive display of the sponsor's logo | Strong advice issued |
| Jan 2015 | Television advertisement | Dettol Hand Wash (滴露潔手液) and Dettol Shower Gel (滴露沐浴露) | Jade and J2 Channels of TVB | Misleading claims | No sanction |
| 24 Apr 2015 | Radio programme | *The Fun Box* (大玩派) | CR1 Channel of Commercial Radio Hong Kong | Indirect advertising | Warning issued |

**Table 15.2**

**Decisions Made Against Broadcasters 2014–2015**

| Decision of the CA | ATV | TVB | now TV | Commercial Radio Hong Kong | Total |
|---|---|---|---|---|---|
| No further action | 0 | 3 | 0 | 0 | 3 |
| Advice | 1 | 3 | 1 | 0 | 5 |
| Strong advice | 1 | 0 | 0 | 1 | 1 |
| Warning | 0 | 1 | 0 | 1 | 2 |
| Serious warning | 0 | 2 | 0 | 0 | 2 |
| Penalty | 0 | 1 | 0 | 0 | 1 |
| No sanction | 0 | 1 | 0 | 0 | 1 |
| Total | 2 | 11 | 1 | 2 | 16 |

**Table 15.3**

**List of Unsubstantiated Complaints handled by the CA**

| Broadcast Date | Programme Nature | Programme Title | Channel | Substance of Complaint | Verdict |
|---|---|---|---|---|---|
| 23 Aug 2013 | Television programme and weather report | News at six (六點鐘新聞)& Main News and Weather (新聞及天氣報告) | ATV Home, Asia, and World | Unfairness, partiality & indirect advertising | Unsubstantiated |
| 2–4 Sep 2013 | Television advertisement | Asia Club ("亞洲會"廣告) | ATV Home and Asia | Identification of advertising material | Unsubstantiated |
| 20 Aug 2013 | Television programme | *Ombudsman Special* (申訴) | RTHK (TVB Jade) | Political advertising | Unsubstantiated |
| 27 Oct 2013 | Television programme | *Financial Magazine* (財經透視) | TVB Jade | Indirect advertising | Unsubstantiated |
| 4, 11 & 12 Dec 2013 and 5, 12 and 13 Dec 2013 | Television programme | *Bounty Lady* (My盛Lady) | TVB Jade, HD Jade, TVBNV and TVB Encore | Indirect advertising | Unsubstantiated |
| 20 Sep 2013 | Television advertisement | ACE Life Insurance Specials ("安達人壽特約:步步安心"廣告) | TVB HD Jade | Identification of advertising material | Unsubstantiated |
| 10 Nov 2013 | Television programme | *City Forum* (城市論壇) | RTHK (TVB Jade) | Unfairness & indirect advertising | Unsubstantiated |

**Table 15.3 (continued)**

| Broadcast Date | Programme Nature | Programme Title | Channel | Substance of Complaint | Verdict |
|---|---|---|---|---|---|
| 19 Dec 2011 | Television programme | After School (放學 ICU) –Doraemon (多啦A夢) | TVB Jade | Violence & indirect advertising | Unsubstantiated |
| 29 Dec 2011 | Television programme | Dolce Vita (港生活‧港享受) | TVB Pearl | Warning caption blocked | Unsubstantiated |
| 7 Jan 2012 | Television programme | Dolce Vita (明珠生活) | TVB HD Jade | Indirect advertising | Unsubstantiated |
| 10 Jan 2012 | Television programme | Scoop (東張西望) | TVB HD Jade | Indirect advertising | Unsubstantiated |
| 16 Jan 2012 | Television programme | Market Place by Jasons Presents: CNY Specialties (Market Place by Jasons 呈獻：品味迎新春) | TVB HD Jade | Indirect advertising | Unsubstantiated |
| 21 Jan 2012 | Television advertisement | Samsung Galaxy Tab (三星Galaxy Tab廣告) | TVB HD Jade | Horror | Unsubstantiated |
| 22 Jan 2012 | Television programme | Wonder Women (女人 本色) | TVB HD Jade | Indirect advertising | Unsubstantiated |
| 7 Feb 2012 | Television programme | Putonghua E-News (普通話娛樂新聞報道) | TVB Pearl | Poor visual quality & indirect advertising | Unsubstantiated |
| 11 Jul 2013 | Television programme | IVE & SBI Student Recruitment Campaign (IVE特約: 放榜星級攻略) | TVB HD Jade | Indirect advertising | Unsubstantiated |
| 14 Dec 2013 | Television programme | Symphony under the Stars (港樂‧星夜‧交響曲2013) | RTHK (ATV World) | Indirect advertising | Unsubstantiated |
| 8 Feb 2014 | Television programme | Dolce Vita (明珠生活) | TVB HD Jade | Indirect advertising | Unsubstantiated |
| 17 Feb 2014 | Television advertisement | Max Chateau Swallow Nest Beverage (大棧有機冰糖燕窩) | TVB Jade | Misleading claim | Unsubstantiated |
| 6 Mar 2014 | Television programme | Pretty Soup Brewers (靚人靚湯) | TVB HD Jade | Indirect advertising | Unsubstantiated |
| 13 Mar 2014 | Television programme | Dolce Vita (明珠生活) | TVB HD Jade | Indirect advertising | Unsubstantiated |

## Table 15.3 (continued)

| Broadcast Date | Programme Nature | Programme Title | Channel | Substance of Complaint | Verdict |
|---|---|---|---|---|---|
| 4 Apr 2014 and 23 May 2014 | Radio advertisement | "Perfect Shape" (必瘦站) | Metro Finance | Insult | Unsubstantiated |
| 22 Jan 2014 and 14 Feb 2014 | Radio advertisement | "Perfect Shape" (必瘦站) | Metro Finance | Denigration & frequency of broadcast | Unsubstantiated & outside the remit of the CA respectively |
| 28 Mar 2014 | Radio advertisement | "Perfect Shape" (必瘦站) | Metro Radio | Contravention of the Disability Discrimination Ordinance | Outside the remit of the CA |
| 25 Apr 2014 | Radio advertisement | "Perfect Shape" (必瘦站) | Metro Finance | Discrimination | Outside the remit of the CA |
| 1, 4, 5 & 8 May 2014 | Television programme | *Travel Expert* ("專業旅運"廣告) | TVB I News | Wrong information in illustration | Minor breach |
| 2 Apr 2014 | Television programme | *Dolce Vita* (明珠生活) | TVB HD Jade | Indirect advertising | Unsubstantiated |
| Apr–Jun 2014 | Television advertisement | BetadineDry Powder Spray (必妥碘乾粉噴霧消毒劑"廣告) | TVB Jade, HD Jade & I News | Disturbing content | Unsubstantiated |
| 12 Dec 2013; 22 Dec 2013 and 9 Mar 2014; 12 Mar 2014 | Television programme | *The Green Room* (今日 VIP), *Jade Solid Gold* (勁歌金曲) & *Extra* (娛樂頭條) | TVB Jade | Indirect advertising | Unsubstantiated |
| 18–20 Feb 2014 | Television programme | *Welcome to the House* (高朋滿座) | TVB Jade | No sponsorship identification | Unsubstantiated |
| 25 Feb and 5 Mar 2014 | Television programme | *Welcome to the House* (高朋滿座) | TVB Jade | No sponsorship identification | Unsubstantiated |
| 5 Apr 2014 | Television advertisement | Lee Kum Kee Soy Sauce ("李錦記醬油"廣告) | TVB Jade & HD Jade | Misleading claim | Unsubstantiated |
| 12–15 May 2014 | Television programme | *Go! Yama Girl* | TVB J2 | No sponsorship identification | Unsubstantiated |
| 19–22 May 2014 | Television programme | *Go! Yama Girl* | TVB J3 | No sponsorship identification | Unsubstantiated |
| 26–29 May 2014 | Television programme | *Go! Yama Girl* | TVB J4 | No sponsorship identification | Unsubstantiated |

**Table 15.3 (continued)**

| Broadcast Date | Programme Nature | Programme Title | Channel | Substance of Complaint | Verdict |
|---|---|---|---|---|---|
| 2 Jun 2014 | Television programme | *Shatin Dragon Boat Races 2014* (甲午年沙田龍舟競渡) | TVB Jade | Indirect advertising & non-programme material | Unsubstantiated |
| 2–5 Jun 2014 | Television programme | *Go! Yama Girl* | TVB J2 | No sponsorship identification | Unsubstantiated |
| 13 Aug 2014 | Television programme | *Koi Kei Bakery Special: The Olden Days And New Age of Macau* (澳門鉅記餅家呈獻：細味時代的巨輪) | TVB Jade | Indirect advertising | Unsubstantiated |
| 16 Aug 2014 | Television programme | *Dolce Vita* (明珠生活) | TVB HD Jade | Indirect advertising | Unsubstantiated |
| 1 Sep 2014 | Television advertisement | Leading brands of the world timepieces (細說名牌名錶匯) | TVB Pearl | Indistinguishable advertisement | Unsubstantiated |
| 13 & 14 Mar 2014 | Television advertisement | Unleash Your Creativity ("2014打開創意天空" 宣傳片) | TVB HD Jade | Non-implementation of conditions of competition | Outside the remit of the CA |
| – | Television advertisement | Advertising on Pay TV | now TV | Objection to placement of advertisements | Outside the remit of the CA |
| 11 Jun 2014 | Television advertisement | Fancl F&H Health Supplements ("Fancl F&H營養補充品" 廣告) | TVB HD Jade | Misleading claim | Unsubstantiated |
| 22 Jun 2014 | Television programme | *Dolce Vita* (明珠生活) | TVB HD Jade | Indirect advertising | Unsubstantiated |
| 17 Sep 2014 | Television programme | News at six (六點鐘新聞) | ATV Home & Asia | Indirect advertising | Unsubstantiated |
| 5, 6 & 9 Sep 2014; and 16, 26 & 28 Sep, 12 and 13 Oct 2014 | Television advertisement | Leading brands of the world timepieces ("細說 名牌名錶匯") | TVB HD Jade & I News | Identification of advertising material | Unsubstantiated |

**Table 15.3 (continued)**

| Broadcast Date | Programme Nature | Programme Title | Channel | Substance of Complaint | Verdict |
|---|---|---|---|---|---|
| 29 Sep 2014 | Television programme | *Hong Kong Connection* (鏗鏘集) | RTHK (TVB Jade) | Partiality, illegal act & political advertising | Unsubstantiated |
| 3 Nov 2014 | Television programme | *Hong Kong Connection* (鏗鏘集) | RTHK (TVB Jade) & RTHK TV 31 | Partiality, illegal act & unsuitable for children | Unsubstantiated |
| 18 Nov 2014 | Television programme | *Metropolitan Consumers* (消費新潮) | RTHK (TVB Jade) | Indirect advertising | Unsubstantiated |
| 15 & 16 Dec 2014 | Television advertisement | Eu Yan Sang ("余仁生"廣告) | TVB Jade and HD Jade; TVBNV TVB Encore; & Cable News | Animal abuse & violence | Unsubstantiated |
| 28 Dec 2014 | Television programme | *Noon Edition* (午間通訊) | Cable News | Political Advertising | Unsubstantiated |
| Jun 2015 | Television advertisement | PPS ("繳費靈"廣告) | TVB Jade, HD Jade, J2 & I News | Horror, Superstition & Bad Influence On Young People | Unsubstantiated |
| Jun 2015 | Television advertisement | Prudential Insurance ("英國保誠保險"廣告) | TVB Jade, HD Jade & Pearl | Disturbing & Discrimination | Unsubstantiated |
| Jun–Aug 2015 | Television advertisement | Broadway (百老匯廣告) | TVB HD Jade, I News & J2 | Indecent & Disturbing Material | Unsubstantiated |

# References

Anderson, W. T., Jr., & Cunningham, W. H. (1972). "The Socially Conscious Consumer." *Journal of Marketing*, 36(3), 23–31.

Chan, K. (2006). *Advertising and Hong Kong Society*. Hong Kong: Chinese University Press.

Communications Authority. (2013). "Generic Code of Practice on Television Advertising Standards". Retrieved from http://www.coms-auth.hk/filemanager/common/policies_regulations/cop/code_tvad_e.pdf.

Day, R. L. (1980). "Research Perspectives on Consumer Complaining Behavior." in *Theoretical Developments in Marketing*, edited by Lamb, C. W. and Dunne, P. M., 211–5. Chicago, IL: American Marketing Association.

Douglas, T. (2002). "The Case for the Self-regulation of Broadcast Advertising — on the ASA model — Is Persuasive". *Marketing Week*, 17–18.

European Commission. (2016). "Unfair Commercial Practices Directive". *A Comprehensive Approach to Stimulating Cross-border e-Commerce for Europe's Citizens and Business*. Retrieved from http://ec.europa.eu/justice/consumer-marketing/files/ucp_guidance_en.pdf.

Freer, R. E. (1949). "Informative and Non Deceptive Advertising". *Journal of Marketing*, 13(3), 358–63.

Greyser, S. A. (1972). "Advertising: Attacks and Counters". *Harvard Business Review*, 50(2), 22–8.

Hanna, R., Rohm, A., and Crittenden, V. L. (2011). "We're All Connected: The Power of the Social Media Ecosystem". *Business Horizons*, 54, 265–73.

Harker, D. (2008). "Regulating Online Advertising: The Benefit of Qualitative Insights." *Qualitative Market Research: An International Journal*, 11(3), 295–315.

Kerr, G., Mortimer, K., Dickinson, S., and Waller, D. S. (2012). "Buy, Boycott or Blog: Exploring Online Consumer Power to Share, Discuss and Distribute Controversial Advertising Messages." *European Journal of Marketing*, 46(4), 387–405.

Lawson, R. W. (1985). "An Analysis of Complaints about Advertising." *International Journal of Advertising*, 4(4), 279–95.

Office of the Communications Authority. (2012). "The Broadcast Complaint Handling Procedures of the Communications Authority". Retrieved from http://www.coms-auth.hk/filemanager/en/content_508/complaint_handling_e.pdf.

Petty, R. D. (1992). *The Impact of Advertising Law on Business and Public Policy*. Westport, CT: Quorum Books.

Phillips, A. (2013). "Journalism, Ethics and the Impact of Competition." In *Ethics of Media*, edited by Couldry, N., Madianou, M. and Pinchevski, A. (255–70). London: Palgrave Macmillan.

Shanahan, K. J., & Hopkins, C. D. (2007). "Truths, Half-truths, and Deception: Perceived Social Responsibility and Intent to Donate for a Nonprofit using Implicature, Truth, and Duplicity in Print Advertising." *Journal of Advertising*, 36(2), 33–48.

Shaver, M. A., & An, S. (2015). *The Global Advertising Regulation Handbook*. Abingdon: Routledge.

Singh, J. (1988). "Consumer Complaint Intentions and Behavior: Definitional and Taxonomical Issues." *Journal of Marketing*, 52(1), 93–107.

# Part V
Communication & Society

# Chapter 16

# Media and Populations in Hong Kong

*Tien Ee Dominic YEO*

## Introduction

Hong Kong has long positioned itself as "Asia's world city" because of its unique history as a former British colony and more recent transformation into a special administrative region (SAR) of China. That nearly 93% of its population is ethnic Chinese belies the diversity of the SAR's 7.32 million residents (Young, 2013). In this chapter, some populations of the SAR—sexual minorities, ethnic minorities, youth and the elderly—are examined in terms of their relationship with both traditional and new media over the last decade.

## The Media and Sexual Minorities in Hong Kong

LGBT (lesbian, gay, bisexual and transgender) individuals are considered sexual minorities in most societies, constituting about 5% to 10% of any population (Vernon & Yik, 2012). There are no official numbers of LGBT individuals in Hong Kong. While homosexual acts between men were decriminalised in Hong Kong in 1991, there have been few efforts to accord legal recognition to same-sex relationships or protect LGBT individuals against discrimination. The courts did not recognise the same age of consent for both homosexuals and heterosexuals until 2006 (Ma, Woo & Tang, 2006). There is no law against discrimination on the basis of sexual orientation in Hong Kong due to strong resistance and political pressure from social conservatives, especially evangelical Christians.

According to a study by the Home Affairs Bureau in 2006, the LGBT community is not generally accepted by the Hong Kong public. It found that nearly half of the participants believed that homosexuality is psychologically abnormal (*Survey on Public Attitudes*, 2006). Even medical students in Hong Kong, the territory's future healthcare providers, might not be as scientifically informed as they should be, as approximately 25% of the 780 medical student respondents to a survey endorsed the notion that homosexuality is a disorder and that therapy for gays and lesbians is needed (Hon et al., 2005) Homosexuality is now considered an alternative lifestyle occurring with some regularity as a variant of human sexuality, rather than a pathological disorder. It is important to understand the attitudes of medical professionals toward homosexuality, as their attitudes may influence their approach to gay men and lesbians as patients. It is also important to understand the current attitudes of medical students who will be the future generation of health care providers. These studies suggest that LGBT individuals in Hong Kong remain largely misunderstood by society.

The social stigma against homosexuality in Hong Kong is exacerbated by the media's negative portrayal of LGBT individuals and issues. LGBT characters have low visibility in local mainstream media and films. When gay men and women do appear in local television programmes or films, they are often represented as distorted, pathologised or voyeuristic (Wong, 2005). Such depictions conjure a negative image of LGBT people and perpetuate public misconceptions about homosexuality, bisexuality and transgenderism.

One of the reasons the local media avoid LGBT issues and characters could be that they expect public controversy to ensue. In July 2006, a Radio Television Hong Kong television documentary, *Tongzhi Lovers* (Tongzhi (同志) is a slang term for "homosexual"), received a stern warning from the Broadcasting Authority after complaints from Christian viewers. The Authority ruled that Tongzhi Lovers was "partial and biased towards homosexuality", "unsuitable for broadcast within family viewing hours" and "promoting [of] acceptance of homosexual marriage" (Tang, 2011). It is unsurprising that broadcasters have tended to shy away from depicting LGBT rights and movements since then.

Another media avenue for public exposure to LGBT issues in Hong Kong is gossip magazines, which have played a dual role of both stereotyping and normalising the image of LGBT groups. They gather details of celebrities' quotidian activities and flamboyantly publish them. Some of these stories have forced LGBT celebrities to come out. Also, the public learn about LGBT lives through such coverage. However, Tang (2006) noted that some media workers "grasped every opportunity to report on lesbian relationships" and intentionally adopted a sensationalist perspective. This kind of coverage, with its eye-catching headlines, affects LGBT groups.

Further contributing to the negative image of LGBT people, the media often associate gay men with sexually transmitted infections (STIs). For example, when reporting the infection rate of HIV, the *South China Morning Post* (*SCMP*) used the headline "'Record-breaking numbers' of HIV cases recorded in Hong Kong as gay men still at highest risk" ("Record-breaking numbers", 2013). To be sure, men who have sex with men (MSM) are more susceptible to HIV infection than their heterosexual counterparts. In 2015, data from the Hong Kong Centre for Health Protection indicated that 53% of new cases of HIV infection were from homosexual contact, whereas only 19% were from heterosexual contact. Nonetheless, the singling out of gay men in the news headlines perpetuates the stereotypical link between HIV and gay men. The resulting stigma directly correlates with delays in testing and initiation of treatment (White & Carr, 2005). It is therefore important for the public to understand that "homosexuality" is not a synonym for HIV and other STIs, not least because misunderstanding the facts gives a false sense of security to non-homosexuals and reinforces stigma and discrimination.

Unlike traditional media, the internet and social networking sites (SNS) present a more socially accessible platform for gay and bisexual men to connect with each other (Baams, Jonas, Utz, Bos & van der Vuurst, 2011; Crowson & Goulding, 2013; Miller, 2015). With features such as anonymity, which may enable greater security and control for users, SNS allow gay and bisexual men to overcome the difficulties of making social connections in unmediated contexts (McKenna & Bargh, 1998; Miller, 2015). The recent rise of location-aware, social networking mobile applications (apps)—such as Grindr and Jack'd—which were created specifically for gay users, further affords a convenient means for gay and bisexual men to locate nearby users with similar relational and sexual preferences (Blackwell, Birnholtz & Abbott, 2015; Miller, 2015; Race, 2015). These affordances, however, have also raised public health concerns about SNS's role in the spread of HIV and other STIs among MSM. A recent study found that the percentage of young MSM—the most-at-risk group for HIV infection in Hong Kong (Yeo & Fung, 2016)—who reported consistent condom use during recent sexual encounters with app-met partners were considerably lower than the general MSM population in Hong Kong (Yeo & Ng, 2016). As for lesbians, their choices are more limited, since there is only one local mobile phone application, called Butterfly, targeting the Hong Kong lesbian community. However, Tang (2015) pointed out that it is important to have apps with local sensibilities and mobile use because social networking will continue to be popular among Hong Kong lesbians.

## The Media and Ethnic Minorities in Hong Kong

The media-related issues faced by LGBT people in Hong Kong are not unique to sexual minorities. Ethnic minorities in the city also experience similar negative media coverage.

Hong Kong has a complex demographic composition. Besides locals who have been living in the city for generations, workers and immigrants from all over the world also live in the city. The term "ethnic minorities" in Hong Kong usually refers to people of South or Southeast Asian origin. Owing to their socio-economic status, Caucasians are typically considered "expatriates" instead of minorities. According to 2011 census, there were more than 451,000 Indonesians, Filipinos, Indians, Pakistanis, Nepalese and other ethnic minorities in Hong Kong, constituting 6.4% of the population. These ethnic minorities in Hong Kong have increased by more than 30% over the past ten years. The majority (75.8%) of the working ethnic minorities were engaged in "elementary occupations," such as domestic work ("Thematic report", 2012).

The media shape people's understanding of the ethnic groups they report on. In a highly diversified society like Hong Kong, the media should shoulder the responsibility of building social relations and deepening mutual understanding. A 2004 survey conducted by the Hong Kong Polytechnic University (Ku, Chan & Sandhu, 2006) revealed that only a quarter of Hong Kong Chinese respondents thought racial discrimination existed in Hong Kong, yet more than 60% admitted to having negative impressions of ethnic minorities. About 40% of the respondents came to their conclusion based on the image of ethnic minorities in the media rather than empirical experience. The survey also revealed that around 41% of the respondents had no acquaintances who belong to an ethnic minority.

The respondents' negative impression of ethnic minorities is closely related to media coverage in terms of the tone used or the subject of stories. While the voices of ethnic minorities are seldom heard in the public sphere, their mention in the media is often related to negative incidents, such as criminal activity, which reinforces public stereotypes. Nevertheless, press coverage is not exclusively negative. News reports have also highlighted the problems faced by ethnic minorities in, for example, learning Chinese, opening bank accounts and obtaining Hong Kong SAR passports. Unfortunately, the recent international media spotlight on "fake refugees" has once again deepened resentment against ethnic minorities in Hong Kong.

The Hong Kong media often portray ethnic minorities in stereotypical menial roles. The racial stereotyping of ethnic minorities in advertisements and school textbooks undermines multicultural harmony in Hong Kong. The positioning of Hong Kong as "Asia's world city", where multiculturalism is embedded, faces increasing conflict with the government's drive to instill ethnic nationalism instead of civic nationalism into Hong Kong people.

## Media Related Issues among Two Age Groups

Media related issues and problems are not limited to minorities. Here, examine two age groups—the young and the elderly— and reveal some problems they face related to the internet.

### The Youth

*Internet Addiction*

According to telecommunications statistics published by the Office of the Communications Authority, more than 80% of the population of Hong Kong has access to the internet, while the local mobile penetration rate exceeded 230%, with over 15.4 million 2.5G/3G/4G mobile subscribers in June 2016 ("Hong Kong internet", n.d.).

A problem that has arisen out of these developments in the last decade is addiction to the internet and its derivatives. Growing numbers of people are spending an excessive amount of time on their computers, tablets and smartphones. Pedestrians who walk along focused on their smartphones without paying attention to the environment are called "smartphone zombies". They "wander the streets, shopping malls and Mass Transit Railway (MTR) corridors, heads down" and seem "oblivious to the world around them" ("Beware the smartphone zombies", 2015). The media in Hong Kong regularly remind people not to gaze at or type on their phones when walking. The

MTR, one of the major means of public transportation in Hong Kong, also changed its announcement for passengers using escalators a few years ago to remind them to not keep your eyes only on their mobile phones in order to prevent accidents and injuries.

Internet addiction is recognised as a newly emergent disorder, which is associated with substance use disorder, attention-deficit hyperactivity disorder, depression, hostility and social anxiety disorder (Ko, Yen, Yen, Chen & Chen, 2012). The process of using digital devices generates neurotransmitters that produce feelings of pleasure. Absence of the substances makes people feel unsafe and uncomfortable, which causes distress (Weinstein & Lejoyeux, 2010), urges or behaviours regarding computer use and internet access that lead to impairment or further distress. Currently, internet addiction is not recognized within the spectrum of addictive disorders and, therefore, no corresponding diagnosis can be made. It has, however, been proposed for inclusion in the next version of the Diagnostic and Statistical Manual of Mental Disorder (DSM). Addiction to the internet has much to do with the popularity of social networking sites such as Facebook. "Facebook" exceeded "Yahoo", "Google", "YouTube" and "Apple" to become the most Googled word in Hong Kong in the first half of 2011 (Cheung, 2011). Hong Kong's social media penetration rate reached 61% in 2015, the second highest in the Asia Pacific region, with an average browsing time of more than two hours per day ("Social media usage", 2015). More than 90% of the online population has access to Facebook. Social networking accounts for 28% of all media time spent online ("Social media usage", 2015).

Internet addiction is particularly serious among teenagers. Shek, Tang and Lo (2008) reported that around 40% of the adolescents who participated in their survey assessed themselves as "addicted to the internet". A three-year longitudinal study conducted by Yu and Shek (2013) collected data from twenty-eight secondary schools in Hong Kong. Using a ten-item test, they revealed that more than 20% of the participants met the criterion of internet addiction, with male students showing more problematic internet use behaviour than female students.

It may be useful to compare the situations in Hong Kong and South Korea. In South Korea internet addiction is considered one of the most serious public health issues. The government estimated that in 2006, around 210,000 South Korean children (ages 6–19) suffered from the addiction. To address the problem, the government trained more than a thousand counsellors specifically to provide treatment for internet addiction by 2007 and also started to introduce preventive measures in schools (Block, 2008). Support for internet-addicted students in Hong Kong is not as well developed as in South Korea. It is basically provided by social workers and counsellors at schools, who have to deal with a host of problems besides internet addiction. More help should be provided for addicts and at-risk individuals. Further, schools and the government could organise workshops and other activities to promote positive youth development and family bonding, which could help prevent internet abuse by youth (Yu & Shek, 2013).

### Cyberbullying

Computers and smartphones have become easily available to teenagers in recent years. The popularity of electronic devices has given rise to a new form of bullying. Cyberbullying (or electronic bullying) is "an aggressive, intentional act carried out by a group or individual, using electronic forms of contact, repeatedly and over time against a victim who cannot easily defend him or herself" (Smith et al., 2008). Cyberbullies disseminate aggression and enmity through email, instant messages, text messages and social network platforms, such as Facebook, Twitter or Weibo. The victims of cyberbullying frequently suffer from psychosocial problems, such as emotional distress or, in extreme cases, mental disorders (Schneider, O'Donnell, Stueve & Coulter, 2011).

The Hong Kong Christian Service's Happy Teens Club conducted a survey on Hong Kong teenagers' experience of cyberbullying in 2009. They targeted local Primary 4 to Form 6 students and received 908 responses. The results indicate that 18% of the respondents had been victims of cyberbullying while 13% had actually been cyberbullies. The top three common bullying acts on the internet reported by the participants were laughing at the victims, spreading rumours about them and forwarding photos, videos or sound clips to embarrass them ("Close to 2%", 2009). The severity and frequency of cyberbullying have continued to surge in recent years. Studies conducted by The Hong Kong Federation of Youth Groups in 2010 indicated that 30.2% of secondary students had been victims and 22% had been bullies (Wong, 2010). The figures of victims and bullies, respectively, increased to 47.3% and 37.2% in 2013, when 5.3% had very frequently been cyberbullying victims and 4.0% had very frequently engaged in bullying (Leung & McBride-Chang, 2013).

The widespread nature of cyberbullying has raised awareness of it. Local media frequently cover the issue and urge the authorities to take measures against it. For example, columnists in the *SCMP* have discussed in detail why cyberbullying is a serious issue and what parents can do to help their children (Lee, 2015). However, the government is slow to regulate cyberbullying. Also, the police do not keep any statistics of cyberbullying acts ("Cyber-bullying", 2012). There could be more victims of cyberbullying than has been reported. More help for those suffering from this form of abuse is warranted.

## The Elderly

### *Accessibility of the Internet to Senior Citizens*

According to statistics released by the government's demographic statistics section, 16% of the city's population was older than sixty-five in 2016, and the percentage of people in this age group will keep rising (Census and Statistic Department, 2016). Studies have revealed that senior citizens have a significantly lower internet use rate than the young and the middle-aged. In 2013, the internet use rate for people aged over sixty-five was merely 18% while the overall rate was 74.2% (Kwong, 2015).

The internet enables easier access to information and social services and shortens the distance between family and friends. Frequent connection to the internet promotes mental and physical health (Newell, 2011), and can enrich the lives of senior citizens. Internet use rates for those aged above 65 were 59% in the United States, 46% in Australia and 42% in the United Kingdom, much higher than that in Hong Kong (Kwong, 2015).

As Kwong (2015) noted, the usual reasons for internet browsing are not as important for senior citizens as younger people. The older folk using the internet are generally reading online news and communicating, mostly by receiving and sending emails. One reason for their not being frequently connected to the internet is that they lack motivation. Many senior citizens do not have the need to use it, nor do they gain gratification from it, giving them little motivation to go online. They will not be gratified unless they grasp the functions of the internet and its accessories, and outside forces are needed to change this cycle if the government wants to encourage senior citizens to take part in online activities.

This problem is compounded by the fact that older people are much less likely to have physical and material access to computers and the internet compared to other age groups. Academics have urged the government and support organisations to provide computers and internet services that are affordable for seniors in order to tackle these physical and material concerns. It has been suggested that the elderly and young people should "work together more", for instance by "bringing senior citizens onto university campuses" so that students can learn from the senior citizens' experience, while the senior citizens can get better access to new technologies and lifestyles (Balakrishnan, 2016).

## A Survey on Public Attitudes toward Homosexuality

In the above sections, we have introduced a variety of issues related to the media in Hong Kong. To gain a better understanding of current public attitudes toward homosexuality and the influence of the media, we commissioned a phone survey, which was conducted between 10 June 2016 and 28 June 2016. It targeted Hong Kong citizens aged eighteen and above. The response rate was 70.6%. A total of 1,008 participants aged between eighteen and ninety-four completed the survey. Among them 455 were male (45.1%) and 553 were female (54.9%). When asked about their sexual orientation, 993 of them identified themselves as heterosexual (92.6%) while 39 participants (3.9%) identified themselves as homosexual (n=12) or bisexual (n=27). Thirty-six participants refused to answer the question (3.5%).

One of the aims of the phone survey was to examine local attitudes toward and acceptance of homosexuality. Three items were used to measure attitudes. The participants were asked to what extent they agreed with the following statements:

- Sex between two men or two women is just plain wrong.
- Homosexuality is abnormal.
- Homosexuality is a natural expression of sexuality in men/women.

The items were measured on a scale of 1 to 5 (with 1 being strongly disagree and 5 being strongly agree). After recoding, the mean scores of the items were used to calculate their attitude toward homosexuality. A higher score indicated a more positive attitude toward homosexuality. Then, the participants were asked to what extent they would accept the following situations:

- Working with gay men or lesbians.
- Being friends with gay men or lesbians.
- Having a homosexual family member.

**Table 16.1**

**Descriptive Statistics of Acceptance of Homosexuality in Hong Kong**

|  | Totally Unacceptable | Unacceptable | Neutral | Acceptable | Totally Acceptable |
|---|---|---|---|---|---|
| Working with gay men or lesbians | 41 (4.1%) | 31 (3.1%) | 91 (9.2%) | 535 (53.9%) | 294 (29.6%) |
| Being friends with gay men or lesbians | 56 (5.7%) | 65 (6.6%) | 107 (10.8%) | 516 (52.2%) | 244 (24.7%) |
| Having a homosexual family member | 222 (23.0%) | 203 (21.1%) | 151 (15.7%) | 311 (32.3%) | 76 (7.9%) |

The items were measured on a scale of 1 to 5 (with 1 being totally unacceptable and 5 being totally acceptable), and the mean score of the items was used to present their acceptance of homosexuality. A higher score indicated higher acceptance of homosexuality. The results suggest that Hong Kong citizens generally have a neutral to positive attitude toward homosexuality, with a similar result for acceptance of homosexuality. The mean score of their attitude toward homosexuality is 3.24 (SD=1.00) and the mean score of their acceptance of homosexuality is 3.57 (SD=0.94).

The level of acceptance changed according to the relationship with the homosexual individual (Table 16.1). While 83.5% and 76.9% of the participants accept that they can work with and be friends with gay men or lesbians, respectively, only 40.3% of the participants accepted having a gay or lesbian family member.

Our findings suggest that age correlates significantly with both attitudes toward and acceptance of homosexuality in Hong Kong. The results of our Pearson's correlation analysis indicate that age has a negative, weak correlation with attitude toward homosexuality (r=−.26, p<.01) and a negative, moderate correlation with acceptance of homosexuality (r=−.45, p<.01), which means that older people tend to have a more negative attitude toward and are less accepting of gay men and lesbians.

Although it seems that Hong Kong people nowadays have a more positive attitude towards these groups, they only have limited real life exposure to homosexual individuals, which could limit their understanding of LGBT

**Table 16.2**

**Frequency of Exposure to Homosexual Content
in Local Traditional Media and Social Media**

|  | Never | Seldom | Sometimes | Often | Very Often |
|---|---|---|---|---|---|
| Local traditional media | 140 (14.2%) | 368 (37.3%) | 425 (43.1%) | 47 (4.8%) | 6 (0.6%) |
| Social media | 173 (23.8%) | 305 (42.1%) | 178 (24.5%) | 62 (8.5%) | 8 (1.1%) |

issues. Within the 1,008 participants, only 386 (38.3%) reported having gay or bisexual friends or co-workers. The majority of these participants (n=199, 51.2%) revealed that they have only one or two gay or bisexual friends and co-workers. In fact, having real life contact with homosexual individuals appears to influence their attitude. Independent sample T-tests show a significant difference between the attitudes of participants who have gay friends or co-workers and those who do not. Individuals who have contact with gay or bisexual people have a more positive attitude towards them than those who do not (M having contact = 3.45, M no contact = 3.10; t (872) = 5.16, p<.05) and a higher acceptance of them (M having contact = 4.00, M no contact = 3.27; t (928) = 12.63, p<.05).

As mentioned above, local mass media provide some of the sources of information from which people learn about homosexual individuals, yet most of the participants who used local traditional media (n=987) indicated that they seldom or never saw homosexual content (51.5%), and 425 of them (43.1%) indicated that they only sometimes saw homosexual content in local mass media (Table 16.2). Even in social media, with its new platforms for online interaction and information exchange, local people receive limited information about homosexuality. Of the 726 participants who reported using social media such as Facebook the majority (65.9%) stated that they seldom or never saw information about homosexuality on those platforms. Only 24.5% of them stated that they were exposed to homosexual content on social media. We can conclude that homosexuals still have limited media exposure, both on local traditional media and social media.

Two key concerns of the LGBT group are introducing anti-discrimination laws to protect the group and legalising same-sex marriage. We asked whether

**Table 16.3**

**Support of Anti-discrimination Laws and Same Sex Marriage**

|  | Strongly Against | Against | Neutral | Support | Strongly Support |
|---|---|---|---|---|---|
| Anti-discrimination laws | 64 (6.6%) | 78 (8.1%) | 336 (34.6%) | 302 (31.1%) | 190 (19.6%) |
| Same-sex marriage | 230 (23.4%) | 157 (16%) | 273 (27.8%) | 221 (22.5%) | 101 (10.3%) |

**Table 16.4**

**Correlations between Homosexuality Content Exposure, Attitudes and Acceptance**

|  | 1 | 2 | 3 | 4 | 5 | 6 |
|---|---|---|---|---|---|---|
| Local traditional media | – | – | – | – | – | – |
| Social media | .332** | – | – | – | – | – |
| Attitude | .037 | .170** | – | – | – | – |
| Acceptance | .282** | .302** | .451** | – | – | – |
| Anti-discrimination laws | .142** | .246** | .498** | .494** | – | – |
| Same-sex marriage | .172** | .281** | .603** | .586** | .570** | – |

**Correlation is significant at the 0.01 level (2-tailed).

the participants supported anti-discrimination laws for LGBT people and same-sex marriage in Hong Kong. More than half of them (50.7%) supported anti-discrimination laws for LGBT, but more participants were against same-sex marriage (39.4%) than for it (32.8%) (Table 16.3).

Table 16.4 shows the correlations between the variables. These suggest that exposure to homosexuality related content on both local traditional media and social media have positive, significant correlations with acceptance and support for anti-discrimination laws and same-sex marriage, but only exposure to homosexuality-related content on social media has a positive, significant correlation with attitudes toward homosexuality.

## Conclusion

This chapter discussed media-related issues and problems that are faced by some minority populations in Hong Kong. Although compared with the past decades, it seems that contemporary society in general holds a more positive and accepting attitude toward gay men and lesbians, the public still have limited exposure to LGBT issues given the lack of coverage in the local media. Nevertheless, with the rise of social media, there are more opportunities for LGBT individuals to connect with each other and possibly raise public awareness of LGBT issues. It should be noted that texts highlighted in this chapter focus on gay men and lesbians, as there is little literature that covers bisexual and transgender people. Nevertheless, readers can still gain insights into LGBT issues as a whole.

Despite its legalisation in various countries (for example, the United States, Canada and many countries in Western Europe), same-sex marriage has gained little support in Hong Kong. Religion is one of the key factors underlying the opposition to same-sex marriage. Traditional Chinese values, especially the emphasis on the importance of having a male offspring to continue the family line, also contribute to the resistance. These factors are formidable barriers against any move towards legalising same-sex marriage in Hong Kong. Furthermore, the negative portrayal of LGBT people in the media perpetuates misconceptions and the significance of marriage equality for them. This chapter also described problems that youths, elderly people and ethnic minorities in Hong Kong are facing, more attention to such problems is needed by both the public and government.

## References

Baams, L., Jonas, K. J., Utz, S., Bos, H. M. W., & van der Vuurst, L. (2011). "Internet Use and Online Social Support among Same Sex Attracted Individuals of Different Ages." *Computers in Human Behavior*, 27(5), 1820–27.

Balakrishnan, N. (3 February 2016). "The Elderly And The Young Should Work Together More." *China Daily Asia*. Retrieved From http://www.chinadailyasia.com/opinion/2016-02/03/content_15382033.html.

Blackwell, C., Birnholtz, J., & Abbott, C. (2015). "Seeing and Being Seen: Co-situation and Impression Formation Using Grindr, a Location-aware Gay Dating App." *New Media & Society*, 17(7) , 1117–36.

Block, J. J. (2008). "Issues for DSM-V: Internet Addiction." *American Journal of Psychiatry*, 165(3), 306–7.

Census and Statistics Department. (2016). *Hong Kong in Figures* (Latest Figures). Retrieved 28 November 2016, from http://www.censtatd.gov.hk/hkstat/hkif/index.jsp.

Cheung, T. (2011). "No surprise: Facebook is More Popular than Anything Else in Hong Kong." CNN. Retrieved from http://travel.cnn.com/hong-kong/life/whats-hot-hong-kong-618023/.

Choi, C. (26 August 2013). "'Record-breaking Numbers' of HIV Cases Recorded in Hong Kong as Gay Men Still at Highest Risk". *South China Morning Post*. Retrieved from http://www.scmp.com/news/hong-kong/article/1366153/record-breaking-numbers-hiv-cases-recorded-hong-kong-gay-men-still.

Crowson, M., & Goulding, A. (2013). "Virtually Homosexual: Technoromanticism, Demarginalisation and Identity Formation among Homosexual Males." *Computers in Human Behavior*, 29(5), A31–A39.

"Cyber-bullying". Hong Kong: The Government of Hong Kong Special Administration Region. (2012). Retrieved from http://www.info.gov.hk/gia/general/201212/19/P201212190360.htm.

"HARiS – HIV and AIDS Response Indicator Survey 2013 for Men Who Have Sex with Men" (2014). Hong Kong: Centre for Health Protection. Retrieved from http://www.info.gov.hk/aids/english/surveillance/sur_report/oth_rep2014_msm_e.pdf.

Hon, K. E., Leung, T., Yau, A. P., Wu, S., Wan, M., Chan, H., & Fok, T. (2005). "A Survey of Attitudes toward Homosexuality in Hong Kong Chinese Medical Students." *Teaching and Learning in Medicine*, 17(4), 344–8.

Hong Kong Christian Service. (14 July 2009). "Close To 2% Youths Experienced Cyber Bullying: We Must Join Hands To Stop The Abusive Trend". Retrieved from http://www.hkcs.org/enews/e064/e06402.html.

"Hong Kong Internet and Telecommunications Reports". (n.d.). Retrieved from http://www.Internetworldstats.com/asia/hk.htm.

Ko, C., Yen, J., Yen, C., Chen, C., & Chen, C. (2012). "The Association between Internet Addiction and Psychiatric Disorder: A Review of the Literature". *European Psychiatry*, 27(1), 1–8.

Ku, H. B., Chan, K., & Sandhu, K. K. (2006). *A Research Report On The Employment Of South Asian Ethnic Minority Groups In Hong Kong*. Hong Kong: Centre for Social Policy Studies, Department of Applied Social Sciences, The Hong Kong Polytechnic University.

Kwong, Y. H. (2015). "Digital Divide: Computer and Internet Use by Elderly People in Hong Kong." *Asian Journal of Gerontology & Geriatrics*, 10(1), 5–9.

Lee, L. (14 April 2015). "Why Cyberbullying Is So Hard on Teenagers, and What Hong Kong Parents Can Do." *South China Morning Post*. Retrieved from http://www.scmp.com/lifestyle/family-education/article/1765529/why-cyberbullying-so-hard-teenagers-and-what-hong-kong.

Leung, A. N., & McBride-Chang, C. (2013). "Game on? Online Friendship, Cyberbullying, and Psychosocial Adjustment in Hong Kong Chinese Children." *Journal of Social and Clinical Psychology*, 32(2), 159–85.

Ma, G., Woo, K. H., & Tang, R.. "Court of Appeal Judgment" (Civil Appeal No. 317 of 2005). (2006). Retrieved from http://www.humandignitytrust.org/uploaded/Library/Case_Law/Leung_v_Secretary_of_Justice.pdf.

McKenna, K. Y. A., & Bargh, J. A. (1998). "Coming Out in the Age of the Internet: Identity "Demarginalization' through Virtual Group Participation". *Journal of Personality and Social Psychology*, 75(3), 681–694.

Miller, B. (2015). "'They're The Modern-Day Gay Bar': Exploring The Uses And Gratifications Of Social Networks For Men Who Have Sex With Men." *Computers in Human Behavior*, 51, Part A, 476–82.

Newell, A. F. (2011). "Design and the Digital Divide: Insights from 40 Years in Computer Support for Older and Disabled People." Synthesis Lectures on Assistive, Rehabilitative, and Health-Preserving Technologies, 1(1), 1–195.

Race, K. (2015). "Speculative Pragmatism and Intimate Arrangements: Online Hook-Up Devices in Gay Life." *Culture, Health & Sexuality*, 17(4), 496–511.

Schneider, S. K., O'Donnell, L., Stueve, A., & Coulter, R. W. S. (2011). "Cyberbullying, School Bullying, and Psychological Distress: A Regional Census of High School Students." *American Journal of Public Health*, 102(1), 171–7.

Sharp, M. (Mar 2, 2015). "Beware the Smartphone Zombies Blindly Wandering Around Hong Kong". *South China Morning Post*. Retrieved from http://www.scmp.com/lifestyle/technology/article/1725001/smartphone-zombies-are-putting-your-life-and-theirs-danger.

Shek, D. T. L., Tang, V. M. Y., & Lo, C. Y. (2008). "Internet Addiction in Chinese Adolescents in Hong Kong: Assessment, Profiles, and Psychosocial Correlates". *The Scientific World Journal*, 8, 776–87.

Smith, P. K., Mahdavi, J., Carvalho, M., Fisher, S., Russell, S., & Tippett, N. (2008). "Cyberbullying: Its Nature and Impact in Secondary School Pupils". *Journal of Child Psychology and Psychiatry*, 49(4), 376–85.

"Social Media Usage in Asia Pacific — Statistics and Trends". (27 January 2015). Retrieved from http://www.go-globe.com/blog/social-media-asia/.

*Survey on Public Attitudes towards Homosexuals*. (2006) Hong Kong: Home Affairs Bureau, Hong Kong Special Administrative Region. Retrieved from http://www.legco.gov.hk/yr05-06/english/panels/ha/papers/ha0310cb2-public-homosexuals-e.pdf.

Tang, D. T.-S. (2011). *Conditional Spaces: Hong Kong Lesbian Desires and Everyday Life*. Hong Kong: Hong Kong University Press.

Tang, D. T. S. (2015). "Essential Labels? Gender Identity Politics on Hong Kong Lesbian Mobile Phone Application Butterfly." In *Routledge Handbook of New Media in Asia*, edited by L. Hjorth & O. Khoo, 263-74. Abingdon, Oxon; New York, NY: Routledge.

*Thematic Report: Ethnic Minorities*. (2012). Hong Kong: Census and Statistics Department, Hong Kong Special Administrative Region. Retrieved from http://www.statistics.gov.hk/pub/B11200622012XXXXB0100.pdf.

Vernon, K., & Yik, A. (2012). "Hong Kong Lgbt Climate Study 2011–12: Attitude To And Experiences Of Lesbian, Gay, Bisexual And Transgender Employees". Hong Kong: Community Business. Retrieved from https://www.home.barclays/content/dam/barclayspublic/documents/news/628-831-230512_HKLGBTClimateStudy.pdf.

Weinstein, A., & Lejoyeux, M. (2010). "Internet Addiction or Excessive Internet Use." *The American Journal of Drug and Alcohol Abuse*, 36(5), 277–283.

White, R. C., & Carr, R. (2005). "Homosexuality and HIV/AIDS Stigma in Jamaica." *Culture, Health & Sexuality*, 7(4), 347–59.

Wong, A. D. (2005). "The Reappropriation of Tongzhi." *Language in Society*, 34(5), 763–93.

Wong, R. (2010). "A Study on Cyber-Bullying Among Hong Kong Secondary Students". Hong Kong: The Hong Kong Federation of Youth Groups. Retrieved from http://benetwise.hk/download/cyberbully_research.pdf.

Yeo, T. E. D., & Ng, Y. L. (2016). "Sexual Risk Behaviors among Apps-Using Young Men Who Have Sex with Men in Hong Kong." *AIDS Care*, 28(3) (2016), 314–18.

Yeo, T. E. D., & Fung, T. H. (2016). "Between '0' and '1': Safer Sex and Condom Use among Young Gay Men in Hong Kong." *Culture, Health & Sexuality*, 18(3), 294–307.

Young, J. (May 30, 2013). "Hong Kong is Multicultural; Don't Let Anyone Tell You otherwise." *South China Morning Post*. Retrieved from http://www.scmp.com/comment/insight-opinion/article/1249135/hong-kong-multicultural-dont-let-anyone-tell-you-otherwise.

Yu, L., & Shek, D. T. L. (2013). "Internet Addiction in Hong Kong Adolescents: A Three-year Longitudinal Study." *Journal of Pediatric and Adolescent Gynecology*, 26(3, Supplement), S10–S17.

# Chapter 17

# An Overview of Health Communication Research in Hong Kong

*Timothy K. F. FUNG, Terri H. CHAN, Yu-Leung NG, Sice WU and Jun LAM*

## Introduction

Hong Kong, once a British colony, is a multifarious metropolis with more than seven million people. It has a medical system of mixed Chinese and Western values (Smith, Bennet & Irwin, 1997). Although Hong Kong has a well established public health system and delivers high-quality health care services (Heung, Kucukusta & Song, 2010; Rodwin, 2011), the city has not only experienced a number of public health crises in the past, such as the epidemics of avian influenza in 1997 and SARS (Severe Acute Respiratory Syndrome) in 2003, but is also facing a number of new public health challenges, such as the potential threats of newly emerging diseases (e.g., Middle East Respiratory Syndrome, Zika virus infection), and an increasing burden from non-communicable diseases and food safety (Rodwin, 2011). Health communication plays an important role in addressing these challenges by contributing to the effort of disease prevention and control, health promotion and health care (Gurman, Rubin & Roess, 2012; Paek, Lee, Jeong, Wang & Dutta, 2010). Because of practical needs, health communication in Hong Kong has received increasing attention.

Although scholars in Hong Kong have been conducting communication research for more than five decades (Chu, 1988; Chan, 1992; Willnat & Aw, 2009), communication in the health domain has been studied in a piecemeal fashion since the legitimisation of the field. Therefore, a systematic review of health communication research in Hong Kong is useful at this stage. It will help us to understand the current status of studies in this area conducted by Hong Kong-based scholars, inform the practices of health communicators and shed light on future health communication studies in Hong Kong. In brief, we aim to shed light on how health communication studies published by Hong Kong-based scholars have evolved and what the current situation is. This work seeks to answer multiple questions, including:

- In what journals did Hong Kong-based scholars publish their health communication studies?
- What theories, methodological approaches and research methods did Hong Kong-based scholars adopt in the health communication studies they published?
- What countries, media and diseases did Hong Kong-based scholars of health communication pay most attention to?

To answer these questions we analysed the content of scholarly articles published by Hong Kong-based scholars from 1992 to 2016. The primary objective was to provide an overall picture of health communication studies published by Hong Kong-based scholars.

## An Assessment of Health Communication Research

### Sampling

The sample consists of scholarly articles on health communication published by Hong Kong-based scholars between 1992 to June 2016. We selected 1992 as the starting point because scholarly articles prior to 1992 are not available in the Web of Science database. Two methods were used to identify the sample. First, we searched for articles on the Web of Science using the keywords "health communication" and "Hong Kong". Since the focus of this study was health communication research in Hong Kong, we only included articles with at least one author who was affiliated with a tertiary institution in Hong Kong. Second, we reviewed each current communication or journalism faculty member's publication list on the websites of the seven tertiary institutions in Hong Kong that have communication or journalism departments. By this method we found journal articles which were not in the Web of Science database as well as books and book chapters. Articles not accessible through our university's library were obtained by emailing the authors. After the sampling process and careful examination of the faculty members' publication lists, 144 journal articles and three books (with thirty-three chapters in total) were identified. In total, our final sample consisted of 177 scholarly articles (both journal articles and book chapters), of which 87.6% (n=155) were written in English and 12.4% (n=22) were written in Chinese.

## Coding Categories

The unit of analysis of this study was an individual article or book chapter, which we analysed using the following twelve coding categories.

Journals—We counted the number of journal articles published in each journal outlet.

Length—We coded the length of each article or book chapter by counting its number of pages.

Number of countries (regions) of focus—This category referred to the number of countries or regions being studied in the research. The codes were 0=none, 1=one country or region and 2=multiple countries or regions.

Specific country (region) focus—This category referred to the country or region being studied in the research. Coders coded an article or book chapter into more than one country or region if it studied multiple countries or regions. Articles or book chapters which did not focus on a country or region were classified as "none".

Type—The types of the articles or chapters were coded as follows. 1=original research, 2=systematic review (e.g., meta-analysis, meta-synthesis), 3=theory paper, 4=commentary and 5=others (e.g., book review, editorial introduction).

Methodological approach—The methodological approaches used in the research were coded into four categories: 1=qualitative, 2=quantitative, 3=mixed (both the two aforementioned approaches were used) and 4=non-empirical research without data (e.g., essays, book reviews, theory paper).

Research method—This refers to the research methods being used in a study. If an article used more than one method, each method was included. We identified the methods by name—for example, laboratory experiment, survey, focus groups, in-depth interviews or content analysis.

Theory—Coders categorised the primary theory or theoretical framework employed in the research. They coded each theory if the article used more than one theoretical framework. We identified the theoretical framework by name—for instance, affective response theory and cognitive-behavioural approach. Articles without a theoretical framework were coded as "none".

Media focus—Articles that examined the content or the effects of the media were coded. The following eleven categories were used: 1=TV, 2=radio, 3=print, 4=out-of-home, 5=direct mail, 6=cinema advertising, 7=mobile communications, 8=internet, 9=all of the above, 10=other than all of the above and 11=none.

Number of authors—We counted the number of authors on each journal article and book chapter.

Affiliation of the leading author and co-authors—We coded the affiliation of the leading author and each co-author based on the country (region) where the tertiary institution is located.

Disease/Illness focus—We adopted Lwin and Salmon's (2015) classification of diseases or illnesses. An article was coded into one of five categories of diseases based on the keywords provided or extracted from the abstract of the article. The five categories were communicable diseases/illnesses, which may be spread interpersonally or infect human beings through non-human sources, such as influenza, SARS and cholera; non-communicable diseases/illnesses, which are unrelated to contacting infectious agents (e.g., cardiovascular diseases, cancers and diabetes); lifestyle health problems, which are health-associated conditions as a result of the way people live (e.g., obesity); environmental diseases/illnesses, which are related to health issues caused by artificial or natural environmental problems (e.g., lead poisoning) and lastly, other diseases/illnesses.

## Coding Procedures

Two trained coders coded a random sample of 15% of the articles to obtain the inter-coder reliability for each coding category. The Krippendorff's alpha of each coding category was ranged 0.54 (theory) to 1.00 (article length, methodological approach). Disagreements were resolved through coordination by one of the co-authors. Meetings were held regularly with the coders in order to address the discrepancies that appeared during the course of coding to minimise their disparities in coding standards and to maximise their agreement. After obtaining inter-coder reliability, the remaining articles were evenly distributed to the coders, who coded them independently.

## Health Communication Research in Journals and Books

Figure 17.1 shows the number of journal articles and book chapters in health communication published in 1992 through June 2016. We analysed journal articles and book chapters separately to better understand the research in each publication type.

### Journal articles

Journal outlets—Hong Kong-based scholars published their work on health communication in diversified journals (Tables 17.1). The 144 journal articles in the sample were published in eighty-nine journals. *Health Communication* (n=9, 6.3%) and *CyberPsychology & Behavior* (n=7, 4.9%) published the largest numbers of articles. The *Asian Journal of Communication* and the *Journal of Health Communication* each published five articles (3.5%). The *Journal of Epidemiology and Community Health* and *Public Relation Review* each published four articles (2.8%).

**Figure 17.1**

**Number of Published Journal Articles and Book Chapters
in Health Communication by Year**

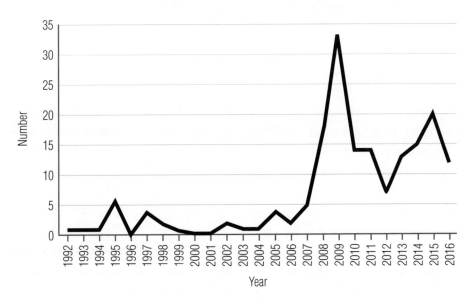

**Table 17.1**

**Journals which Published Three or More Articles in the Sample**

|  | Number | Percentage (%) of Sample |
|---|---|---|
| *Health Communication* | 9 | 6.3 |
| *CyberPsychology & Behavior* | 7 | 4.9 |
| *Asian Journal of Communication* | 5 | 3.5 |
| *Journal of Health Communication* | 5 | 3.5 |
| *Journal of Epidemiology and Community Health* | 4 | 2.8 |
| *Public Relations Review* | 4 | 2.8 |
| *European Journal of Disorders of Communication* | 3 | 2.1 |
| *Journal of Applied Communication Research* | 3 | 2.1 |
| *Journal of Consumer Marketing* | 3 | 2.1 |
| *PloS ONE* | 3 | 2.1 |

Length—The average length of the articles in the sample was 15.3 pages (SD=9.3; min=2; max=63).

Number of countries (regions) of focus—Most articles were focused on one country or region (n=110, 76.4%). Sixteen articles (11.1%) involved more than one country or region, and eighteen articles (12.5%) do not focus on a particular country or region.

Specific country (region) focus—As shown in Table 17.2, about two-fifths of the articles (n=70, 41.4%) were studies that focused on Hong Kong. The United States (n=31, 18.3%), Mainland China (n=16, 9.5%), Taiwan (n=9, 5.3%), South Korea (n=8, 4.7%), Singapore (n=6, 3.6%) and Australia (n=5, 3.0%) were also frequently studied.

Type—The majority of the articles in the sample described original research (n=122, 84.7%). The rest were theory papers (n=7, 4.9%) or systematic reviews (n=4, 2.8%).

Methodological approach—A quantitative approach (n=99, 68.8%) or a qualitative approach (n=24, 16.7%) was used in the majority of articles in the sample. Four articles combined qualitative with quantitative approaches (2.8%). Seventeen articles were non-empirical studies (n=17, 11.8%).

**Table 17.2**

**Specific Countries (Regions) of Focus in the Journal Articles and Book Chapters**

|  | Journal Articles | | Book Chapters | |
|---|---|---|---|---|
|  | Frequency | Percentage (%) | Frequency | Percentage (%) |
| Hong Kong | 70 | 41.4 | 16 | 38.1 |
| U.S. | 31 | 18.3 | 2 | 4.8 |
| Mainland China | 16 | 9.5 | 11 | 26.2 |
| Taiwan | 9 | 5.3 | 3 | 7.1 |
| South Korea | 8 | 4.7 | – | – |
| Singapore | 6 | 3.6 | 2 | 4.8 |
| Australia | 5 | 3.0 | – | – |
| Denmark | 2 | 1.2 | – | – |
| Germany | 2 | 1.2 | – | – |
| UK | 2 | 1.2 | – | – |
| Asia | 1 | 0.6 | – | – |
| Japan | 1 | 0.6 | – | – |
| Canada | – | – | 1 | 2.4 |
| Malaysia | – | – | 1 | 2.4 |
| None | 16 | 9.5 | 6 | 14.3 |
| Total | 169 | 100.0 | 42 | 100.0 |

Research method—Table 17.3 shows that survey was the most frequently used research method (n=58, 36.7%), followed by content analysis (n=19, 12.0%), laboratory experiment (n=13, 8.2%), focus group (n=12, 7.6%) and secondary data analysis (n=7, 4.4%).

Theory—Ninety-eight articles (64.5%) did not adopt any theory. Among those with theoretical frameworks, the theories employed were diverse. The top five were the theory of planned behaviour (n=5, 3.3%), social cognitive theory (n=5, 3.3%), framing (n=4, 2.6%), social capital theory (n=2, 1.3%) and expectancy value theory (n=2, 1.3%).

**Table 17.3**

**Research Methods in the Journal Articles and Book Chapters**

| | Journal Articles | | Book Chapters | |
| --- | --- | --- | --- | --- |
| | Frequency | Percentage (%) | Frequency | Percentage (%) |
| Survey | 58 | 36.7 | 2 | 5.6 |
| Content analysis | 19 | 12.0 | 8 | 22.2 |
| Laboratory experiment | 13 | 8.2 | 1 | 2.8 |
| Focus group | 12 | 7.6 | – | – |
| Secondary data analysis | 7 | 4.4 | – | – |
| In-depth interview | 5 | 3.2 | 2 | 5.6 |
| Meta-analysis/ synthesis | 4 | 2.5 | – | – |
| Time series analysis | 4 | 2.5 | – | – |
| Discourse analysis | 3 | 1.9 | 3 | 8.3 |
| Ethnography | 3 | 1.9 | – | – |
| Quasi- experiment | 3 | 1.9 | – | – |
| Conversation analysis | 2 | 1.3 | 1 | 2.8 |
| Field experiment | 2 | 1.3 | – | – |
| Textual analysis | 2 | 1.3 | 3 | 8.3 |
| Case study | 1 | 0.6 | 1 | 2.8 |
| Genre analysis | 1 | 0.6 | – | – |
| Historical analysis | 1 | 0.6 | – | – |
| Observation | 1 | 0.6 | – | – |
| Sediment biogeochemical analysis | 1 | 0.6 | – | – |
| Social network analysis | 1 | 0.6 | – | – |
| Non-empirical study | 15 | 9.5 | 15 | 41.7 |
| Total | 158 | 100.0 | 36 | 100.0 |

Note. Percentages do not add to 100% due to rounding.

**Table 17.4**

**Media of Focus in the Journal Articles and Book Chapters**

| | Journal Articles | | Book Chapters | |
|---|---|---|---|---|
| | Frequency | Percentage (%) | Frequency | Percentage (%) |
| Internet | 28 | 17.5 | 2 | 5.6 |
| Print | 14 | 8.8 | 8 | 22.2 |
| TV | 10 | 6.3 | 2 | 5.6 |
| Mobile communications | 9 | 5.6 | 1 | 2.8 |
| Radio | 2 | 1.3 | 0 | 0 |
| All of the above | 8 | 5.0 | 6 | 16.7 |
| Other than all of the above | 9 | 5.6 | 3 | 8.3 |
| None | 80 | 50.0 | 14 | 38.9 |
| Total | 144 | 100 | 36 | 100 |

Note. Percentages do not add to 100% due to rounding.

Media focus—The largest number of articles in the sample examined the internet (n=28, 17.5%), with print media being the next largest (n=14, 8.8%). Ten articles examined television (6.3%) and nine articles examined mobile communication (5.6%). About 50% of the sample did not study any media channels (Table 17.4).

Number of authors—The number of authors per article ranged from one to ten. The average number of authors per article was 3.1 (SD=2.1).

Affiliation of leading author—About 70% of the leading authors were affiliated with Hong Kong institutions (n=102), followed by U.S. affiliations (n=22, 15.1%). Others were affiliated with institutions in Australia (n=3, 2.1%), Austria (n=3, 2.1%), Singapore (n=3, 2.1%) and Taiwan (n=3, 2.1%).

Affiliation of co-author(s)—Most co-authors were affiliated with institutions in Hong Kong (n=87, 42.0%), followed by those in the United States (n=31, 15.0%), Singapore (n=11, 5.3%), the United Kingdom (n=10, 4.8%) and Mainland China (n=7, 3.4%).

Disease/Illness focus—Studies of communicable diseases/illnesses (n=15, 40.5%) formed the bulk of the journal articles related to diseases/illnesses. A considerable number of communicable diseases/illnesses related articles were on HIV/AIDS (n=6, 40%) and influenza including H1N1 and H5N1 (n=6, 40%). Two articles (n=2, 13.3%) studied SARS, and one article examined fungal diseases (n=1, 6.7%).

Fourteen studies examined a specific non-communicable disease or illnesse, with depression being the most discussed (n=4, 26.7%). Cancer, suicide, language delay and speech disorders were each discussed in two articles (13.3%). The remaining five articles on non-communicable diseases/illnesses were devoted to chronic diseases (e.g., diabetes), cleft palate, end-stage renal disease and reperfusion injury.

## Book Chapters

We identified three books related to health communication authored by Hong Kong-based scholars:

- *How Much Do You Know about Doctor-patient Communication?* (Ma, 2009a);
- *Health Communication and Public Health* (Ma, 2009b); and
- *The Social Construction of SARS* (Powers & Xiao, 2008).

The first two were part of the 2008 Health Communication Series, which was published after the conference organised by the Department of Communication Studies at Hong Kong Baptist University (HKBU) and the Hospital Authority. We analysed each of the thirty-three chapters in these three books.

Number of countries (regions) of focus—Of the thirty-three chapters, twenty-one (63.6%) were single-country studies and six (18.2%) were multiple-country studies.

Specific country (or region) focus—The largest number of chapters were focused on Hong Kong (n=10, 30.3%) and Mainland China (n=6, 18.2%). Four (12.1%) studied both Hong Kong and Mainland China. One quarter of the chapters (n=8) were multiple-country studies (Table 17.2).

Type—Nearly half the book chapters were original research (n=16, 48.5%). Theory papers accounted for 21.2% (n=7) and one chapter (3.3%) was a commentary.

Methodological approach—More book chapters used the qualitative approach (27.3%, n=9) than the quantitative approach (15.2%, n=5), unlike journal articles. Two book chapters (6.1%) used mixed methods. Seventeen book chapters (51.5%) were non-empirical studies.

Research method—Unlike journal articles, content analysis was the most frequently used research method in book chapters (n=8, 22.2%), followed by discourse analysis (n=3, 8.3%), textual analysis (n=3, 8.3%), surveys (n=2, 5.6%) and in-depth interviews (n=2, 5.6%). Case studies, conversation analysis, and laboratory experiments were used in one book chapter each (2.8%). The research method used in fifteen chapters (41.7%) was non-empirical study (e.g., reviews, essays) (Table 17.3).

Theory—Of the book chapters, 84.9% (n=28) did not employ any theoretical framework at all. In the five book chapters with a theoretical framework (30.3%), the elaborated likelihood model/heuristic systematic model, protection motivation theory, symbolic convergence theory, information game theory and the model of strategic management of public relations were used.

Media focus—Three book chapters studied more than one media channel, so we coded each media channel in these. As a result, we had thirty-six samples in this category. Traditional media were the main focus in the book chapters. Eight of them (22.2%) focused on print media and two (5.6%) on TV. Two chapters examined the internet (5.6%) and one (2.8%) studied mobile communications (Table 17.4).

Affiliation of the leading author—Twenty-three book chapters (69.7%) were written by single authors. The book chapters were mainly written by scholars in Hong Kong (n=20, 60.6%) and the U.S. (n=8, 24.2%). Mainland Chinese leading authors wrote two chapters (6.1%). Leading authors from Taiwan, Singapore and Australia accounted for one chapter (3.0%) each.

Affiliation of the co-author(s)—There were thirteen co-authors in total. The majority were affiliated with institutions in the U.S. (n=4, 30.8%) and Hong Kong (n=4, 30.8%) and two were affiliated with institutions in Singapore. Each of the other co-authors was affiliated with an institution in Mainland China, Taiwan or Denmark.

## Limitations

Before we discuss our findings in detail, it is important to note that the aim of this study is not to provide a comprehensive examination of health communication research in Hong Kong, our sample being subject to a number of limitations. First, this analysis mainly includes health communication studies from the Web of Science database. Although health communication is a multidisciplinary area, we only include studies from the communication and journalism disciplines. Health communication studies in other related disciplines such as psychology, sociology, nursing and public health were not included. Second, health communication studies that were published before 1992 were not included because these journal articles are unavailable in the Web of Science database. Third, some communication and journalism faculty members did not provide a complete list of their publications on their web pages. Finally, the search for published books related to health communication is not exhaustive and health communication-related academic books published by Hong Kong-based scholars from other disciplines such as health psychology, and public health were not included in the analysis. Another limitation is the issue of inter-coder reliability. Although the inter-coder reliabilities of most coding categories reached 0.70 or above, those of two categories—disease/illness of focus and theory—were below 0.70. However, the coders met regularly to resolve coding disagreements. Despite these limitations, our findings provide a useful reference for understanding the trend of health communication research in Hong Kong over the last two decades.

## Conclusion

A notable trend found in this review is that academia in Hong Kong has produced a growing literature on health communication. The number of scholarly articles being published by Hong Kong-based scholars increased between 1992 and 2016. Plausible factors for this rise include the need for risk and outbreak communication during health crises and health warnings, the rising concern over health issues and increasing attention to health communication from the international scholarly community and international health agencies (e.g., the World Health Organization).

An important but alarming finding in this review is the lack of theoretical base in Hong Kong health communication research. More than 60% of journal articles and book chapters did not report using any theory. This restricts knowledge advancement and theoretical contribution. Theory-building efforts are important for advancing knowledge in health communication at large and for developing more culture-specific, indigenous knowledge in particular.

Another noteworthy phenomenon is the diversity in terms of journal outlets. This reflects the multidisciplinary nature of health communication. Authors worked in institutions in many different countries; Hong Kong-based scholars collaborated with researchers in Asia, Europe and North America.

The findings reveal that communication scholars in Hong Kong have paid relatively little attention to the use of communication technology, such as the internet and mobile phones, in health-related issues. With the increasing use of communication technology, scholars in Hong Kong should pay more attention to its potential in healthcare and health promotion. Furthermore, these findings show that the quantitative approach is dominant in health communication studies in Hong Kong. Surveys, content analysis and laboratory experiments were the most frequently used research methods.

The majority of the studies focused on a single country or region, and Hong Kong, the U.S. and Mainland China were the most frequent country/ region of focus. However, about 10% of the studies in journal article and nearly 20% of book chapters involved more than one country/region. This suggests that scholars in Hong Kong conducted some comparative studies in health communication. We recommend more comparative studies across regions or cultures in the future because they may enhance our understanding of the factors that foster the identification of universal principles that transcend cultural boundaries (Lwin & Salmon, 2015).

A noteworthy finding is the lack of studies on diseases that matter most in Hong Kong. For example, malignant neoplasms, pneumonia, heart diseases, cerebrovascular diseases, dementia and chronic lower respiratory diseases were the major leading causes of death in Hong Kong in 2014 (Department of Health, 2016a), but there was no study which examined communication-related issues of these diseases and illnesses. Although some scholars studied communication-related issues of cancer, diabetes and renal diseases, the number of their research articles was limited. Some scholars examined communication-related issues of HIV/AIDS, influenza (H1N1, H5N1) and SARS, but some notifiable communicable diseases such as chickenpox, food poisoning, scarlet fever and tuberculosis are largely overlooked (Department of Health, 2016b).

To address the need for communicating health-related issues in a Chinese society, a balance between contextual- and cultural-specific factors and universal principles is needed in health communication research (Lwin & Salmon, 2015). Communication scholars in Hong Kong can make an important contribution on how to communicate health effectively in Chinese cultural contexts. Meanwhile, scholars in Hong Kong should pay more attention to theory building and comparative research, which may potentially make significant contributions to knowledge advancement in health communication.

# References

Chan, J. M. (1992). "MassMedia and Socio-political Formation in Hong Kong, 1942–1992". *Asian Journal of Communication*, 2, 106–29.

Chu, G. C. (1988). "In Search of an Asian Perspective of Communication Theory". *Media Asia*, 13, 3-5. http://dx.doi.org/10.1080/01296612.1986.11726201.

Department of Health, HKSAR. (2016a). "Public Health Information and Statistics of Hong Kong". Retrieved from http://www.healthyhk.gov.hk/phisweb/plain/en/healthy_facts/disease_burden/major_causes_death/major_causes_death/.

Department of Health, HKSAR. (2016b). "Number of Notifiable Infectious Diseases by Month in 2016". Retrieved from: http://www.chp.gov.hk/en/data/1/10/26/43/5128.html.

Gurman, T. A., Rubin, S. E., & Roess, A. A. (2012). "Effectiveness of Health Behavior Change Communication Interventions in Developing Countries: A Systematic Review of the Literature". *Journal of Health Comuunication*, 17(Suppl/ 1), 82–104. doi:10.1080/108107 30.2011.649160.

Heung, V.C.S., Kucukusta, D. & Song, H. (2010). "A Conceptual Model of Medical Tourism: Implications for Future Research". *Journal of Travel & Tourism Marketing*, 27(3), 236–51.

Lwin, M. O., & Salmon, C. T. (2015). "A Retrospective Overview of Health Communication Studies in Asia from 2000 to 2013". *Asian Journal of Communication*, 25(1), 1–13. http://dx.doi.org/10.1080/01292986.2015.1009265.

Ma, R. (Ed.) (2009a). "Jiankang chuanbo yu gonggong weisheng" [Health communication and public health]. Hong Kong: Hong Kong Educational Publishing Co.

Ma, R. (Ed.) (2009b). "Yi bing goutong zhi duoshao" [How much do you know about doctor-patient communication?]. Hong Kong: KAI Education.

Paek, H., Lee, A. L., Jeong, S., Wang, J., & Dutta, M. (2010). "The Emerging Landscape of Health Communication in Asia: Theoretical Contributions, Methodological Questions, and Applied Collaborations". *Health Communication*, 25, 552–559. Retrieved from http://dx.doi.org/10.1080/10410236.2010.496705.

Powers, J. H., & Xiao, X. (Eds.), (2008). *The Social Construction of SARS: Studies of a Health Communication Crisis*. Philadelphia, PA: John Benjamins Publishing Company.

Rodwin, V. G. (2011). "Health in Hong Kong: An International Urban Perspective". Retrieved from https://lsecities.net/media/objects/articles/health-in-hong-kong-an-international-urban-perspective/en-gb/.

Smith, D. H., Bennet, K., & Irwin, H., (1997). "Hong Kong Patients' Preferences for Participation in Medical Decision Making" in *Working Papers on Health Communication and China*, edited by Smith, D.H. Hong Kong, HK: David C. Lam Institute for East-West Studies.

Willnat, L., Aw, A. (2009). "The Big Unknown: Political Communication in Asia" in *Political Communication in Asia*, edited by Bryant, J. & Zillmann, D. New York, NY: Routledge.

# Chapter 18

## Post-Democratic and Pre-Democratic Movements:
### From "Sunflower" in Taiwan to "Umbrella" in Hong Kong

*Ringo MA*

## Introduction

The year 2014 witnessed large protest movements in Taiwan and Hong Kong in which students played major roles. Both were opposed to the Chinese government, both have had profound effects on their respective places of occurrence and both were important events in Chinese history. The first to occur was the occupation of the Taiwanese Legislative Yuan by protesters from 18 March to 10 April 2014, during which the Executive Yuan was also occupied briefly. Then, from 28 September to 15 December, protesters in Hong Kong occupied a number of places on main thoroughfares. The former movement is called the Sunflower Movement, and the latter is called Occupy Central (since their plan was to occupy Central District, a main commercial area, although when the movement began, protesters actually occupied areas outside the district). Since participants of Occupy Central used a yellow ribbon as their symbol while their opponents used a blue ribbon, the two groups became referred to as "yellow ribbons" and "blue ribbons". As protesters used umbrellas to protect themselves from the tear gas and pepper spray used by the police against them, an umbrella, especially a yellow one, also became a symbol of the movement, hence the name "Umbrella Movement".

The two movements drew great attention in both places, and the public was polarised by the events. As a result, neutral comments on them are rare.

In each case, one group totally supported the movement and the other was totally opposed to it. Some passionate people seem to have forgotten basic differences between Taiwan and Hong Kong. For example, the president and the Legislative Yuan in Taiwan are democratically elected, and Taiwan is a democracy, whereas Hong Kong is a special administrative region of China.

## Theories of and Research on Social Movements

Let us begin with a definition. According to the *Encyclopedia Britannica*, a social movement is a "loosely organised but sustained campaign in support of a social goal, typically either the implementation or the prevention of a change in society's structure or values" (Social Movement, 2015). We see from the definition that it contains two ideas:

- Participants of a social movement are different from people who happen to be on a street or members of a formal organisation.
- The main aim of a social movement is to either implement or prevent some social change.

According to the research of Staggenborg (2011), all scholars of social movements should take into consideration "historical context and cultural differences." His book mentions two groups of theories of social movements that arose in the United States: the collective behaviour theory, and resource mobilisation and political process theories. Following traditional points of view, the collective behaviour theory considers a social movement to be a result of discontent that arises because of problems in society. Resource mobilisation and political process theories, on the other hand, stress that a social movement is a continuous political process that transforms collective actions outside established structures into actions inside them. The theories consider participants of social movements as rational actors. In other words, past social movements created the generally unquestioned status quo of society (Macionis & Plummer, 2005).

Besides the above theories, which originated in the United States, there is the new social movement theory, which originated in Europe. It is a theory of social movements in post-industrial societies. Based on viewpoints similar to those put forward in the theory, some scholars distinguish conventional social movements from new social movements. The former occurred during the industrial revolution, when the working class fought for better economic conditions. The latter occur in the era after the mid-1960s, in which the new middle class fight for social changes regarding, for example, homosexuality, the environment and free trade. In the context of social developments in post-industrial society, new social movements occur in a consumer society, an information society or a communication society. These social movements are different from their predecessors, which were predominantly blue collar. The well-known sociologist Alain Touraine (2002) pointed out that the terms "social movement" and "class conflict" differ in that the former is about the participants as actors, or their consciousness of active participation, as opposed to economic determinism. According to Wilkinson (1971, p. 13), "[the] word 'movement'... implied autonomy, self-generated and independent action, control and leadership."

The mass movements that started in 2011 in Egypt, Spain, Tunisia and the United States broadened the horizons of social movements. For the first time, social media and mobile communication devices played a major role in mobilising participants. The profound impact of the internet on mobilisation may be studied from the following two perspectives: the internet as a fast, inexpensive means of communication and mobilisation; and its role as a new framing tool and the "change that it has effected as a new setting for political dialogue and discourse" (Turner, 2013).

Traditionally there are three approaches to researching the mobilising power of a social movement (Jiloka, 2012) which focus on: the opportunities of and constraints on developments of the movement, the network and resources with which organisers can mobilise supporters and how participants define a movement and the frames with which they use to view the movement. Now that mobile communication devices are considered essential personal gear, the second approach is obviously out of date.

The effects of a social movement on society may be considered in relation to the answers to two questions: who is changed? and how much change is there? Their answers may be combined in the following four ways, according to the type in which social movements may be classified (Macionis & Plummer, 2005):

- alternative social movements (the answers to the above two questions being, respectively, specific people and limited change);
- redemptive social movements (the answers to the questions being, respectively, specific people and radical change);
- reformative social movements (the answers to the questions being, respectively, all people and limited change); and
- revolutionary social movements (the answers to the questions are, respectively, all people and radical change).

This method of classification enables us to find the difference in the ease with which social movements accomplish their aims. For example, an alternative social movement is obviously less difficult than a reformative one.

Although social movements occur in very different places and times, and very different technology may be available to their participants, the factors that lead to their success or failure are not very different. Foremost among these factors is the number of people who are willing to devote time and money to a long movement which is usually in opposition to the authorities and in which they willingly follow the orders of its leaders. Since a social movement does not have official membership, the number of its participants fluctuates constantly. It is impossible to find their number with any accuracy. The turnout for an important event, however, is often an indicator of the importance the public attaches to a social movement and if this number is high, it can be a bargaining chip in negotiations with authorities.

Research into social movements shows that their development follows a general pattern. The earliest stage of a social movement often depends on charismatic leaders who articulate the ideals of the movement. By expounding their beliefs these thinkers lead their supporters. As the movement grows and establishes a social and economic base, charismatic leaders will be replaced, a bureaucratic structure gradually emerges and accommodation to society occurs (Zald & Ash, 1966). The *Encyclopedia Britannica* has the following to say about social movements, "If a movement endures and grows for any length of time, administrative leaders arise who are concerned with the practical matters of organisation and strategy." (Social Movement, 2015).

Some scholars believe that research into the causes of social movements, such as the reasons for discontent, belong to the realm of sociologists, and that communication scholars should study rhetoric (Golden, Berquist & Coleman, 1992, p. 419). Some scholars, however, stress that rhetoric cannot be dissociated from its causes and effects. For example, Bitzer (1972, p. 41) wrote, "A work of rhetoric is pragmatic; it comes into existence for the sake of something beyond itself; it functions ultimately to produce action or change in the world; it performs some task."

In general, a social movement is basically a large scale rhetorical act. Its participants hope that it will draw attention to an important issue. They try to change the opinions of a lot of people. Cathcart (1978) stated in clear terms that "a movement is primarily a symbolic or rhetoric act." He added: "Movements are carried forward through language, both verbal and non-verbal, in strategic [ways] that bring about identification of the individual with the movement." Golden, Berquist and Coleman (1992) wrote, "Any social movement... requires a man of words who manages the 'language.' These are the rhetoricians who weave a discourse which captures the urgent feelings and desires of the movement."

Some communication scholars classify the discourse of social movements into two main types: agitation discourse and revolt discourse (Golden, Berquist & Coleman, 1992). The former advocates an important social change, resistance to which has to be dealt with by extraordinary means of persuasion. The latter publicly advocates using violence to overthrow the current government. Both this classification and the one based on the answers to the questions who is changed, and how much is changed, have their strengths. Both classify social movements according to their degree of radicalism.

Fox and Frye (2010) examined social movements from three perspectives: the functional approach, frame analysis, and visual and embodied rhetoric. Stewart, Smith and Denton (2012) discussed the following functions of persuasive communication which may be applied in various social movements:

- transforming perceptions of reality;
- altering the self-perceptions of protesters;
- legitimising the movement;
- prescribing courses of action;
- mobilising for action; and
- sustaining the social movement.

## Comparisons between the Sunflower Movement in Taiwan and the Occupy Central Movement in Hong Kong

### Causes of the Movements

On 17 March 2014, during a meeting of the Internal Administrative Committee of the Legislative Yuan, presiding chair of the committee, Kuomintang (KMT) legislator Chang Ching-chung, was considered to have been the force behind the pushing of the Cross-Strait Service Trade Agreement (CSSTA) through the committee in thirty seconds. The then-ruling KMT and the opposition Democratic Progressive Party (DPP) disagreed on the nature of the CSSTA. Therefore, they disagreed on its review process. By 17 March, the committee review of the CSSTA had gone on for more than three months. Chang Ching-chung considered the CSSTA an executive order and reviewed it accordingly. According to the law, a committee has to finish its review of an executive order in three months. If not, the order is considered to have passed the committee and it is submitted to the legislature "for record". The opposition maintained that the CSSTA was a treaty because it is an agreement reached with a political entity (Mainland China) and it involves rights and obligations of the people. As a treaty, it should be submitted to the Legislative Yuan for review and passage.

Hong Kong's movement started following the 31 August 2014 decision by the Standing Committee of the National People's Congress of the People's Republic of China regarding the 2017 chief executive election in Hong Kong. According to the Basic Law, the chief executive is elected by a 1,200-member election committee. The Standing Committee decision stipulated that candidates for the 2017 election should first be nominated by at least half of the members of a 1,200-member nominating committee similar to the election committee. The nominating committee would nominate two or three candidates, and these selected candidates would then be elected by universal suffrage. This form of election was very different from what most Hong Kong people considered universal suffrage.

The two social movements have fundamental differences. The one in Taiwan occurred because in a multiparty legislature the treatment of an important issue by a democratically elected legislator of the ruling party caused serious controversy. The one in Hong Kong was caused by an autocratic decision by a committee in a one-party system. A lot of people in Hong Kong considered the decision to be a breach of a promise of universal suffrage, hence the cause of their great discontent.

Although the places, time and issues of the two movements were different, they shared a common sentiment. To put it simply, it was mistrust of the Chinese government. Supporters of the movements believed that they had been oppressed and controlled by the Chinese government, so although the movements were apparently different their followers would morally support each other, boost each other's morale and even pass on strategies. To understand their discontent it is necessary to review some historical events.

## Origins of the Anger in Taiwan and Hong Kong

The relationship between the Republic of China ("Taiwan" in the following) and the People's Republic of China ("China" or "Mainland China" in the following) is complicated, covering decades of hostility. When China and the

United States announced that they would "normalise diplomatic relations" in 1978, the Chinese Army stopped shelling Kinmen on alternate days and cross-strait relations began to thaw. Still, in the mid-1990s, verbal and military threats made by China to Taiwan angered the Taiwanese people. During the eight years from 2000, when Chen Shui-bian of the DPP was in office, cross-strait relations further deteriorated. The then-general secretary of the Chinese Communist Party, Hu Jintao, improved relations with the KMT. When Ma Ying-jeou of the KMT came to power in the 2008 elections, cross-strait economic and trade exchanges flourished rapidly.

The end of martial law in Taiwan in 1987 had seen "the beginning of hostility and resentment between the two main political parties [in Taiwan]" and "a decline of political confidence year by year" (Wu, 2015). The KMT's policy stresses that cross-strait exchanges should be based on equality and the "one China" principle, but the meaning of "one China" is interpreted differently on the two sides of the straits. Internationally, China refuses to recognise Taiwan as an independent political entity, maintains that Taiwan is a part of China and opposes any country having formal diplomatic relations with Taiwan. The mixture of friendliness and hostility towards Taiwan makes it difficult for its two main political parties to arrive at a compromise about their cross-strait policies. Gradually the whole of Taiwanese society became polarised regarding cross-strait relations.

One faction believes that Taiwan should face reality and, in order to maintain good cross-strait relations, should learn how to deal with a formidable adversary to create a win-win situation. The other faction believes that dignity is of utmost importance and rejects what it sees as wishful thinking and economic overdependence on Mainland China, fearing being tricked into unifying with China. Members of the former faction, broadly referred to as "blue camp" or "pan-blue," even if they are anti-communist, in some ways identify with China, while the latter faction, or the so-called "green camp" or "pan-green," make a clear distinction between Taiwan and China. The relative power of the factions fluctuates over time. The factions are not evenly distributed across age groups. In general, the number of people belonging to the latter faction is increasing, and young, educated people tend to identify strongly with Taiwan. They think that Taiwan is oppressed internationally by China, but the Ma Ying-jeou administration, which ended in 2016, was tolerant of this and compromised too easily. Moreover, the administration was generally considered incompetent, and Taiwan entered an economic downturn, so there was general discontent with the government leading up to the demonstration in 2014.

Party politics in Taiwan have some similarities and differences with other countries. With the popularity of social media, a salient feature of new movements in the United States, Italy, Spain and Portugal is "a rejection of parliamentary and representative politics, deemed as excessively corrupt and influenced by corporations" (Turner, 2013). This feature is seen in the Sunflower Movement in Taiwan, which emphasised its intention "to correct the shortcomings of the representative system of government." Taiwan differs from other countries in that it has the aforementioned cross-strait situation and the related problem of national identity. These problems translate into a cut-throat zero-sum game, and enable a lot of political figures to reap rewards. The past two presidents of Taiwan, for instance, suffered from the "second-term curse" of their American counterparts, but their curses were different. The third year of Chen Shui-bian's second term, 2006, saw the campaign "A Million Voices Against Corruption, President Chen Must Go", which went on for more than a month and participants of which were claimed to number close to a million. The third year of Ma Ying-jeou's second term, 2014, saw the three-week Sunflower Movement, which had about half a million participants. Besides the many more immediate causes, prolonged resentment of the losing party in the previous general election also contributed to the eruption of these large-scale movements. Since popular resentment was partly due to national identity, it did not easily subside after the election.

In Hong Kong, anti-communist activities and pro-communist activities have been a part of the history of the past sixty years. The riots on Double Ten Day (10 October) in 1956 by pro-KMT factions and those by leftist labour unions in 1967 are well known, but they are now long in the past. These earlier struggles between anti-communist and pro-communist forces are not helpful for understanding the Occupy Central Movement because a lot of young people who took part in the latter were born in the 1990s or after. In other words, they grew up after 1997, when Hong Kong returned to Chinese sovereignty. To understand the movement, we need to understand the situation in Hong Kong after returning to China. According to the current system, the chief executive is elected by a 1,200-member election committee. In the legislature, about half of the legislators are elected by functional constituencies, each of which is a professional or special interest group. For example, insurance and tourism are functional constituencies. The electoral bases of many functional constituencies consist of corporations and legal entities instead of individuals. They often elect business owners or members of senior management. Although they may not be traditional supporters of the communists, they may have investments on the Mainland or are conformists. So when Beijing announced that in 2017 candidates for chief executive would be nominated by a 1,200-strong committee similar to the present election committee, a lot of people believed that it would screen out opposition candidates and felt betrayed by this.

In recent years, the Chinese government has greatly disappointed a lot of Hong Kong students. Examples of such disappointments are extensive, but we can mention a few which are related to the focus of this chapter. The first is the rough treatment that journalists sometimes receive on the Mainland. For example, in 2008, when Hong Kong journalists were trying to film the hectic crowd of ticket buyers at the Beijing Olympics, they were stopped, some with violence. In July 2009, when Hong Kong journalists were reporting on the Urumqi riots, some were threatened with guns, beaten up, or had their hands tied behind their backs and were made to kneel on the street.

The second relates to political conflicts at universities. The council of a university is responsible for senior personnel management and is controlled to a large extent by the chief executive and pro-government parties. A lot of university students clash with these councils over a range of issues. The students are most influenced by universal values and they highly prize democracy and freedom. The number of conflicts has been increasing in recent years, and heated confrontations have been frequent. For example, the Hong Kong Blue Book, edited by one professor, claimed that the general education curriculum of another university was dominated by United States influence and received funds from them, while the university in question denied the unwarranted charge of infiltration by a foreign government in no uncertain terms. Hongkongers have also been unhappy to see Hong Kong officials becoming more like officials in Mainland China. Passing the buck and corruption have become common. Even the Independent Commission Against Corruption (ICAC), whose success in suppressing corruption Hong Kong is proud of, had a commissioner who was discovered to have spent public funds to treat Mainland officials to lavish meals and to give them expensive gifts.

These events keep occurring, causing many Hong Kong people to lose confidence in the Chinese government and to identify less and less with China. At the same time, there are signs that China is trying to rein in Hong Kong.

When Hong Kong first returned to Chinese sovereignty, the Liaison Office of the Central People's Government in the Hong Kong Special Administrative Region was relatively uninvolved. It seldom commented on Hong Kong politics. In recent years, it has become more aggressive; its officials have openly criticised researchers at universities and members of the Legislative Council. These have further contributed to the growing estrangement of some Hong Kong people from China.

In the internet age, young Hong Kong citizens know a lot more about global politics. Many Hong Kong students go to universities abroad via exchange programmes. Recent data show that Mainland China is one of their least favourite places for such exchanges, while Taiwan is high on the list. The presidential election in Taiwan once every four years attracts Hong Kong students as observers. Democratic practices outside Hong Kong contrast sharply with China's one-party autocracy.

## Aims of the Social Movements in Taiwan and Hong Kong

Since the aim of a social movement is to effect or to prevent social change, to understand the differences between the social movements in Taiwan and Hong Kong we need to compare the changes that they aimed to effect or prevent. The aims of the Sunflower Movement in Taiwan were to return the CSSTA signed on 21 June 2013 to the Executive Yuan and to set up a mechanism to monitor cross-strait agreements. It expressed its discontent with the Legislature and requested legislators to listen to public opinion instead of following their party line. It also demanded political parties not punish legislators who did not vote according to their party line.

The aim of the Occupy Central Movement in Hong Kong was to fight for true universal suffrage, including the removal of functional constituencies from the legislature. True universal suffrage meant rejecting the decision by the Standing Committee of the National People's Congress regarding political reform and press for the right of citizens and political parties to nominate candidates for chief executive.

The two social movements seem to be similar, but the difficulty in accomplishing their aims was rather different. Taiwan has a multiparty democratic system. If a social movement has the support of the majority no one can stop it from realising its aims. An opposition party often takes advantage of public discontent with the party in power and makes promises that are easy to fulfil. Regarding cross-strait relations, the DPP and the KMT have sharp differences, and the DPP disagreed with signing the CSSTA. The crucial issue was public opinion. In the absence of censorship, the main objects of persuasion were the masses. According to resource mobilisation and political process theories (Staggenborg, 2011), a social movement is a continuous political process that enables actions outside established structures to be transformed to actions inside them. If the public is convinced and the next general election reflects public opinion, then ideas outside established structures will be transformed into ideas inside established structures. The difficulty the Sunflower Movement faced was how to answer its critics. For example, how should Taiwan deal with a hostile Mainland China?

The social movement in Hong Kong in 2014 was almost doomed to fail. Participants of the Occupy Central Movement wanted to reverse a decision of the Standing Committee of the National People's Congress. The committee was not democratically elected and its decision was an instruction of the Chinese core of power after its deliberation. It is extremely difficult to reverse such a decision. That is why during the movement the terms "movement" and "revolution" often co-existed in slogans. After the movement ended, the then-president of the Hong Kong University Students' Union, Fung Jing-en, said during an inauguration ceremony for new students that the "unprecedented" Umbrella Revolution had "sparked heated discussion of our identity amid current doubts and future uncertainties. The independence of Hong Kong and Hong Kong as a nation are only some of the recently developed ideologies."

In the classification of Macionis and Plummer (2005), the Sunflower Movement in Taiwan was an alternative social movement. It affected specific people by effecting limited change. Its immediate aim was to put pressure on legislators, so that they would not pass the CSSTA. Its long-term aim was to attract the attention of that part of the public that did not belong to the green camp and to win them over. The intended change was to bring about a comprehensive review of Taiwan's policy towards Mainland China. The Occupy Central Movement involved fundamental changes. In the occupied areas the slogans "Down with one-party dictatorship" and "Down with the communist party" were ubiquitous, so it may be regarded as a revolutionary social movement. It affected all people. The change was to be radical. Thus, the difficulties the two movements faced are vastly different.

## Communication Strategies of Social Movements in Taiwan and Hong Kong

Since the two social movements in Taiwan and Hong Kong occurred in different political environments, their communication strategies were also different. Taiwan, being democratic, is used to social movements. Many members of the public were familiar with the arguments against the CSSTA, so the movement emphasised the following questions: why should the review process of the Legislative Yuan be negated? Why should the Legislative Yuan or the Executive Yuan be occupied to force the executive branch to withdraw the CSSTA from consideration? The movement drew wide attention to the slipshod review by the Legislative Yuan and succeeded in blocking the passage of the CSSTA. Occupying the Legislative Yuan and the Executive Yuan obviously drew wide attention but was not met with wide approval. Leaders of the movement failed to handle some negative reports and situations. For example, when social movements all over the world emphasised peace, rationality and non-violence, how should they explain the unprecedented vandalism in the Legislative Yuan and theft in the Executive Yuan? Why did they fail to come to an agreement and sever ties with the protesters who occupied the Executive Yuan under the leadership of Wei Yang?

In September 2012, Spanish protesters' attempt to occupy the country's legislature was thwarted by riot police firing rubber bullets, but protesters of the Sunflower Movement were able to occupy the Legislative Yuan. Were the police in Taiwan too weak to stop them or was the situation in Taiwan more severe than that in Spain, so that protesters had to pull out all the stops to occupy the Legislative Yuan? If we analyse the movement using the persuasive functions of social movements that Stewart, Smith and Denton (2012) discuss, it was effective regarding transforming perceptions of reality, altering self-perceptions of protesters and mobilisation. However, in terms of prescribing courses of action and legitimising the movement it might be found wanting.

The Occupy Central Movement in Hong Kong was organised with the awareness that it would fail, but participants wanted to uphold universal values. Universal suffrage itself was not controversial, but the masses may not have understood its importance. Therefore, there were many layers of purpose in the movement. First, the movement instilled hope in the participants, pushing them to believe that they could effect change. Many of them likely thought "If there are enough of us and we are vocal enough, then maybe we will win some democracy." Next, the movement provided a vent for frustrations. Participants were largely disatisfied with the current state of affairs, the movement gave them a channel to voice their opinion that "Beijing may be hell-bent on clamping down on democracy but we are not going to take it quietly." Third, it had essential elements of a revolution against violence, but was euphemistically called a "movement", which at least would not be suppressed by force.

The main propaganda thrust of Occupy Central was that the political reform proposed by the central government was "fake universal suffrage" and that a lack of democracy was extremely harmful to Hong Kong society. During the movement, communist propaganda used the slogan "peace and democracy" to highlight the disturbance caused by the movement and its rejection of so-called universal suffrage. In this way, the pro-communist side made a new "frame" to counter Occupy Central's "frame" for fighting for universal suffrage. On Hong Kong's streets, various groups opposed to Occupy Central confronted its supporters. In the occupied areas there were frequent altercations and violence. A few weeks later some supporters began to doubt whether it was necessary to prolong the movement. For example, retired Cardinal Joseph Zen, a long-time supporter of democracy, appealed to students to leave about two weeks after the movement started. He said that it was "foolish" to continue the occupation. He accused students of "hijacking" Occupy Central. Apparently, the occupiers were in a serious dilemma. If they left then they would have accomplished nothing. If they did not, then how could they persuade other people to persist without hope? The organisers of Occupy Central needed to communicate with the masses to spread their ideas, but it seemed they failed to do so carefully due to internal discord, so the movement petered out and the government was able to clear the occupied areas one by one.

If we examine the movement according to the six persuasive functions of Stewart, Smith and Denton (2012), it was relatively effective regarding transforming perceptions of reality, altering self-perceptions of protesters and mobilisation, but fell short of the mark regarding legitimising the movement, prescribing courses of action and sustaining the social movement.

## The Fundamental Differences between the Social Movements in Taiwan and Hong Kong

Superficially, the large social movements in 2014 in Taiwan and Hong Kong were very similar. They opposed the Chinese Central Government. Students played important roles in them. Since they had no political resources they resorted to boycotting classes and occupying public places.

If we consider their political contexts and aims, however, we see that they had fundamental differences. In 2014, Taiwan was a democracy. It had experienced party alternation twice. Local elections began to be held regularly in the 1950s. The Sunflower Movement was triggered by discontent with the parliament and legislators, but its basic cause was cross-strait issues which were related to national identity. Similar discontent may happen in any democratic country. A recent example is the passage of an extremely controversial piece of military legislation on 16 July 2015 by the Japanese House of Representatives despite a boycott of the vote by most members of the opposition. An earlier example was the attempt in September 2012 to occupy the Spanish parliament, noted previously. National identity was also an issue in the referenda in Scotland, in the United Kingdom (2014) and in Quebec in Canada (1980 and 1995). In a democracy, a social movement mainly communicates with the entire electorate. If the consciousness of the electorate is raised, then the ruling party will usually give in. If it refuses to give in, the worst that can happen is to wait until the next general election, which will reflect public opinion.

Hong Kong is a special administrative region of China. It does not have a democratic system. Important political decisions are made by the central government. Although some legislators are democratically elected they are hampered in their role by the constraints of the political process. Occupy Central was effectively a direct challenge to the Chinese central government. In the current circumstances, although this may be tolerated, Beijing always tries to find ways to tighten up control. Participants of the movement knew that their demands were made in vain, unless the communists fell from power. So it was essentially a revolutionary movement. Its participants faced difficulties totally different from those faced by social movements in democracies, and were more like Sun Yat-sen and his supporters who opposed and eventually overthrew the Qing Dynasty. If we apply the agitation discourse and revolt discourse with which Golden, Berquist and Coleman (1992) classified social movements, then the discourse of the Sunflower Movement was essentially the former while that of Occupy Central was essentially the latter.

The participants of the two movements were also different. Although leaders of the Sunflower Movement claimed that they transcended party lines, their ideology was the same as that of the green camp and their background was steeped in the green camp. Few people would deny the special relation between the movement and the camp. So a lot of people considered it a "blue-green" conflict like the movement against Chen Shui-bian in 2006. Participants of Occupy Central were teachers and students who supported democracy along with supporters of the pan-democrats. They had different backgrounds. They supported different political parties or had no party affiliation. Besides supporting democracy and opposing one party dictatorship they had no complex ideology. As far as experience was concerned, student leaders of the Sunflower Movement were older than their counterparts in Occupy Central by a few years and had more experience in social movements. They were, therefore, able to handle their work in the movement independently. The student leaders of Occupy Central were university undergraduates. Some of their passion arose out of their participation in the movement against the moral and national education curriculum, which fuelled their discontent with the government. These young, passionate students and other older proponents of democracy, such as Tai Yiu-ting, Chu Yiu-ming and Chan Kin-man (the "trio of Occupy Central"), formed an army of defenders of universal values.

Both movements faced challenges when they tried to unify their supporters. In other words, they had problems issuing their agendas for action. Both movements gradually petered out. Leaders of the Sunflower Movement Lin Fei-fan and Chen Wei-ting decided to sever ties with Wei Yang, who occupied the Executive Yuan. It was reported that when the Legislative Yuan was occupied Lin had the privilege of a private bathroom. Chen Wei-ting tried to ride on the success of the movement to become the youngest legislator in history, but withdrew from the election because of a sexual harassment scandal. In Hong Kong, Tai Yiu-ting, creator of the idea of Occupy Central, told the media in early September 2014 that the strategy of pressuring Beijing to give way on political reforms in Hong Kong had failed, and support for the movement was declining. Then, it was reported that he had misused donations.

The reputation of both movements may or may not be tarnished, but they left an indelible mark on local history. The Sunflower Movement confirmed that the local identity of the new generation was getting stronger, and cross-strait relations were heading toward a new low. Occupy Central made some Hong Kong people disillusioned with "one country, two systems" and brought them to the realisation that Hong Kong is emphatically now a part of China.

## Conclusion

When the United Kingdom ruled Hong Kong, there was little communication between young people in Taiwan and Hong Kong. Seventeen years after Hong Kong's return to Chinese sovereignty there was frequent communication between the young people of the two places. They supported each other in the large social movements they organised with the objective of breaking loose from the control of Mainland China. The movements had a lot of similarities, which made some people think that one was a replica of the other. In fact, they had some basic differences.

The Sunflower Movement in Taiwan may be considered a reaction by some citizens to shortcomings of the representative system of government in a democracy. Its aims were to draw the public's attention to certain specific issues, to "awaken" the citizenry, to put public pressure on the administration, and to canvass support for the opposition party in the next election so as to escape from Chinese influence. The Occupy Central Movement in Hong Kong may be considered a democratic movement in a dictatorship. The movement in Taiwan was, therefore, a post-democratic movement, while that in Hong Kong was pre-democratic. As a result, their chances of success and the effects they had were different.

The two movements occurred at different stages of democratic development, but their demands were similar. To a certain extent they had the same objectives. This rare coincidence has turned a new page in the history of social movements and provided a special case in the study of multi-society social movements.

# References

Bitzer, L. F. (1972). "The Rhetorical Situation." in *Contemporary Rhetoric: A Reader's Coursebook*, edited by D. Ehninger. 39-78. Glenview, IL: Scott, Foresman and Company.

Cathcart, R. S. (1978). "Movements: Confrontation as Rhetorical Form." *Southern Speech Communication Journal*, 3, 233–47.

Colvin, G. (1 April 2015). "Intrepid Guides for a Messy World." *Fortune*. Asian Pacific Edn. 171(5), 44–6.

Fox, R. L., & Frye, J. J. (2010). "Tensions of Praxis: A New Taxonomy for Social Movements." *Environmental Communication*, 4, 422–40.

Golden, J. L., Berquist, G. F., & Coleman, W. E. (1992). *The Rhetoric of Western Thoughts*, 5th edition. Dubuque, IA: Kendall/Hunt.

Jiloka, S. (2012). *Global Social Movement*. Delhi, India: Signature Books International.

Macionis, J. J., & Plummer, K. (2005). *Sociology: A Global Introduction* (3rd edition). London: Pearson.

"Social Movement". (2015). In *Encyclopædia Britannica*. Retrieved from http://global.britannica.com/topic/social-movement.

Staggenborg, S. (2011). *Social Movement*. New York: Oxford University Press.

Stewart, C. J., Smith, C. A., & Denton, R. E. Jr. (2012). *Persuasion and Social Movements* (6th edition). Long Grove, IL: Waveland.

Touraine, A. (2002). "The Importance of Social Movements." *Social Movement Studies*, 1(1), 89–95.

Turner, E. (2013). "New Movements, Digital Revolution, and Social Movement Theory." *Peace Review*, 25, 376–383.

Wilkinson, P. (1971). *Social Movement*. London: Macmillan.

Wu, R. (吳榮鎮). Betrayal: Down With the Wall of Shirking, Greed and Jealousy. (背叛─推倒卸責、貪婪、嫉恨的高牆). Taipei: Zhiku (智庫), 2015.

Zald, M. N., & Ash, R. (1966). "Social Movement Organizations: Growth, Decay and Change." *Social Forces*, 44(3), 327–341.